Touchstone
A Division of Simon & Schuster, Inc.
1230 Avenue of the Americas
New York, NY 10020

First Touchstone paperback edition June 2013

TOUCHSTONE and colophon are registered trademarks of Simon & Schuster, Inc.

For information about special discounts for bulk purchases, please contact Simon & Schuster Special Sales at 1-866-506-1949 or business@simonandschuster.com.

The Simon & Schuster Speakers Bureau can bring authors to your live event. For more information or to book an event contact the Simon & Schuster Speakers Bureau at 866-248-3049 or visit our website at www.simonspeakers.com.

Designed by Akasha Archer

Manufactured in the United States of America

10 9 8 7 6 5 4 3 2 1

The Library of Congress has cataloged the hardcover edition as follows:
Moceanu, Dominique, 1981–
    Off balance / Dominique Moceanu with Paul and Teri Williams.
      p. cm.
    "A Touchstone Book."
1. Moceanu, Dominique, 1981– 2. Women gymnasts—United States—Biography.
3. Gymnastics—Social aspects. I. Williams, Paul. II. Williams, Teri. III. Title.
    GV460.2.M63A3 2012
    796.44092—dc23
    [B]
                                                    2011040276

ISBN 978-1-4516-0865-6
ISBN 978-1-4516-0866-3 (pbk)
ISBN 978-1-4516-0867-0 (ebook)

A MEMOIR

Off
Balance

DOMINIQUE MOCEANU
WITH PAUL AND TERI WILLIAMS

A TOUCHSTONE BOOK
PUBLISHED BY SIMON & SCHUSTER
NEW YORK   LONDON   TORONTO   SYDNEY   NEW DELHI

ABOUT THE AUTHOR

Largely considered one of the greatest and most accomplished gymnasts of the modern era, Dominique Moceanu, born in 1981, is the youngest American gymnast, male or female, to win an Olympic gold medal (at age fourteen), and the youngest to win a Senior National All-Around title (at age thirteen!). She was also the youngest gymnast to compete at the World Championships, to earn a spot on the US National Team, and the youngest athlete ever featured on a Wheaties box!

Born to immigrant Romanian parents, she started her gymnastics career at the ripe old age of three.

Today Dominique is happily married to Dr. Michael Canales, a gymnast turned foot and ankle surgeon. The couple lives in Cleveland with their two children, Carmen and Vincent.

To my dear husband, Michael, you have shown me that
old scars can heal and have helped me reignite my passion
for gymnastics. My love for you is timeless.

To the city of Cleveland, for accepting and treating me as one of your
own, and providing the ideal backdrop to raise my family.

To the gymnastics fans who have stood by me, I am honored
by your continued support. Your loyalty has been one of the highlights
of my career. To those who have always told me to write a book,
well, here it is!

—Dominique

Table of Contents

Contents

Off Balance

Chapter 1

SISTERS

When you have traveled the world, won Olympic gold, *and* gone through a very public court battle against your parents all by the age of seventeen, surprises don't come easy. Discovering my sister Jennifer, though—*that* was a surprise.

On December 10, 2007, I found out that I had a second sister. I was nine months pregnant and about to take my college semester finals. With swollen feet and body parts bigger than I had ever imagined possible, I couldn't even squeeze into a school desk anymore. But earning a college degree was a promise I had made to myself—and third trimester or not, I was going to get those finals done.

Cleveland was cold, rainy, and gray in a bona fide Ohio winter way. All I wanted to do was finish my exams, cuddle up under a blanket with some hot chocolate, and wait for the imminent arrival of my firstborn. But alas, that was not yet in the cards. I was headed for a study session right after a quick stop at the post office.

Earlier in the week, I'd missed the delivery of a piece of certified mail, and the notice had been sitting on my desk for several days. Lugging my backpack full of business textbooks to my car, I felt baby give me a stern kick. I almost lost the certified letter notice in a cold gust of wind and rain. Little did I know, this tiny three-by-five-inch piece of paper would turn my life—past, present, and future—upside down.

As a competitive gymnast, my life has always been filled with challenges that would ultimately define my future. From day one, I was taught to be prepared at all costs. And yet, pulling into the post office parking lot that day, I couldn't have been more unarmed, unguarded.

After finding my place in line, I did finally wonder *who* might have sent me a registered letter. Only my family and personal friends used my home address. Looking out a nearby window, I saw that the rain was getting heavier. I needed to get home. I couldn't afford to dawdle at the post office. The holiday season lines were longer and slower than usual, and I was getting antsy just standing there when I had so much to do. It seemed that everyone but me was sending packages or cards to relatives across the globe.

I finally got to the front of the line, received my package, and walked out into the rain.

As I awkwardly tried to dodge puddles, I stole a peek at the label on the envelope. The bubbly cursive letters seemed so personal, but the name on the return address was completely unfamiliar to me. Back in my car I tore open the package and pulled out a cluster of items: a typed letter, a bundle of photos, and some court documents. *Please tell me I am not being sued!* Then I caught a glimpse of something familiar on one of the documents—my mother's and father's handwriting.

The cover letter was a page and a half of cleanly typed words, unequivocal in meaning, straightforward in sentiment. But my head began to spin as I struggled to make sense of even the simplest words.

> *I've known my whole life that I was adopted . . . and that my biological last name was Moceanu.*

I read the letter slowly—again and again. Breathless and stunned, I sat behind the wheel, staring out the window at the cars driving in and out of the parking lot—a stream of mothers, grandmothers, uncles hurrying in the rain with their holiday packages.

Her name was Jennifer and apparently she was my long-lost sister given up for adoption by my parents in 1987. The letter explained that Jennifer had always known that she was of Romanian heritage, but that it wasn't until she was turning sixteen that her adoptive parents decided to share the details of her birth. They revealed to her the names of her biological parents, and me, her biological sister. She wrote that she had been waiting four years to contact me directly.

> *I feel that I have one chance to show you and prove to you that I'm not some crazy person . . . I'm sure after seeing all of the papers, you'll see that I'm serious.*

Is this possible? I thought. I tried to think back to 1987. I would've been six years old when Jennifer was born. Was my mother even pregnant? Why couldn't I remember? My life has been one bizarre adventure, filled with highs and lows, one head-line after another . . . but a secret sibling? I sat in my car for what seemed like hours, repeatedly examining the contents of the pack-age. The information was presented meticulously, like a jigsaw puz-zle, each piece carefully and intentionally placed next to the other. The evidence was overwhelming.

The photographs hit me the hardest. The girl in the images looked exactly like my younger sister, Christina, born in 1989 when I was almost eight years old. Eventually I could see that while it was definitely not Christina, there was no doubt that she was a sis-ter nonetheless—*my* sister. The resemblance was uncanny.

I have another sister!

How could something like this be kept a secret?

I was an only child for the first eight years of my life. My par-ents, Romanian immigrants, struggled to provide me a better life than the ones they had left in their homeland. They worked hard to give me every opportunity in life, and once I showed natural talent as a young gymnast, they spent every last penny on my training. My father ("Tata") often worked several jobs just to meet the financial burden of my escalating coaching and gym costs. My parents even relocated our family from city to city and state to state whenever necessary to meet my evolving gymnastic needs. According to Tata, I was destined for greatness, so I did my best not to disappoint my parents. By the age of seven I was a serious, committed gymnast, and by the age of nine I was receiving national attention and re-garded as one of America's hopefuls. Standing on the podium at the 1996 Olympic Games in Atlanta and receiving a gold medal was the crowning jewel in a successful gymnastics career and, most certainly, the confirmation that my parents' sacrifices were not in vain.

I took another look at the photos, took a deep breath, and called my parents in Houston.

"Hello?" Mama answered groggily.

"Did you give up a baby for adoption in 1987?" I blurted out. I knew I caught her by complete surprise and gave her a morning wake-up call she'd never forget, but sitting in my car, in the rain outside the post office, I needed answers.

Silence.

I felt a strange combination of emotions whirling out of control. I looked at my belly, my unborn baby, while images of my own childhood raced through my head. My parents were devoted to me and worked tirelessly to provide me with everything they possibly could. They wanted me to have every opportunity in life. But what I longed for most in my early childhood was a bigger family—brothers and sisters. The birth of my sister Christina in 1989 was one of the happiest days of my life. I remember Mama bringing her home from the hospital and how everything instantly seemed sweeter. A baby sister—she was everything to me. We did everything together and today remain the closest of friends. How could it be that Mama had another baby before Christina? Another sister? This didn't make any sense.

"Mama, you have to tell me—is it true?" I pleaded.

"Yes, it's true," she said quietly in a voice I hardly recognized. I had been so close with my mother my entire life and truly thought that I knew everything about her. I suddenly felt a distance from her, and I didn't like it one bit. I couldn't understand how or why she would keep this from me and Christina. I'd expect something like this from my father, who is a born salesman and a master at gently twisting the truth when it suits his needs. He never had a real need to lie outright, since he could wrap you up in his stories in a heartbeat. What he omitted was oftentimes more telling and more important than what he actually said. But *not* my mother. Mama was a straight shooter, honest to the core. Or at least, that's the Mama I knew.

"How could you have kept this from me?" I cried into the phone, both of us knowing there was no possible answer that would satisfy me. Tears flowed down my face; the floodgates had opened and I couldn't stop. I was a complete mess.

I heard my mother crying on the other end of the phone, too. Mama has always been my rock and confidante, and her pain has always been my pain. But at that moment, I felt a total disconnect, which made me feel confused, angry, and alone.

I had so many questions, so few answers. My emotions were running in every direction, moving so quickly I could barely keep up. The raindrops hit the car roof like little metal hammers.

I felt paralyzed, retracing the steps of my life. Every photo ever taken, every holiday spent, all of our childhood memories—there should've been *three* sisters. My life reshuffled, restructured in a matter of minutes.

Just like that, with the rip of an envelope, I had a sister and her name was Jennifer. She was born October 1, 1987, the day after my birthday. We are exactly six years and one day apart.

Jennifer would have been the *middle* sister. Why was she given up for adoption when Christina and I were allowed to stay?

Jennifer had provided contact information, and I was tempted to call her right away, but first I had to learn more. Anyway, I was in no mental state to talk at that point.

"I wanted to tell you, and I almost did many times. I just couldn't find the words," said Mama.

I was disappointed for so many reasons, but most of all I felt betrayed that she had kept this from me all these years. She had been the one I could trust and the one I relied on to always tell me the truth. I felt angry, sad, deceived, and vulnerable. I had always been open with Mama and confided in her things I have never shared with anyone else. And prior to receiving Jennifer's letter, I had thought she had done the same with me.

Even though my mother had kept this from me, at least I was able to communicate with her. As for my father, I couldn't bring myself to speak to him for several weeks; I knew, deep down, that he was likely responsible for how things were handled, or mis-handled. After all, he had played a key role in virtually all the most painful moments in my life up to then.

My father was not a man of the modern age, and even though he loved the United States, he was very much an old-school Ro-manian. As a father and husband, he ruled our house with an iron fist. Decisions were made by him, obeyed by us, and explained by nobody. To question my father's reasoning as a child was invitation for punishment, and as an adult was invitation for outbursts.

Starting with my teenage years, I had clashed with my father many times but had never really been angry with my mother, not in this way. I always felt sorry for my mother; she had such a difficult marriage and wasn't treated the way I believed a wife should be treated—with love and respect.

My home life throughout my childhood was turbulent, at best. Tata's rage and temper tantrums took a toll on my family. We often found ourselves hiding in separate rooms. I can barely recall a single holiday when my father didn't make a scene or create some kind of chaos. We were *always* walking on eggshells. As a child, I never understood his rage, and I still struggle to understand why he did such horrible things to the family he was supposed to love.

But things had started to soften between my father and me at the time I received Jennifer's package. We still clashed on many is-sues, but his battle with a rare form of eye cancer had significantly shifted the dynamics of our relationship. He took a big leap when he allowed himself to get emotional and melancholy in my pres-ence. However, all the old feelings of frustration and alienation returned when I discovered that he and my mother had kept this huge secret from me for twenty years.

Despite being physically weakened by the cancer treatment, my father's retelling of Jennifer's birth was matter-of-fact and decidedly old-school.

"You must remember, Dominique, we were very poor, struggling to survive and put food on the table. When she was born, the doctors told me that we wouldn't be able to afford her medical bills. I saw her, and she was born with no legs. We had no money and no insurance. We could barely take care of ourselves and you."

No legs?! What does that mean, no legs? I thought. My father had a knack for embellishing, so I never quite knew what to believe.

"That's what I remember."

And that was it. Nothing more. I'm sure the finer details after twenty years in the vault were a little fuzzy, but I expected more—something, anything. I needed more of the story, more pieces to a puzzle that was becoming more confusing with each new detail, but my father had said his piece and offered no more.

Once again, it was my mother who tried to help me understand.

"I was given an ultrasound," she began. "It was the only ultrasound of my entire pregnancy. We had no insurance and I had not even seen a doctor prior to delivery. I saw the way the technicians looked at the ultrasound, and I knew something was wrong, but they would not say a word, and I left the clinic with no one ever explaining what they saw. I remember feeling scared and uneasy, but tried not to worry. Months later, when I went into the hospital to deliver the baby, they took me to the operation room to perform a C-section. I was without your father, and it seemed as though they put me to sleep with anesthesia almost immediately. All I remember was waking up in a fog—and with no new baby. Your father said that our little girl was born with no legs. I never saw my baby. I never held her, never touched her, never even smelled her. I desperately wanted to, but your father told me we had to give her up and that was that. We never looked back because it was too painful. You know your father—once a decision is made, that's the end of it.

"He never asked me how I felt after all of that happened. It was such a horrible time in my life. After I came back from the hospital

I cried for a very long time in the emptiness of the streets. No one even noticed my sadness."

It seems crazy and tragic that this could happen in the United States in the 1980s, but in my family's universe, it made sense. My father controlled my mother; every meaningful decision was made by him alone. She had no friends or family in this country and spoke limited English. My mother depended entirely on him, and that's how he liked it.

My mother spent twenty years hiding the pain and agony of this secret, but on December 10, 2007, it finally came out.

Tormented, betrayed, and still in shock, I knew I had to contact Jennifer.

Chapter 2

CAMELIA

To better understand my parents today, we have to look back to their homeland, Romania. Situated north of the Balkan Peninsula in Central Europe, Romania is a country well known for its history of hard-line communism. It fell under communist control in 1947, after the previous ruler, King Michael, was driven into exile. My parents grew up under the brutal dictatorship of Nicolae Ceauşescu, who rose to power in the 1960s and continued to rule until the Romanian Revolution in 1989. Romania's economy fell apart under Ceauşescu's reign, leaving most citizens starved for food, work, and a sense of hope. Meanwhile, Ceauşescu himself lived lavishly and misappropriated the country's resources for his own benefit. Ceauşescu's secret police agency (the Securitate) regulated almost every aspect of daily life—from deciding who could have children to who was permitted to own a typewriter. Human rights violations under Ceauşescu were legendary.

It's not every day you meet someone who was raised in a communist country during a period referred to as the "reign of terror," let alone when they happen to be your parents.

In November of 1980, on the day of my parents' engagement party, my father's family presented a dowry—a few wool dresses, a gold cross, and a handful of other gifts, in exchange for my mother's hand in marriage.

At the age of nineteen, my mother, Camelia, would marry my father, Dimitry Moceanu, a man she'd never met and whom she had seen only in a photograph. When my mother describes the events leading to her marriage, it is as though she is watching someone else's life unfolding in front of her: yes, she *was* the bride, but unlike brides of the western world, decisions about the flowers, the wedding gown, church, day, time, and even the *groom* did not belong to her. It's not that she completely opposed the marriage—options for a young woman in Romania at that time were pretty bleak—but she felt like a pawn being pushed, pulled, and maneuvered.

My father's family, the Moceanus, made the arduous 350-mile journey from Bucharest to my mother's home in Dudestii Noi to attend the engagement celebration for their youngest son. Noticeably missing from the entourage was my father. To his credit, he had been in America looking for work and planning for his future, but he was denied a visa to leave the country in time for the celebration.

So their son could at least *see* what his bride-to-be looked like, the Moceanus had announced that they would have a professional photographer at the celebration to memorialize the engagement and take formal photos of my mother. At this time in Romania, money was scarce and times were tough. Excess was frowned upon; in fact, it was practically sinful. But weddings were still considered a special, once-in-a-lifetime event. It was okay to splurge a little on a celebration with a photographer and maybe even a visit to the salon. On the day of my mother's engagement party, she had her long, black locks perfectly curled and set to impress the mysterious man she was about to marry. It was important to look her best in the photos, even if she hadn't chosen the man who would be her husband. A first impression lasts a lifetime.

It didn't take long to notice that my father was not the only one missing that night. The professional photographer never materialized. No real explanation was ever provided, either—it just didn't happen. There, in her own home with the celebration swirling around her, my mother felt alone—no fiancé and not even a photographer to capture the moment or at least lend an air of importance to the event. In the end, she did not remember a single photo being taken that day.

"Beautiful, smiling Camelia" would not dare voice or even hint at her overall disappointment that night. She was the product of a traditional Romanian upbringing. The youngest of her siblings, my mother was born in Timişoara on October 19, 1961. In her generation, Romanian women were expected to know their place in society. The rigid environment didn't leave much room for questioning any of the rules, much less breaking them. A woman's role was exclusively in the home as wife and mother. Subservience, obedience, and unquestioning loyalty to the husband were a must. My mother was taught first and foremost never to bring shame to the family and that the man was head of the household, period.

Off Balance

The head of my mother's household had been Spiru Staicu. Born on the border of Albania and Greece, my grandfather ("Papu") was a typical old-world disciplinarian. Obedience was well ingrained in my mother from the time she was a young child. Papu made all of the family and household decisions, no matter how big or small. He lacked a higher education from a traditional standpoint, but he was an avid reader and devoured books about history and geography. He especially loved reading the Bible. Positioning himself as the rule maker, Papu seemed to make a conscious decision not to get too close to his children. My mother cannot remember Papu ever showing warmth or affection toward her or her siblings. His explosive temper and booming voice didn't help. As the baby of the family, my mother mostly kept her distance.

Papu met and married my grandmother ("Maia") Domenica in his later adult years, and they immediately started their family. Brothers Nelu and Mircha and sister Katarina came first, then my mother. However, before my mother was born, tragedy struck. As the story has been told to me, one afternoon, Mircha followed Nelu into the fields of their farm. Nelu climbed up onto a tractor in the fields and began to play around. As he pretended to drive, swinging the huge steering wheel from side to side, he didn't notice Mircha behind him struggling to climb up into the huge machine. Tiny Mircha wasn't strong enough to hoist himself onto the tractor and, mid-climb, he lost his footing and slipped. He tumbled down and landed with a thump, his head smashing into a rock. Poor Mircha, only five years old, died instantly. Maia was so overcome with grief over Mircha's passing that she convinced Papu that they should have one more child. So, with the loss of Mircha came a new beginning: my mother was born.

The family lived on a small farm in Dudestii Noi, just outside Timişoara, Romania. They tended sheep to make milk, feta cheese, and wool, and would sell these goods at local food markets. It provided enough to support the family during the early 1960s prior to Ceauşescu gaining power.

The wide plains and rolling grass hills of the small village provided a perfect playground. The siblings and village kids played tag and running games as well as Hide and Seek and the popular Romanian ball game One and a Life, which is similar to American dodgeball. After an afternoon of play, my mother would race home for a dollop of *orez cu lapte*, a traditional rice pudding. On special days, she'd have homemade *cozonac*, a fluffy, sweet bread made with milk, eggs, butter, and nuts.

Childhood games and special treats were wonderful, but they placed a distant second to competitive sports. Romania is well known for its nationwide passion for sports, especially soccer and gymnastics. It introduced the world to legendary gymnastics superstar Nadia Comaneci, who brought international fame and honor to Romania by dominating women's gymnastics at the 1976 Olympics in Montreal. Nadia captured the hearts of the world in the Montreal games, when she took home three Olympic gold medals, one silver medal, and one bronze. In the process of winning her medals, Nadia became the first gymnast in history to receive a perfect score of 10 in modern Olympic gymnastic competition, which she achieved on the uneven bars. What's more remarkable, Nadia went on to repeat that feat and received a score of 10 in six additional events during the same games. Prior to that time, it was considered almost inconceivable for a gymnast to receive a perfect score in any event. The highest mark the scoreboard was set up to display was a 9.9, so Nadia's 10 had to be shown as 1.0 simply because there was no space; it became a memorable sight in itself.

Nadia's performance at the Montreal Olympics, and again at the 1980 Olympics in Moscow, where she earned two more gold medals and two silver medals, helped catapult gymnastics' popularity on an international scale. Nadia Comaneci became a household name across the globe and today, Nadia is still one of the most famous and highly regarded gymnasts in the history of the sport.

Nadia's rise to success came at a dark time in Romanian history and provided a much-needed symbol of hope for her country and its people, including my mother, a teenager at the time and the same age as Nadia. Most Romanians had endured years of oppression and extreme poverty during the communist reign of terror from 1945 to 1989. Nadia's Olympic victories in 1976 gave Romania a rare opportunity to bask in positive international attention. In her wildest dreams, my mother would have never imagined that twenty years later, she'd be friends with *the* Nadia Comaneci, and that they both would be cheering for me as I won my very own gold medal in gymnastics at the 1996 Olympics in Atlanta, Georgia.

My mother was a natural athlete, and there wasn't a sport she didn't love. From handball to gymnastics to running, she excelled in most of the sports offered at school, but track was her favorite. It was her dream to be accepted into the prestigious High School of Sport in Timişoara, but admission into this well-respected school was extremely competitive, and only those students who possessed elite athletic talent and were able to pass an entry exam were invited to enroll. She felt confident about the entry exam since she was already a standout student, achieving stellar academic grades. She set high athletic goals for herself, trained, and worked herself to exhaustion just to get closer to her dream of attending the school and going on to compete internationally in track and field.

Finally, it seemed, her hard work paid off. She had been accepted into the High School of Sport. My mother couldn't speak and was so overwhelmed with pride and joy that she could barely breathe. She'd done it. She was one of the few, one of the chosen. Going to the High School of Sport was the only thing that she had ever really wanted and dreamed of. Now it was no longer a carrot merely dangling in front of her—it was actually hers. Or was it?

"She will not go," Papu announced.

They were only four little words, but my mother knew deep in her gut that they were absolute. The decision to decline enrollment was made with no discussion or input from my mother or Maia, but its long-lasting effects would alter the course of my mother's life.

Papu said it was improper and refused to pay to further the education or athletic career of a daughter. Her place as a young woman, he insisted, was in the home.

The acceptance offer was officially declined, and my mother's education and athletic dreams were gone forever. She found very little to smile about. She tried to maintain a brave face around the house, for fear of annoying her father, but found herself sobbing quietly under the covers.

It was at about this time that Papu drew a very specific outline of my mother's future. He decided that once she finished eighth grade, she would move to Bucharest to live with her brother, Nelu, and his wife, Nina, and complete high school there. She would not be permitted to attend university, so after graduating from High School #21 in Bucharest, she was to be paired with a husband. Papu believed a woman of that age was to marry and settle down, so that's exactly what she did.

My paternal grandfather, Stere Moceanu, arranged for his youngest son, Dimitry, to marry my mother. Radiantly beautiful, she was a catch by anyone's standards. Before and after being sent to marry my father, she caught attention from countless men for her silky black hair, dark eyes that sparkle like black diamonds, smooth olive skin, and slender hourglass figure. To this day, she never has to wear any makeup to be beautiful. I remember men and women turning their heads to admire her beauty when I was a child. Despite these physical gifts, I never once saw her gloat or even consider herself above the ordinary. She always stayed true to her humble nature. She had the wisdom of an old soul and carried herself with dignity and class in public and in private. And, like any "good Romanian woman" of that time, she had an unwavering work ethic.

My mother finally got to meet my father in December 1980, a few weeks prior to their wedding. She had seen a murky photo of him, shown to her by the Moceanus the night of their engagement party, so she recognized his big smile and handsome face. On January 28, 1981, wearing a long-sleeved crimson dress, she married him in Sérres, Greece, with no parents or family members present, just the priest and a couple of distant cousins of my father's who served as witnesses. She worked to appear confident and calm, but for my mother, who'd never before been away from her family or country, it was a frightening step into the unknown.

"It all happened very quickly," my mother has told me. She was innocent, naïve, and nineteen; everything was new and exciting, but also very scary. After a brief stay in Greece following their wedding ceremony, my parents boarded a plane bound for the United States and waved good-bye to Europe forever.

Through centuries of arranged marriages, many have resulted in beautiful unions. However, after living through my parents' turbulent relationship, I told my mother at a very young age that I would pick my own husband. He might not even be Romanian or Greek, for that matter. I made it clear that an arranged marriage, even if Tata (my father) insisted, would *not* be in my future.

Today, as a wife and mother, I understand the adjustments of being newly married. Two people used to doing things their own way suddenly have to learn how to be united as one. The smallest thing has the potential to become an issue. It takes a lot of patience and compromise, but it is usually tempered by the fact that you are doing it with someone you love. Thankfully, I was able to choose my husband, someone I had known well and loved for years before. I can't imagine how scared Mama must have felt having to go through all of that with a husband she'd known for only a matter of weeks, especially since she had to leave everything familiar behind and start anew in a foreign land without any family or friends.

Tata always believed that in America all of his dreams would come true. He desperately wanted to be in the United States, which he felt epitomized freedom and opportunity. He wanted to escape the communism and oppression of Romania. Living and thriving in Romania was getting increasingly harder. The government was beginning to seek more control over the everyday lives of its citizens. The Romanian people were struggling terribly and living in a virtual police state. It seemed there were no jobs or money to be made, and every word and action was being monitored. My father, born with a passionate entrepreneurial streak, felt perpetually stifled. His response to the brutal regime was to get out of Romania and seek a better life. Now that he had a wife by his side, he was on his way to conquer America, "the land of the free," and to make something of himself.

To this day, I specifically remember my family's joy at the collapse of Ceauşescu's communist regime in 1989. Ceauşescu had ruled Romania with an unforgiving iron fist for decades, and in return, his countrymen had the last word—he was driven from power on December 22, 1989, tried, and then executed by firing squad only three days later. A new era ushered in a series of economic and political reforms, and now Romania has made a positive transformation. Its population of approximately 21.5 million is experiencing economic growth as a democratic nation. I have come across many Romanians who are hopeful and proud of the development. For most, no matter how far you roam, part of your heart is always home. Despite this progress, Tata never spoke about wanting to return to his homeland.

After their Olympic Airlines flight landed in New York, my parents boarded a Greyhound bus and made the journey to Hollywood. In California, they could stay with my father's brother, Costa. Tata is one of four children: his oldest sister, Maria, was followed by brother Iani, then brother Costa and, finally, Tata. They were all born in Romania, most in Constanţa, and then spent their childhoods in Bucharest, the capital. Tata had been inspired to move to Hollywood—the land of sunshine, entertainment, and opportunity. He knew it was where he could stake his claim.

Shortly after they arrived in Hollywood, my mother's hunch that she was pregnant, which she felt even before leaving Greece, was confirmed. My parents were in a foreign country without a dime to their name, unable to speak the language, and had no home. To make ends meet, Tata took odd jobs, anything he could find to make a few dollars. He found steady work in the cafeteria at an English-language school and was in charge of preparing and serving coffee, danishes, small candies, chocolates, sandwiches, and so on. Although it was a far cry from his entrepreneurial visions, it was work. He and my mother relied on every penny and didn't buy anything except absolute essentials that first year. In a good month, it was just enough to get by.

They stayed with Tata's brother Costa and his new wife when they first arrived in Hollywood, but soon realized the tight quarters wouldn't last forever. After a few months, they moved out and were transient for most of that first year, living with friends, often sleeping on spare beds or sofas. From time to time, they'd have to sleep in their car, a Volkswagen Beetle, until they found a new place to stay.

All the while, my pregnant mother was frightened deeply by the uncertainty of their safety and future. She ached to return home to Romania, but she knew my father did not consider it an option. Everything felt so foreign to her; she felt isolated and alone. No friends, no ability to speak the language, no driving. She cried every day but was careful to hide it from Tata. She turned to the one thing she could afford and that brought her the comforts of home: prayer. She prayed they'd have a place of their own even if it was a shack. And she prayed for the health and safety of her family back in Romania.

My mother relied exclusively on my father's advice and approval for everything. She was an inexperienced and sheltered teenager who knew the world only from what she'd read in books and seen in the movies. Growing up on her parents' farm with her siblings, she never imagined she'd end up in Hollywood, the land of movie stars, freeways, and high-rises. She did the only thing that was familiar: she plunged into books to learn about her new culture and, most important, started teaching herself English. She relied on a dog-eared Romanian-English dictionary she had brought from home. At first it was difficult, but through practice and watching children's television shows, she gradually began to pick it up. Her confidence grew slowly until she felt comfortable enough to speak in public.

Throughout her pregnancy, prayer was the only form of health care my mother received—she constantly prayed for a healthy delivery. She received zero prenatal care and never once visited a doctor prior to giving birth. My parents had no health insurance and really didn't understand the risks, complications, or overall protocol of giving birth. They were poor immigrants but somehow managed to stay alive and have food and shelter. Although they had been strangers when they met and married only months prior, the challenges and struggles definitely brought my parents closer and forged a bond between them. My mother began to feel an attachment to Tata in a way she had never before experienced. She relied on him for everything. In retrospect, he didn't know much, either, but between them, he was undoubtedly more experienced when it came to street smarts and basic survival skills. He'd at least traveled some of the world and lived on his own before their marriage.

My mother's prayers were answered, in part at least, when they finally saved enough money to rent an apartment just before I was born. It was a studio apartment on Whitney Street, just off Hollywood Boulevard. It may have been tiny and not in the best neighborhood, but to my parents, it was a castle—finally, a place of their own.

Despite the complete lack of prenatal care, my mother had no complications during her pregnancy, and I was delivered the old-fashioned way with no birthing drugs. The only drama came prior to my delivery while my mother was in labor. My parents were forced to travel to two different Los Angeles hospitals before a third one, Hollywood Presbyterian Hospital, finally accepted an uninsured, pregnant woman in active labor. My father stayed in the waiting area during the delivery, leaving my mother alone in a room full of doctors and nurses. After only a handful of months studying English, she could understand only half of what they were saying and was forced to communicate, in part, through gestures.

I was born on September 30, 1981, at 1:27 p.m., weighing in at seven pounds, six ounces. As she tells it, my mother pushed a few times, and I came quite quickly without a fuss. Although exhausted, she felt a wave of peace wash over her as she held her baby girl in her arms for the very first time.

Now, as an adult and a mother, I better understand my parents' overpowering urge to give me everything the world had to offer, and then some. I still remember holding my own children for the first time—that moment when I realized I'd do *anything* for them. My parents had left their homeland, their families, and everything familiar to them to build a better life in the United States. Looking back, I can appreciate my mother and Tata both determined in their own way to make my life count. I can see how my parents' growing up in a dictatorship and my mother's oppressive upbringing and crushed dream of a future in sports culminated in an intense need to give me everything *they* could not have. Sadly, the line between what is best for a child and what a parent *thinks* is best for the child is often blurred, even by good intentions. This was a lesson I'd learn, but not soon enough.

Chapter 3

AWAKENING

It's taken the better part of three decades, but it's safe to say that I've finally come to terms and fully accepted that my childhood wasn't normal—in fact, wildly *abnormal* would be more apt. As I was growing up with parents plucked straight out of communist Romania and plopped down in the fast-paced American culture of the 1980s, it didn't take much to see that my home life was "different." Not only was our language different, our food, religion, holidays, customs, and even our clothes screamed *"outsider."*

Growing up, I was considered odd by the other kids in our neighborhood and at school. I was a straight-A student, excelling in my classwork, but I was extremely shy and quiet and didn't become more talkative until my teenage years. In elementary and middle school, I was simply "the European kid" who spoke a strange language that nobody understood and ate weird foods like ground meat rolled up in cabbage leaves, called *sarmale* (s-ah-rh-mha-leh), with braunschweiger—a creamy type of liver spread from Germany—and pâté, ground meat minced into a spreadable paste. Mama used to put it on bread, sometimes toasted in the mornings for breakfast and sometimes on sandwiches she packed for my school lunch. What kid eats liver paste? Me and no other American schoolkid, I can assure you that. Mama would say it was a highly nutritious source of iron, protein, and vitamin A, but what kid cares about that? The other kids only cared that it looked "gross," and as long as I ate those foods, nobody wanted to exchange lunches with me, which excluded me from the social game of lunch hour.

After a while, I didn't want to bring lunch from home and instead asked Mama for the $1.10 so I could buy a school lunch and a chocolate milk in its own tiny carton. Mama had no problem giving me lunch money a couple times each week, and I was relieved. I learned what other kids ate and asked Mama for those foods—bologna sandwiches, potato chips, and cookies. Oddly, I didn't try the American classic PB&J until I was much older—after the Olympics at age fourteen! I loved it! Eating strange foods was part of who I was, but I believed eating the same foods as my classmates would help me fit in, and I needed all the help I could get.

I was sometimes singled out by other students at school, leaving me even more self-conscious and insecure about who I was. Who was I, after all? I didn't even really know back then. I struggled daily to fit in. I remember one day in third-grade gym class when the instructor selected two students as team captains to pick squads for kickball. I wasn't close with anyone in my class, but I truly felt like an outcast that afternoon when everyone else's name in the class was called one by one and I was left standing all by myself looking from side to side uncomfortably and somewhat mortified. It was clear that neither wanted me and they simply refused to choose me. The PE teacher finally came to my rescue and named me to a team to break the awkward silence. It felt like an eternity as I walked in shame to stand in line with my team. I felt so unwanted. I didn't belong anywhere.

In retrospect, incidents like that just added fuel to my isolation and made me feel out of place in a time when I was trying so hard to find myself. All I really knew was that I had a strange last name and parents who were from a country that no kids, and few adults, could find on the map. My parents had heavy accents when they spoke English, and nobody could ever pronounce our last name correctly. I avoided saying my last name as much as possible when I was younger because I was embarrassed when people would ask me to repeat it over and over and still weren't able to pronounce it correctly. It only reminded me of how awkward and weird I was among my peers.

Believe it or not, I still had anxiety about saying my last name in public as teenager after I had already become an internationally known gymnast. I remember panicking when I was thirteen years old at a USA–Belarus–China gymnastics competition called the Visa Challenge in 1995. In a televised interview, the reporter asked each member of Team USA to introduce herself by saying her first and last name into the cameras for the viewers at home. As she went down the row of my teammates standing in a line beside the balance beam, I quickly tried to rehearse how I should pronounce "Moceanu." I must've said it five different ways, trying to figure out which pronunciation would be easiest to understand. I could hear Tata's voice rattling in my head, as he would say our family name proudly—our name is "M-oh-chee-ah-noo!" He said it with such certainty and such finality, but I still thought it sounded funny when I said it out loud. I wasn't comfortable for some reason.

Off Balance

I wasn't nearly as nervous to compete in the meet as I was during these introductions. As the cameraman went down the line, one by one my teammates said their names with confidence: "Dominique Dawes," "Katie Teft," "Kellee Davis." When he got to me in the middle of the group, my mind jumped and I intentionally mispronounced my name "Dominique M-oh-*sey*-noo." I couldn't believe I had just changed my name on national TV to make it easier for people to say. It sounded so silly once it came out of my mouth, and immediately I realized I had made a mistake and probably greatly disappointed my family, too. I felt awful.

I guess I was still haunted by my earlier years when I was ashamed of my name during roll call at school. I'd be so nervous as I squirmed at my desk waiting for the teacher to scroll down the alphabet and finally get to my name. There was always a pause after my first name, the teacher unsure how to pronounce my name. They'd give their best crack at it, but it would *always* end up butchered.

I rarely went on playdates or invited anyone home to play in those early elementary years, which didn't help in the friend department. I was nervous that Tata would say or do something to scare them off for good. Tata could be charming and friendly, but he could also be aloof and act suspicious of "outsiders." Romanian was all I spoke at home. Mama and Tata were multilingual, speaking Greek, Romanian, and English fairly fluently. English took the most effort, though, so they would resort to what made them most comfortable around the house, and that was speaking Romanian. I am thankful and grateful now that I learned it, but when I was young I resented that I was forced to speak Romanian at home. It was yet another reminder that I was different.

It was a constant struggle for me to make friends. I didn't feel, act, or look like anyone else at school or in my neighborhood, but once I put on my leotard, stepped into the gymnasium, and felt that mat under my feet, all of those feelings of being an outsider vanished. Gymnastics—the amazing sport it is—became my outlet and gave me confidence.

My life as a gymnast actually began at the age of three, shortly after Tata moved the family to Illinois in pursuit of a new business opportunity. My parents enrolled me in tennis and gymnastics classes at Northbrook Square Gymnastics in Chicago, near where we lived. Tennis lasted for only one lesson, and that was the end of that, but I took to gymnastics immediately. When I close my eyes, I can still recall my earliest memory of gymnastics class, watching a group of kids bouncing on the trampoline in the corner of the gym. The trampoline—the apparatus every kid loves most—was like a magnet for me. I didn't know what it was, had never seen anything like it, but I knew I wanted to do it. I wanted to be one of those little kids in a leotard and tights, laughing and jumping and waiting in line for another turn.

I felt an instant connection with gymnastics, a connection that has stayed with me and provided my childhood with a desperately needed sense of belonging. The gym was my haven, the one place where I could fit in. Beyond the ethnic and cultural issues that ostracized me, I was also physically different. I was awkward looking with huge brown eyes, dark brown, pencil-straight hair styled into an old-school Romanian bowl haircut from the 1980s. And I was very, very small. I was always the tiniest kid on my street and in my classes at school. While the average five-year-old girl is about 3' 8" tall and 45 pounds, I was nowhere near that size until I was almost ten. It wasn't until I was nine years old that I reached 3' 10" and 50 pounds. Even as an Olympian in 1996, when I was fourteen, I measured only 4' 4" and weighed in at 70 pounds. Because my size made me look younger than my actual age, I was sometimes teased by the other children. They'd call me "shorty," "small fry," and "shrimp."

The gym was the one place I didn't have to worry about feeling awkward for being so petite. It was where I felt most at home.

Gymnastics was challenging and often hard work, but I loved the movements, the stretching, rolling, flipping, twisting, and bending. And although I didn't know exactly what it meant at the time, it made me feel good when my instructors kept nodding their heads and telling me I was a "natural."

By the time I was five, Tata decided the family should leave behind the brutal winters of Chicago and move to the warmer climate of Florida. Another new city, new neighborhood, new kids, new job for Tata, and a new gym. I remember the first day Mama and I walked into LaFleur's Gymnastics in Tampa. The gym was a good forty-minute drive from my family's apartment in Temple Terrace, but Mama didn't seem to mind, especially since we spent most of the drive talking and listening to the radio. I squeezed Mama's hand tightly as we made our way through the gym's doors and lobby. I loved the warmth I felt from Mama. I always felt so close and so safe with her. I loved her so much.

As Mama and I sat in the waiting area watching more children arrive with their mothers and some with their fathers, I kept peeking at the gym through the viewing window. I remember thinking that the gym was so much bigger than my first gym back in Chicago and was set up differently. I began to wonder if they did the same kind of gymnastics in Tampa as they do in Chicago. And then I saw it. There it was, on the right-hand side of the gym . . . the trampoline. But it wasn't just one; they had *three* trampolines connected one to the other, built up on a podium surrounded by carpet. The trampoline was my favorite, and I never grew tired of it. I sat in my white leotard with little sparkles, counting the minutes for class to start!

And so it began: Our routine of driving to LaFleur's several times each week for my gymnastics classes. The gym's owners, Jeff and Julie LaFleur, along with Beth Hair, made up my new coaching team. It was the beginning of a wonderful and nurturing relationship with a triad of coaches: Jeff as my primary coach, Julie as my dance coach and floor choreographer, and Beth as my balance beam coach. Most of the skills I learned from them I carried with me for the rest of my career. With their guidance, I excelled quickly and developed a true love affair with the sport of gymnastics. I am forever grateful that we landed at the doors of LaFleur's Gymnastics when we moved to Florida.

These unjaded early years of gymnastics were magical for me and hold some of my purest and most inspiring memories of the sport. Putting on my leotard, packing my bag, and climbing into the car with Mama was invigorating and symbolized my path to something wonderful and safe. Every time I walked through the doors of that gym, I felt alive and excited. I knew this was the sport for me, even at the young age of five. There wasn't anything in my life that I felt so strongly about or, aside from Mama, that I loved so much.

By the time I was seven, I started to realize that I didn't just love gymnastics, but also that I had a special gift for it. I started to notice that I learned quickly and picked up new maneuvers faster than the other girls in my classes. It was as if I were born to do gymnastics. A big plus in my favor was that I had no fear. Even at six, I was a daredevil, relishing challenges and more than willing to try any new somersault, back bend, or flip. Fear only set in much later, when my surroundings and pressures changed in the sport and in my life, but as a child I was virtually carefree when I learned and performed. I would overhear my coaches telling my parents in serious tones that I had true natural ability for the sport and that they were very excited to be working with me. I could feel the energy from their excitement. I noticed that the coaches spent extra one-on-one time working with me and that they appreciated my fearless approach.

My parents believed early on that gymnastics would be my future and were determined to do whatever it took for me to succeed. The high priority they placed on my gymnastics explains their willingness to spend money on my classes and training even though most months we lived hand-to-mouth. In their eyes I was destined to be a meaningful contributor to the sport that meant so much to their home country. My parents often used to tell a story about the moment they *knew* I'd become a champion gymnast. I've heard them tell it so many times, I can recite it in my sleep: "We put Dominique on a clothesline at six months old to see how long she could hang on and test her strength. She didn't let go until the clothesline broke!" It still makes me laugh when I picture Tata telling it with the same level of enthusiasm each time. He'd actually act out the story, fists over his head pretending to imitate me holding on to that clothesline. He was so proud that he was almost giddy when he shared this story over and over throughout the years.

As I grew more skilled and more serious about gymnastics, my training and the number of hours I spent at LaFleur's gym increased dramatically. By the age of seven, I was training with Jeff, Julie, and Beth five to six days per week, logging twenty-five hours, often more, each week. When I first started working with them, I was a compulsory level gymnast, so I spent my days practicing and perfecting predesigned routines with a series of required moves. The compulsory routines are dictated by USA Gymnastics (USAG), the organization that governs competitive gymnastics in the United States. During compulsory levels 4 through 6, gymnasts perform the same routine with the same movements to the same music. I looked forward to completing my compulsories and moving on to "optionals," the next level, where I'd get to flex my own creative muscles and create my individualized routines with my coaches to reflect my own style and personality, especially for balance beam and floor exercise routines. I was excited for the day I'd get to pick my own floor music and show my customized routines. I knew the harder I worked, the faster I'd move through compulsories, so I followed my scheduled calendar diligently.

Granted, my daily routine was quite different than that of the average seven-year-old, but it was the only life I knew and I embraced it. Each weekday I went to public school until early afternoon, then off to LaFleur's for four hours of training. Plus, I was at the gym training Saturdays from 9:00 a.m. to 1:00 p.m. During the summer, my daily workouts were from 9:00 a.m. to 4:00 p.m. Often on Friday nights, I would stay late, until 9:00 p.m. for "Open Gym" to play and have extra time to do whatever I wanted.

Jeff LaFleur was a demanding and structured coach. He expected a lot from his athletes, and I never wanted to disappoint him. I was in a group that varied in age quite a bit, and I worked extremely hard to get Jeff's praise and approval each and every day. I'd later come to understand the intricacies of successful student-coach relationships and just how fortunate I was to start my career with a demanding yet empathetic coaching presence and mentor. Jeff is still among my favorite coaches I've had the privilege to work with, which says a lot considering I have had the help of more than twenty coaches throughout my athletic journey. Looking back, what I loved about his coaching style most was that he always brought a great sense of balance to our training sessions. He demanded more out of me when necessary, but, as a father himself, he seemed to have an innate sense of when to show a more nurturing side. Jeff treated all his gymnasts with a level of respect and caring that I valued even as a young girl. I felt so comfortable with his coaching style and direction. I always felt that he cared about me as a person as well as my progress in the sport, which meant the world to me. I cannot recall a single time Jeff lost his temper or even yelled at me, yet he always had my utmost attention and respect.

Jeff had competed as a collegiate gymnast at the University of Minnesota, where he majored in physical education and minored in child psychology. Maybe this mixture of disciplines explains why he has such an incredibly easy way with kids. As an Elite-level gymnast, he competed internationally and represented the United States, which helped him relate to his gymnasts on an athletic level as well. Having actually gone through the rigorous training himself and experiencing firsthand what it was like to compete as an Elite gymnast I think made him an even more understanding coach. He had been there and knew exactly what it was like. He pushed us because he knew what was required to reach the next level, and he never wanted his gymnasts to settle when he knew they could achieve more.

Jeff was super strong and worked hard to stay fit, even for coaching standards. I was always amazed that he could pull off his trademark one-arm handstand on the men's parallel bars with his legs in a straddle position at any given time. I thought that was the coolest thing ever.

I spent so much time with my coaches that they became like family to me. I looked to Jeff as a positive male role model and somewhat of a father figure as well as a coach. At this point, Tata was gone most days, working long hours to provide for us. Often frustrated and exhausted, he was temperamental and moody when he was home, sometimes blowing up at Mama or me for no apparent reason. At the gym, I appreciated Jeff's steady, reliable nature.

I believe my rapid early progress during those formative years was a testament to Jeff's coaching skills. After only a year and a half of compulsory gymnastics, I moved up to the optional level, which in turn increased my training to a minimum of thirty-two hours per week. I was on my way to the bigger and bolder gymnastics skills. By the time I was nine, Jeff had already taught me a triple back dismount, which is three consecutive flips in the air; a Tsukahara, also known as a full-in (two consecutive flips in the air with a 360-degree twist in the first flip), on the floor, and a Yurchenko-style vault, which is a round-off entry onto the board with a backward motion, landing with my hands on the vaulting horse, followed by flips and twists off of the horse into a landing.

At the time, I had never seen anyone else my age complete this vault with a 360-degree twist in a tucked and layout position. Jeff was also the first to teach me a release move on the uneven bars called a Gienger, named after the German male gymnast Eberhard Gienger. This skill begins in a handstand on the high bar, then moves into a giant swing and on the rise three-quarters of the way through, as the toes come up above the high bar, the gymnast releases the bar into a straight body layout (or hollow position) into a half twist (180-degree turn), and ends with a regrasp of the high bar. I would go on to compete this release move in the 1996 Olympics.

Julie, Jeff's wife, who majored in physical education and minored in dance, was my floor choreographer at the gym. She was as sweet as honey and always seemed to have the patience of a saint. I will never forget working with her on my very first optional floor routine for level 8. Mind you, I was no dancer at this stage in my career. I could flip, twist, and swing on the bars with no problem, but dance—forget it. I couldn't keep a beat or even find it. Maybe it was because I was never exposed to much music outside of some traditional Romanian songs and what little radio I heard. Dancing was completely foreign to me, and it showed. I'm sure that, deep down, Julie must have thought she was choreographing a routine for an uncoordinated Smurfette, but she remained patient and kind until I eventually got it. It was a learning experience that came much less naturally than the other skills and moves I was learning, but I needed it to grow and develop within another realm of my sport. It was a challenge, but Julie worked and worked with me until it was just right. Ironically, years later, I'd become a choreographer myself and teach other gymnasts how to dance and perform their floor routines. To this day, I'm still learning from Julie as I remind myself to have the patience with my students that she once had with me.

Beth Hair, my beam coach, was the belle of our gym. Well,

in my eyes, at least. She was beautiful, with dark brown eyes, bouncy brown curls, and a slender, fit figure. Her fingernails were always perfectly manicured and painted a bright scarlet color that matched her lipstick. She'd sometimes have jewelry and rhinestones on her nails, which I thought was so chic. I'd see her miniature gold ring dangling from her thumbnail while I was on beam or when she helped stretch me during flexibility training.

Despite all her glamour and my impression that everyone in Tampa must have had a crush on her, Beth was a no-nonsense beam coach whom I respected immensely. When she would get frustrated with a student's performance, she'd make it clear who was boss. She demanded a positive attitude and the highest work ethic from her gymnasts and would get on our cases if she thought we weren't putting in our best effort. She required seemingly endless series of repetitions during her beam workouts. Most gymnasts dislike this about the balance beam, and the fact that it's only four inches wide becomes more and more intimidating as you grow tired. I know that Beth's strict style of coaching made me a tougher competitor. Beth had a purpose for what she did when she did it, and I liked that. When I began training with Beth at the compulsory level, I didn't like the beam at all, and it was my least favorite rotation. I hadn't mastered it, and if I did fall during competitions in my early years, it was usually on beam. Beth was tough but fair, and she clearly recognized my weakness on the beam; however, she also believed I had potential, so she pushed me until it finally began to click.

Beth taught me my very first optional beam series. After I mastered a walkover back handspring I moved on to a back handspring back handspring, which was a common flight series for an optional gymnast. I then went on to a back handspring layout step-out, which is a backward motion—jumping from my feet to my hands, and then my feet again—with my legs passing in a 180-degree split while in vertical, followed by the same movement with no hands touching the beam on the second flight. By the time I was eight, Beth had me doing a three-part series that consisted of a back handspring, a layout, and another back handspring.

For my second series, Beth had me do an unconventional round-off back handspring step-out on the four-inch-wide beam. It was more bold and daring than my other series, especially for my age. I remember that two of my other teammates were doing this same type of series, but I hadn't seen it performed much at competitions, so I knew it was unique. I took pride in doing it even though it was a little scary.

I loved gymnastics. I loved it so much I'd sometimes just say the words to myself like a declaration: "I love gymnastics." I craved the excitement of learning new tricks and threw myself into working to be better than every other gymnast I trained with. A fierce competitive spirit was there in full force before I hit the third grade. I longed to be the best in every aspect of the sport—from the discipline to the most difficult skills to winning in competitions. I found myself at this very young age driven to achieve superiority in everything I did. The hard work and long hours all seemed like a part of the process necessary to achieve the goals of pleasing my coaches, my parents, and myself. At that time, there was no cynicism—just an all-out belief in big dreams and championships. No one shut those dreams down, either. Least of all Tata, who made no secret of the fact that I, Dominique Moceanu, was "an Olympic champion in the making." Those early years made up my most free and happy period as a young girl and a young gymnast.

Mama and Tata were also pleased with my progress and development at LaFleur's, and when I was nine, Tata decided to call Channel 10 News in Tampa Bay to let them know about how "special" his little girl was at gymnastics and that I was doing things very few people in the world at my age could do. Tata was always thinking about his next move and always up to some wild scheme or another. Sometimes his plans would work out and other times they would fail spectacularly. Whatever he said to the good folks at Channel 10, it worked because the local sports desk actually decided to come out and film a feature segment at LaFleur's gym, with a spotlight on me as the most promising gymnast of a promising bunch.

This news story may seem like no big deal to most people, maybe even trivial, but it was a turning point. It was the first time I saw the outside world show an interest in what went on inside our gym. I was so happy that people, real grown-ups, actually cared enough about our sport to film it and put it on TV. And it was the first time anyone other than my coaches and parents had taken an interest in my talent.

I was so excited the morning of the news shoot. Mama's parents, Maia and Papu, had recently arrived in the United States from Romania and were living with us at the time. We were all crammed into this little apartment, but for Mama it was a taste of familiarity and comfort, so it was nice to have them there even though we were practically on top of one another. Maia helped take care of my younger sister Christina and me while Tata pulled Mama in every direction insisting she go with him to car auctions throughout Southern Florida to help him bring cars back to his auto dealership in Tampa. Tata loved cars, and he had a knack for selling anything, so as a car salesman he worked long hours. He did what he had to in order to support us, and that "us" now included Mama's parents. I know he wasn't thrilled about having to support Maia and Papu on top of the four of us, as I'd overhear him complain to Mama.

It was nice to have Papu with us, too. He'd mostly linger in the background, in the living room or in the little bedroom he, Maia, and I shared, often singing Macedonian tunes with his deep, steady voice. He was balding and had little patches of white hair on the sides of his head. He was already eighty-five years old when he came to the States, so he never learned English, or Romanian, for that matter. A true Macedonian, he spoke only Macedonian. It's no wonder I couldn't understand what was being said in my house sometimes; I never knew exactly what language was being spoken because Maia, Papu, and my parents would mash up his and their languages in the same sentence, confusing me entirely!

Even though I never fully understood the words of Papu's songs, it always made me feel happy when I'd hear his rich voice. It was a tiny apartment, so I could hear him sing whether he was eating breakfast or bathing. I loved that he never cared what anyone thought about him and never bothered to ask whether any of us liked his singing.

On the "Channel 10 Day," I could hear Papu singing throughout the house as I was in my room trying to focus on one important thing: "What leotard am I going to wear for the news piece today?" If only such things remained my biggest dilemmas in life. I dug through my closet looking for the right leotard, throwing several maybes that I'd collected over the years onto my bed while the automatic rejects got tossed back into the closet in a pile. I was looking for my "lucky leo." Every gymnast has one. They also have their "bad luck leo," the leo they got hurt in and some vow to never wear again. A few more searches through my basket of clean clothes and finally, way down at the bottom, there it was, my pot of gold at the end of the rainbow: my black leo with big green leaves and pink, purple, and orange flowers—that was the one. It reminded me of the jungle, and I'd had lots of good workouts when I'd worn it. *My good luck charm*, I thought, and I pulled it on. I was ready!

Both Mama and Tata took me to the gym that day, which was rare. I remember sitting in the backseat quietly just watching the road unfold in front of us. I was a little on edge and getting more nervous as we got closer to LaFleur's. I wanted everything to go well. Tata was buzzing with an excited energy and talking nonstop about what an important day this was. He was wearing one of his special white button-up shirts, had his straight brown hair slicked back with gel into a mini-mullet, and his wiry mustache tightly combed. Mama, in typical fashion, was calm and quiet. She didn't like a fuss made over her and never wanted to be the center of attention, so it was no surprise when she declined to be interviewed by the news crew later that afternoon. Tata, on the other hand, was front and center, ready to go from the moment we stepped into the gym.

When we arrived, the camera crew and news reporter were already at the gym setting up. I tried to act normal and get ready for my warm-ups, but I was so excited and a little nervous because I didn't want to make a mistake in front of this new and very special audience. I especially didn't want to disappoint my coaches or Tata, and I wanted people to be impressed with what we were doing at LaFleur's.

My teammates, other coaches, and a handful of parents would stop by every so often to peek at the cameras and see what we were doing. I had butterflies fluttering in my stomach at first, but as the day went on, I became more relaxed and the butterflies disappeared. Generally speaking, I was a particularly shy little nine-year-old, but the gym could always draw me out of my shell. I truly loved being there and was always able to lose myself in the physicality of the sport. When I performed in the gym, the rest of the world just sort of blurred around me, and I felt at peace with myself.

Jerry Johnson, the local sports news anchor for Channel 10, covered the story and started the segment very generously:

"Right here in our Bay Area lives a little girl with even greater vision. You see, Dominique Moceanu is just nine years old, and that means she'll be just old enough for the 1996 Olympic Games in Atlanta. She's a gymnast with extraordinary talent and a dream that began even before she was born in the heart of her father amid the communism of Romania. . . . At the tender age of nine,

Dominique already has the look of a world-class gymnast. She has the poise. She has the determination."

The camera crew recorded all of my events that day—vault, bars, beam, and floor—and Jeff had me demonstrate all of my most difficult skills for each event.

On the vault, I did a Yurchenko tucked full, which is a round-off entry vault with backward motion into a block off the vaulting horse and into a flip backward in a tucked position with a 360-degree twist. It's an expected skill from an Elite senior-level gymnast, but was an advanced skill for my age, especially in the early 1990s. I was actually able to do this skill in a layout position onto a small eight-by-twelve-inch mat over the pit, which I did in practices with relative ease, but I felt most comfortable that day doing it tucked, and Jeff agreed.

As the cameras caught this vault on tape, I remember Tata front and center about halfway down the runway on the right side watching me with his arms crossed, beaming with pride. Tata had been working so much, he would only come to see me perform at the gym occasionally. Which was typically fine with me—I didn't like him there, hovering over me and watching and critiquing my every move. But on this special day I figured it was okay. In a way, it was his day, too, since he had orchestrated the whole event. I know Tata was full of pride and pleased to no end that people were taking an interest in *his* daughter. He held his chin high as he stood close to the vaulting horse and then on to the bars. Being able to please him in this way—to be the source of his pride—felt like a significant achievement in itself.

The news story wouldn't have been complete without an interview with Tata. Looking pleased to have the reporter and news camera's attention, he explained that he was a gymnast himself back in Romania. In the final news story, Tata's name appears in captions under his image, misspelled as "Dimetrius Moccano," instead of "Dimitry Moceanu." Tata was comfortable in front of the camera and his words, despite the thick accent, came easily:

"In the capital Bucharest, I practiced almost eleven years until I was in eleven grade in the high school. It was very important to me to be gymnast. I mean gymnast was my profession, was to be my career . . . but I cannot finish it because the government doesn't let me. I came to the United States in about '79 because of the regime in Romania, the communism. You know, it was very hard. I escape through the airport. I took a plane. I flew in Vien . . . Vienna. I stayed six months and then after, I came here. Everybody knows that United States is the best country in the world [w-oo-rhl-dh]."

Animated and emphatic, Tata was a charmer. He had the news reporter and crew laughing and hanging on his every word and sweeping hand gesture. He went on:

"I said to myself if I ever have a child, I like to be a gymnast. . . . My heart is jumping with every movement, every step she does on the floor, or beam or, you know, parallels."

At that point, the camera panned out with perfect timing to catch me doing a press handstand on the balance beam.

I was the focus of the piece, but my part was to perform my skills, leaving everyone else to comment. I did manage to squeak out a few sentences:

"I was little, three and a half when I started gymnastics. I've been doing it for six years. My goal is to reach the 1996 Olympics."

"How come?" Jerry asked.

"Because I wanna win a lot of medals," I said with a smile and shrug of my shoulders, "and be on TV a lot."

It almost seemed scripted, but it wasn't. Definitely not the words of the shy little girl I was outside those gym doors. I was feeling the moment and gaining more confidence with each word I spoke.

"It's absolutely realistic." Coach Jeff followed up, in support.

"When I look at Kim Zmeskal and Betty Okino and some of the kids that are in the top three of our country right now . . . [Dominique's] way ahead of where they were four years before the Olympics . . . she's milestones ahead of them and, so barring injury or, you know, unforeseen mishaps, she's got a tremendous shot at the Olympic team, and perhaps an Olympic medal."

Jeff, always focusing on developing the complete athlete, made sure my efforts outside the gym were acknowledged:

"She's extremely quick and a straight-A student . . . all three terms last year she had straight A's in conduct and achievement, so she's extremely bright intellectually, as well as extremely fast and strong and powerful, so she can grasp the concept and make it work."

I remember Tata being particularly proud, practically bursting with joy, when I did my triple back dismount off of the uneven bars. It was one of the highlights of the day and was emphasized on Al Keck's "Sportsline" segment on the Channel 10 evening news that night.

Tata, with his chin held high, would call it "The Triple" like it was this work of genius. With his dramatization and heavy accent it sounded more like "*Th-uh Tr-e-e-pole*." Indeed, for my age this was a gigantic skill well beyond my years of experience. As it turned out, I really was one of very few gymnasts in the world at the time who had even attempted this skill, much less at the young age of nine. In retrospect I am so grateful to Jeff for allowing me to excel in a rapid yet safe manner. He fed my talent by safely allowing me to do daring skills that I desperately wanted to try, but always was there to spot my every move and not let me do it on my own until I was truly ready. It was my favorite dismount, and I loved doing it partly because it was so unique.

On the day Channel 10 was there, Jeff decided it was safest to assist me by lightly spotting my triple dismount. Jeff didn't see the need to show off for the cameras by pushing me to do the dismount without a spotter and risk injury. He was a wise coach, and I respected and trusted him completely.

I stood at the chalk tray, powdering my hands after warming up on the bars. I tried to ignore the cameraman circling around trying to catch me from different angles. That part was all so new to me. It was hard not to look directly at the lens, and I did my best to pretend I didn't notice the camera. As I chalked up, I even winced once after catching myself staring straight into the camera. In future years, that news camera would become a constant companion and familiar presence as I traveled the world to compete at high-profile gymnastics meets. But for now, it was still a new distraction that I had to try to tune out as I prepared for my triple dismount.

I climbed the steps to reach the high bar that stood alone over a loose foam pit. As I stood on top of the wooden step, which Jeff would later use to spot me, I looked down at my chalked hands. Beneath the chalk, my hands were pretty beaten up. I was one of the few gymnasts who didn't wear grips on the bars. Grips—leather two-inch strips that support the middle of the palm with two holes for the second and third fingers, with a strap around the wrist for support—help gymnasts grip the bar better while offering some protection to the skin. Most US gymnasts wore grips at the time, while gymnasts from Europe and Asia rarely wore them. After lengthy practices on the bars, my hands were more torn up and callused than those of my teammates who used grips, but I didn't mind. I was comfortable not wearing them, and I figured it made me tough. I felt I had a better hold on the bar without a layer of material in my way. Later in my career I did learn to use grips, but as a young gymnast of Romanian descent, it seemed part of my birthright not to.

I rubbed my hands together and quickly glanced around the gym. Everything and everyone seemed so still, practically frozen with most eyes on me. I could see Mama peering out from the viewing balcony, Tata standing proud next to the bars, my teammates, coaches, a smattering of parents, the reporter Jerry Johnson, and his crew all waiting to see what I could do.

I took a deep breath and focused on doing the best triple dismount I possibly could. I grasped the bar, hung straight down, and moved my hands side by side to get to the middle of the high bar so I could land in the middle of the mat. I pulled myself over the bar and placed myself in a support position and waited for Jeff to climb up and spot me. Once he was ready to go, I casted to a handstand with my legs slightly apart and a little loose, but as soon as I reached my handstand position, my body remained tight and straight. I wound up with two giant swings over the dismount bar, gaining tremendous speed and making sure my legs stayed glued together. As my legs reached above the bar on my final swing, I released the bar underneath. I didn't have to think, I just floated through the air. I did what naturally felt easy to me—I flipped: three consecutive flips in a tucked position with my legs at 45 degrees and slightly separated. I landed soundly on the soft twelve-inch mat. I remember Jeff jumping off the spotting table and being there for me throughout my triple, with his hand lightly tapping my back for reassurance and safety. By the time I completed the three flips, Jeff was to my left on the mat and watched me roll out of the dismount with room to spare. I did it with such ease.

It still amazes me today that I went for such a challenging skill while the cameras were rolling. I can understand now why Tata was so proud. I relished being one of the few gymnasts in the world who could perform a particular skill at that age. I liked that. It made my desire and fire burn harder to be the best. It also served to heighten my competitive spirit while making the world seem so much smaller—knowing that only a handful of others anywhere else in the world could even attempt what I could do. And sure enough, beating the rest of the world became a part of Tata's mantra from that day forward. I can still hear my father's voice in my head saying, "You *have* to be the best!" With his broken English it sounded more like "Y-o-o h-ah-v t-o-o b-he d-uh b-eh-s-t!" And he'd give two fist pumps, as if pumping confidence into both of us. Sometimes it would make me laugh out loud, and Tata would stop and say, "What? It's true, you have to believe!" Although I would act like his exaggerated mannerisms were over the top, I knew deep down he was right. I did have to believe in myself and in the possibility of going to the Olympics one day, and perhaps even winning a medal—maybe even a gold!

The Channel 10 segment closed with a Jerry Johnson comment:

"Dominique Moceanu, very, very talented and only nine years old, headed for the 1996 Olympics Games in Atlanta, no doubt. There are senior Elite-level gymnasts all over the world who cannot do a triple, and that's a triple somersault on the dismount from the uneven parallel bars, and Dominique *M-ahr-cee-ah-no* can do one."

I still value that first news story and never underestimate what it did for my career. I'm thankful for the memories and footage, and thankful, in particular, to Tata for making it happen. I already knew I loved the sport of gymnastics, but something unspoken, some new level of belief in myself, just clicked that day. I realized that beyond loving my sport, I *thrived* on performing gymnastics, especially under pressure. I relished the aspect of others taking notice of my hard work. *This is awesome!* I thought. In my mind, I was no longer the small, skinny, awkward European kid; I was a 1996 Olympic hopeful! A fire had been lit under me. I knew I wanted to be an Olympic champion.

Chapter 4

THE LETTER

December 2007

Hi Dominique,
My name is Jennifer Bricker. I'm not sure whether or not you have read the papers I sent you, but if you have, let me explain what they are all about. I've known my whole life that I was adopted and that my heritage was Romanian. Ever since I was about six years old, I've been obsessed with gymnastics and I always watched you on TV. In fact, you were kind of my inspiration to start competing myself! Anyway, right before I turned sixteen, I was asking my mom if

there was anything she had not told me about my adoption, and I was expecting her to say "no" because they (my parents) never kept any secrets from me, but she said "yes." There was something she had not told me yet. She said that I would never believe her, so she told me that my biological last name was "Moceanu" and proceeded to show me the papers I sent you.

I almost could not believe it myself. You had been my idol my whole life, and you turned out to be my sister! I was in extreme disbelief, and my immediate thought was that I wanted to meet you and let you know! So my whole family had known for quite a while, but they had to wait until I was older for a lot of different reasons to tell me, which was the right thing to do.

My uncle is a retired private investigator, and he got in contact with Dumitru, your father. He talked to your father, and he did not deny that I was their biological child, but he would not return my uncle's phone calls after that. So we stopped trying to contact you for a while because I did not want to seem pushy and I wanted to do this right. I feel that I have one chance to show you and prove to you that I'm not some crazy person, but I'm sure after seeing all of the papers, you'll see that I'm serious. I've been a member of your website almost since the day I found out. I saw pictures of Christina, and you would not believe how much we look alike, it's so crazy. The first time I saw a picture of her I got chills; my friends and family thought it was me on the computer!

I realize this must be a lot for you to take in right now, I mean, it is a lot for me too, but I've had a lot of years to soak it all in. I've been trying ever since I was sixteen (I'm now twenty) to think of the right way to get in contact with you. I thought about it almost every day. I would see different things on your website and see pictures of you and Christina and think, I wonder if they even know about me? I really hope we can get in contact; I would love that more than anything in the world!!

If you still for some reason do not believe me and the papers,

I would even take a DNA test if you wanted, just to prove it. I'm up for anything; I just have already lost all of these years without ever meeting or knowing my two sisters. If you want to call me my number is [redacted]. *Please do not hesitate to call, I would really LOVE to hear from you, and I hope all is well!!*

Jennifer

I lost count of the number of times I read Jennifer's letter. I'd see her bubbly cursive writing on the envelope when I closed my eyes at night, and I could practically recite the letter from memory. When I first sifted through her package in the parking lot of the post office, I remember looking outside the tinted windows of my SUV to see if there was anything suspicious—a clue perhaps to make sense of everything. As silly as it sounds, I was halfway expecting Ashton Kutcher to jump out and say I'd been "punk'd!" Of course, that didn't happen, but it seemed more likely at the time than what I was actually reading.

As brave and tough as I thought I was, I couldn't bring myself to pick up the phone and dial Jennifer's number. I was numb. I needed time to talk it over with my husband and Christina, and I most definitely needed face time with Mama and Tata so I could get the real story. I needed answers. Why had they kept this from me? How could I not know? I had questions swirling through my head so quickly, I couldn't finish one thought before the next question jumped in. Here I was, finally enjoying the most "normal" stage of my life so far—happily married, inches from my college degree, and about to give birth to my first child. I didn't want to cause Jennifer further pain by making her wait and wonder, but I needed time to digest this craziness. I was gaining a daughter and a sister all in a matter of weeks.

For my daughter, Carmen, I was prepared. I had been counting the days since I got pregnant and could hardly wait to meet her. Mentally and emotionally, I had never been more prepared for anything. I had read every pregnancy and parenting book I could get my hands on, took my prenatal vitamins religiously, exercised, drank my daily water, and carefully monitored every stage of my pregnancy. I even wore compression stockings to limit swelling in my legs and feet. Every last detail of the nursery was complete and perfect, ready and waiting for Carmen's arrival. The new cherry-wood crib, dresser, and changing table had been carefully placed, then moved and moved again until they were just right. We painted the walls a pretty light blue that reminded us of a cloudless sky on a warm summer day. Tiny onesies, newborn diapers, wipes, diaper cream, blankets, and baby books filled every corner of the room. We were ready.

But Jennifer, I wasn't ready for her at all. To say I felt blind-sided would be an understatement. On the one hand, one of my childhood dreams had finally come true. I had always fantasized about having a big family when I was younger. I figured having siblings who shared the same family, DNA, and lifestyle as me would be a godsend and would fill some of my loneliness, especially when it was just Mama, Tata, and me. After years of praying and begging, I was blessed with my sister, Christina, who was born August 24, 1989, one month before I turned eight years old. Oh, how I had wished for her, and she was the best birthday present ever. I couldn't believe I had a sister, and I treasured her from the day she was born. Christina was my everything, and I was so happy to have her. She actually kick-started my desire for an even bigger family. I knew it was a bit greedy asking Mama for yet another sister, but Christina was so lovable with her big brown eyes and warm smile that I wanted more Christinas. I thought there was hope, but nothing ever happened. Years later, Mama confessed to me that she didn't want any more children with Tata. *She didn't want any more children with Tata.* Her words hit me like a ton of bricks. She longed for more children and would have been in her glory with an entire houseful, but "not with Tata." Not with Tata's violent temper and unpredictable mood swings. His hot temper made raising a family very challenging, oftentimes unbearable, and it eventually drove a wedge between them. It saddened me to see Mama grow more distant from Tata throughout my childhood.

It felt like hours before I could pull myself together enough to start my car and leave the parking lot after reading through Jennifer's package. I kept glancing down at the papers and photos piled on my lap and the passenger seat as I drove toward home. I just couldn't get my head around the fact that since 1987, I'd had a biological sister in this world and I had absolutely no clue. I tried to do the math, backtracking nine months from Jennifer's birth to get a picture of what was happening in our family, in my life, at that time. It just wasn't adding up. Jennifer was born October 1, 1987, exactly six years and one day after I was born. All that time I was wishing for a sibling before Christina was born, I already had one! Mama delivered Jennifer the day after my sixth birthday. How could I not even remember Mama being pregnant? I was going in circles trying to retrace that period from five to six years old. I was always with Mama, hugging and snuggling with her. How could I not realize she was pregnant? I had spent endless hours at the gym, but Mama was there, too. Could I have been so focused on my own life that I missed something this big? Mama has always been petite, and I know she was quite small during her pregnancy with me, gaining only twenty pounds, but she must have been particularly small and hardly showing at all with Jennifer for me not to see or feel the change in her belly. Carmen kicked and repositioned herself as I pulled into the driveway of our home. The irony was overwhelming.

I made my way up the walkway and through our front door, which seemed to be growing narrower by the day, and plopped down at the kitchen table to sift through the papers and photos yet again. I thought about how Tata always made sure I was kept from "adult talks" when I was younger. Both he and Mama believed children should be children and didn't feel it was necessary for me to know too much, leaving me in the dark on many topics. Gymnastics kept my focus after school, and since I never hung out with the "cool" crowd at school, I was never privy to playground tales about the birds and the bees. I was so sheltered and naïve that I didn't even know where babies came from until many years later as a high schooler. I'm sure I was completely out of earshot any time they discussed Mama's pregnancy, especially after she delivered Jennifer. Also, my parents had continuous financial and marital troubles, so oftentimes I simply tuned out, just trying to stay out of the way. Perhaps I simply wasn't present enough to notice Mama was expecting.

I sat in the kitchen, looking around the house, taking stock of how things had changed since I walked out my front door that morning. My dog and longtime companion Princess danced at my feet trying to get my attention. She sensed something was different and finally jumped on me and crumpled the papers on my lap to reach my face. I stroked her, but my mind was a million miles away. Here I was on the verge of motherhood, supposedly one of the most fulfilling and miraculous experiences of my life, and I was completely turned inside out. I had already been on emotional overload trying my hardest to keep my pregnancy hormones in check and eke out a solid ending to my semester before going into labor. Now, nothing felt normal, and I had a nagging feeling that nothing would until I reached out to Jennifer. She had just put her heart in a package and shipped it off to a complete stranger. I knew she'd want to hear from me, but was she expecting me to just pick up the phone and call her *today*? It was probably the decent thing to do since she had already been waiting four years, but I hadn't even had four hours, and I just wasn't there yet. She sounded so grounded and at peace in her letter, yet I couldn't help wondering if she was actually angry or harboring some deep resentment toward me—Mama and Tata didn't give *me* away, after all. *I* was angry and resentful already; why wouldn't she be? There were so many layers to this story, I didn't know where to start or how. My own hurt and anger kept me from picking up the phone that afternoon. I wasn't ready to hear her voice and have no place to hide if I couldn't answer her questions.

I decided on a letter—a happy medium of sorts. I'd be reaching out to let Jennifer know that I received her package, but I'd maintain a bit of space, a buffer, so I didn't have to bare my soul completely just yet. The letter got my message across loud and clear: I believe you, Jennifer. I also told her that I looked forward to talking with her, but it would have to wait. For now, my obligation was a healthy delivery for Carmen. Along with the letter, I sent a bouquet of flowers.

A sense of relief washed over me once I mailed the letter. It was much more difficult to write than I'd expected. I was an emotional mess and could barely see the computer screen through my tears. I was confused and angry. I couldn't process the deep hurt I felt that Mama and Tata had kept this secret for twenty years. It took all of my strength to stop my tears for any length of time. I found myself crying most of the day, every day, for the following weeks. I literally had to will myself to school to complete my final exams. I remember looking around thinking how none of my classmates or professors had the slightest clue what was happening in my life, and I wondered if they were going through difficult times in their own lives. So strange how you can feel like you know people, yet so much remains hidden. We talked, exchanged pleasantries, and discussed the course material, but I never let them in on my little secret and I never learned any of theirs. I'd wondered how my few good girlfriends in my classes would have reacted had I shared my story, but it wouldn't have been fair to distract them with my own family drama right before their final exams anyway.

I'll never forget my husband Mike's face when he walked through the door after work and saw the photos of Jennifer for the first time. He did one of those double takes you see in the silent movies. He looked as shocked as I've ever seen him. Mike has seen and heard his share of interesting stories and, as a surgeon, has met people from all walks of life, so he takes most things in stride and is not shocked by much. The photos, more than anything else, threw him for a loop. I practically gasped on the phone earlier that day when I tried to describe how Jennifer looked spookishly like my younger sister Christina. Jennifer and I definitely have a very strong resemblance, but she and Christina looked almost like twins. Like Christina and myself, Jennifer strongly resembled Tata's side of the family, but after a closer look, I realized that Jennifer looked more like my father than any of us—it was unreal. It was difficult to get my head around the fact that someone else in this universe could look so much like us. The round face, straight dark hair, big brown eyes, pronounced chin—she was 100 percent Moceanu.

With final exams over and my official to-do list almost clear, the plan was to rest and wait for Carmen's arrival. It proved valuable space for me to regroup. I couldn't help obsessing about how difficult it must have been for my parents when Jennifer was born. Rubbing my belly and feeling the warmth of Carmen inside me, I felt sadness and even pity for Mama and Tata, feeling they had no choice but to give away their own flesh and blood. I could almost understand that that time was just too painful, so they coped by pretending it never happened.

Christmas Eve 2007, I lay in bed with my eyes wide open while the house slept soundly: Christina on the couch, Mike's parents in our guest bedroom, and Mike beside me. We were all gathered to celebrate the holidays and await Carmen's birth. I had a hunch that my little miracle was going to be a Christmas baby, and the sporadic contractions I'd had over the prior two days fueled my certainty. As I tossed from side to side trying to find a comfortable spot, there it was. A strong contraction followed by another and another. I just lay there, listening to my body. I wanted to make sure it was the real deal and dreaded the thought of being that first-time mom who rushes to the hospital only to be sent home with "false labor." My overnight bag was packed and I was ready to go, but I had to be *sure* it was the right time. When a contraction would start, I'd freeze and wait out the pain in silence, counting the seconds until it started to fade. I stayed calm between contractions, which is typical of how I've always dealt with physical pain in the gym or anywhere else. I go inward and just try to work through it myself. I didn't want to disrupt anyone's sleep until it was absolutely necessary, so I tried hard not to make any noise at all.

By the time the contractions were coming every five minutes or so, I was doubled over in pain in our bed. Mike was trying to comfort me and waited calmly for me to give the signal that I was ready to get into the car to go to the hospital. He granted my wish for one last call to the doctor to make sure this was really it, then he, Christina, and I were off, driving through Cleveland's early-morning darkness on Christmas Day. I remember seeing the patches of snow on the road outside the window between contractions.

It gave me the extra strength I needed to have Mike and Christina beside me for the delivery, and I was grateful to share the beautiful moments of Carmen's birth with them. Mike has been my partner, my motivator, and the most loving and supportive husband I could have asked for, and he didn't disappoint when I needed him most that day.

My sweet sister Christina was almost silent during the entire labor and delivery. I am pretty certain it scared her to death. Her eyes were wide, mouth agape, and she said she'd "never seen anything like it." I really don't think she knew what to expect next, but she stayed by my side the entire time, holding my hand, and even my leg, when I needed her. I fed off of her love and encouragement.

Carmen made her debut on December 25, 2007, around 3:06 p.m. After the final push, a silence gripped the room, which made me nervous. I realized I hadn't heard her cry. Mike rubbed my arm and said everything was okay, but it was in his doctor voice, which made me worry more. I could see my doctor looking and assessing the situation, and I held my breath until I finally saw a smile spread across her face. Only later did I learn that Carmen had the umbilical cord wrapped around her neck and there was some concern, but it was fleeting. I was so relieved once I heard her cry a minute later. It was the sweetest sound I'd ever heard.

We were blessed with this little miracle. She truly was a marvel. I was in awe and felt so fortunate, so happy. She was the most beautiful and precious being I'd ever seen—with a full head of jet-black hair, dark brown eyes, and a cherub round face with Mike's Filipino button nose. I was at such peace holding her in my arms tightly swaddled with her pink-and-blue-striped hospital beanie on her head. I kissed her and held her to my chest. It was the absolute best feeling in the world.

It was January 14, 2008, a good five weeks after I had received Jennifer's package, when I finally picked up the phone to call her. My stomach was a bundle of nerves, but I sat at the desk in my office and promised myself that I wouldn't get up until I had completed my mission. It was around 9:00 a.m. and Carmen was down for her morning nap, so I knew I had to take advantage of the quiet while it lasted. I took one last sip from my coffee mug, drew a deep breath, and dialed. Once the line started to ring on the other end, I felt less nervous and actually got more excited with each ring, wondering why she was taking so long to answer.

"Hello?" Her voice was raspy.

"Hi, Jennifer. This is Dominique. How are you?"

She seemed a bit startled, clearly not expecting a call from me or apparently from anyone else at that time in the morning. I glanced at the clock quickly to make sure I wasn't calling obnoxiously early. *Nine a.m. That's decent*, I thought. I had been on "mom time" for the past three weeks, which meant I ran on a twenty-four-hour clock dictated by my little Carmen. To me, 9:00 a.m. wasn't much different than two in the afternoon or two in the morning, so I made a habit of checking the clock before calling or texting family or friends on a whim.

"Oh, hi," she said after a pause.

"Christina and I had the biggest shock of our lives. Our parents never told us about you. I definitely have a lot of questions myself," I said matter-of-factly.

Silence.

"I want to thank you for going about this the way you did, Jennifer. I respect you so much for that."

"I didn't know what else to do, but I knew I had one shot to show you that I was for real," she jumped in.

"There was no question in my mind from the photos that it was for real. My mouth just dropped when I saw my mother's handwriting and then my father's signature on those legal documents you sent with your letter. I just about dropped the papers from my hands. I was totally overwhelmed with emotion when I read everything, but I really do appreciate the way you went about it—there was no question in my mind that this was true."

I had little sticky notes spread across my desk reminding me of things I wanted to ask or tell Jennifer. I figured they'd provide some backup help if I got nervous or if there were awkward silences. Mike added his extra support by poking his head into the office every few minutes while keeping an ear out for Carmen. What do I say to the sister I have never met before?

Turns out Jennifer and I had plenty to say to each other, and I really didn't need my sticky notes at all. Our conversation seemed to open up and flow quite easily and pretty soon we were chatting away. I felt like I was talking one hundred miles a minute. We both had so much to say, and I remember both of us saying, "This is so crazy" several times. It was just so bizarre. The entire situation felt like a strange dream that was still hard to wrap my head around, even as I was talking with her.

"Talking to you is something I've been dying for since I found out that we were sisters," she said. "When I got your letter saying that you believed me, I almost passed out. I had no idea how you were going to react, but I knew I had to write to you. I figured the truth was something you should know if you hadn't already been told."

I made a point to reiterate to Jennifer that I really didn't know about her prior to receiving the package. I didn't want her to think, even for one second, that I had known about her all these years and had simply chosen not to contact her. She said she had a feeling that was the case but had always wondered.

"I have had real dreams about meeting you, and in them you reacted horribly, and I was so worried. I didn't know how you'd react—if you'd be accepting or not," she said.

I had Jennifer on speakerphone with the volume set to max so I could really hear her voice and not miss anything. I was so immersed in our talk that I hadn't noticed that Mike had grabbed our video camera and was filming the conversation. I shot him a serious look and gestured to stop, but he ignored me and kept filming. I am thankful now that I have parts of our first conversation recorded. There was so much said between us that I could barely remember half of it after I hung up. That's my husband, thinking ten steps ahead as always. He knew that one day we would all want to look back on this moment—and he was right.

"This has been very difficult and emotional for my family also," Jennifer said. "I mean, they've known since I was very little that *you* were my sister, but they never told me until much later, when I was older, which was the right thing to do."

"You're lucky that your parents were honest with you," I said. "That's the best gift they could've given you—their honesty. I was very upset with my mother and father for not being open with me and my sister. It came as a complete shock when we found out."

"This October will be five years that I've known about you, but it's still surreal for me, too," she said. "Ever since I was a little girl, I was always hooked on you. I don't know why. I loved gymnastics and I knew that we were both Romanian, and you know, your birthday is the day before mine."

"Yeah, I saw that on the court documents. So, you are going to be twenty-one this October. Wow! Maybe soon we can start making up for lost time somehow. I look forward to meeting you," I said and meant it, but inside I knew I was not ready to meet. That would have to be down the road a bit.

"By the way," Jennifer blurted out, "you know I have no legs, right?"

Excuse me, did I hear correctly? I thought to myself. I remembered how Mike sometimes pokes fun at my bad hearing—probably a result of listening to blaring music in my teenage years.

"What? What did you say?" I asked.

"I was born without legs. You didn't know?" she asked.

Hearing it from her hit me like a ton of bricks, and I immediately welled up but tried my hardest not to let her know I was crying.

"Well . . ." I searched for the right words, but I'm not sure what the right words would even sound like. "Well, my dad did say something about it, but I thought his memory might've been a little fuzzy or that he was exaggerating . . . I guess not." I realized as soon as the words left my mouth that they sounded really bad. Definitely not the right words.

I tried hard to remember exactly what Tata had said about the birth. I do remember him saying that they wouldn't be able to afford to take care of the baby because she was born with "no legs." I certainly didn't take him literally. It's the way Tata talked when he wanted to emphasize something. He had a way of twisting things to fit his purpose, so I never really knew what was true and what was exaggerated. I guess I interpreted Tata's version of "no legs" to mean that Jennifer was born with a minor disability or other health issue. Besides, in her letter, Jennifer had said she did gymnastics and volleyball, and I never in my wildest dreams pictured her doing those sports without legs.

Things got so crazy after Carmen's birth that I still hadn't had the opportunity for a true family summit on Jennifer. Christina and I had talked about it for hours on our own, but my face time with Mama and Tata was limited to their visits after Carmen's birth. They were glowing as first-time grandparents, and it never seemed like the right time to bring up those painful memories and a part of their past that they had kept deeply hidden for twenty years.

Now, sitting here talking to Jennifer, I was kicking myself for not getting better answers when I drilled Tata and Mama immediately after I received Jennifer's package. Maybe I was in denial and really didn't want to know everything yet. Perhaps I just couldn't process all of that information at once—a sister I never knew of *and*, by the way, she has no legs.

"People forget about me having no legs within minutes of meeting me," she said.

I was fascinated with this girl. She had so much confidence and positive energy. I was drawn to her and wanted to know her.

"I think it was just a hard time for my parents in their lives," I said, realizing that I sounded almost silly defending Mama and

Tata. But I couldn't stop. I explained that they were poor immigrants who came to this country with very little in their pockets and struggled for a long, long time. I remembered Tata saying that they didn't have any money or insurance, and that's why they went all the way to Salem Hospital for the delivery.

"Supposedly, there was a Romanian doctor at Salem Hospital who told my parents that they wouldn't be able to afford the medical care you needed. I believe my parents wanted to give you a better life. That's how everything happened," I said, almost cringing at how matter-of-fact I make it sound.

I added, "I hope you had a good childhood."

Taken out of context, my comment may sound trite, but it was, in fact, one of the most sincere moments of our discussion. Christina and I didn't have a good childhood in many respects. We lived in fear of Tata's wrath much of our youth, and I was hoping that Jennifer was adopted into a loving family and that her childhood was better than ours. I breathed a sigh of relief when I heard Jennifer talk about her "great" childhood.

"Oh yeah, I did," she said without hesitation. "I am very fortunate. I could've been somewhere horrible, but it was pretty much a miracle. My parents called in specifically for me at the right time. I was adopted at three months old, but it was official at one year. The social worker said she'd never seen a couple call in for a specific child and get her in such a short time."

Jennifer went on to say that her parents never treated her like she was adopted and certainly never treated her like she was disabled. They taught her that she could do anything. She said they raised her "well" and that she had a great childhood, and I could tell she genuinely meant it.

"We missed out on a lot of years of our lives together," I said. "My sister Christina and I have a special bond and are so close. To know that I had another sister that I could've been an older sister to years ago, that would've been very nice, but now it's not too late.

We still have the rest of our lives to get to know each other and to build that relationship. I am glad that we still have time to make it right . . . that's the positive part."

"Definitely, I agree, I mean we're all still so young," she said. Her positivity was contagious, and I couldn't help but smile.

With that, Jennifer said she had to get ready for work but looked forward to talking again soon. I glanced at the clock and was surprised to see that we'd been talking for an hour. I had to laugh at myself for being so nervous to call in the first place—that was, hands down, the fastest one-hour phone call I'd ever had. Jennifer was warm, outgoing, and friendly, and certainly very easy to talk to even under the circumstances. And, when I asked where she worked, her reply somehow didn't surprise me at all.

"Disney World," she said.

The happiest place on earth, I said to myself.

Chapter 5

TINY DANCER

Never could I have been prepared for what I was about to go through when I moved to Houston to begin training with Bela and Marta Karolyi at the age of ten.

In Tampa, LaFleur's gym had been a haven—my home away from home. I loved it there. Loved the atmosphere, my fellow athletes, the gym friends and extended family I'd made, and most of all, I loved my coaches. Jeff LaFleur was the first coach, and really the first person outside of my family, who had believed in me. He told me that I could achieve great things in gymnastics. For an eight-year-old giving it all she's got, that goes a long, long way. I was excelling as an athlete, and my confidence both in and out of the gym was higher than ever during my training with Jeff. It was one of the happiest times of my childhood, the first time I was comfortable in my own skin. I felt strong, ready for anything.

The move to Texas happened so quickly. In the spring of my third-grade year, my parents announced that I was going to Houston to be evaluated by Bela and Marta Karolyi, and if they accepted me as one of their gymnasts, our entire family would move to Texas for my training.

Apparently, Tata had contacted Bela Karolyi a few years prior, when I was very little, around five years old. In typical Tata fashion, he told Bela how talented I was and that one day I'd be a great Olympian. Bela was a world-famous coach and no doubt had received many, many calls from parents just like Tata.

"She's too young right now. Let her get some training in and bring her for an evaluation when she's nine or ten," Tata remembered Bela saying.

Not surprisingly, Tata followed through and called Bela from Tampa when I was nine years old to tell him I was "ready" to be evaluated, and that was that.

I wasn't involved in any decision making in our family, and it was no different with my gymnastics. Mama and Tata took care of all of the planning, phone calls, and arrangements. I didn't know anything about Texas except that it was far away from Tampa and LaFleur's gym. As far as the Karolyis, I only knew what I saw on television—the big teddy-bear-looking man with dark brown hair with hints of gray and a thick mustache who gave big bear hugs to his gymnasts after they nailed a performance. I remember feeling a sense of familiarity and comfort when I heard his thick Romanian accent during his interviews. His wife, Marta, had very tanned skin and a stern pout, and I remember noticing that she always stood straight and tall, with her chin pushed up in the air. She had short dark brown hair with blondish frosty tips. She never really smiled and actually looked a bit scary to me, even through the television. I remember thinking Bela would be the nicer of the two.

I was glued to the TV whenever gymnastics was on, and I'd watch the Karolyis interact with their gymnasts, especially when an athlete came off the floor after a performance. I knew exactly how it felt finishing an event and walking to my coach to either celebrate or be comforted if I hadn't done as well as expected. It *looked* like the Karolyis cared about their gymnasts; they'd give them a hug or pat. As a viewer, I, like most, was clueless as to what actually happened behind closed doors of the Karolyi gym.

Mama and Tata made their first trip to Houston in May 1991, leaving Christina and me at home in Florida with Maia and Papu. They wanted to get a feel for Houston, scout out the location of the gym, talk to Marta and Bela in person, and possibly look at potential neighborhoods to live. It still seemed unreal to me, and I didn't think we would actually leave Tampa.

When they returned from Houston, Mama and Tata laid out the plan: if all went well, trip number two to Houston would be my audition with the Karolyis, and trip number three would be our family's official move to Texas. We didn't have money for plane tickets, so each of these journeys would be by car—a whopping 1,500 miles round trip from Tampa to Houston.

Before trip number two a few weeks later, Mama and Tata met with Jeff LaFleur to deliver our good news, which was bad news for him. Tata told him the decision had been made; I was leaving LaFleur's to go train for the Olympics with the Karolyis in Houston. Tata had our plan mapped out and said we owed it to Jeff to be up front from the start. I was confused but afraid to ask too many questions. I hadn't even met the Karolyis yet, much less been evaluated by them, so, at the time, I couldn't figure out why my parents were already planning our move to Houston. What if the Karolyis didn't think I was good enough to train with them? In hindsight, I realize that alongside my hard work, it was my parents' unwavering confidence in me, year after year, that propelled my success and allowed me to reach my goals. It's a trait that I see in myself as a parent today—believing in my children and supporting their efforts 100 percent in whatever they do is one of the greatest gifts I can provide. My parents believed I was good enough to train with the best at the Karolyis' gym, so that's where they were taking me.

During our last few months in Tampa, Mama had found a part-time job as a cashier in a small cafeteria. She tells a story of when she told a coworker that she was planning to move to Houston to support her daughter to train for the Olympics. The woman literally laughed in Mama's face and said Mama was crazy to pick up her entire life and move the family just for a daughter's pipe dream. The woman did have a valid point. I mean, how many child athletes actually make it? The slots are very few. The woman wished Mama good luck but warned her, "It's not going to happen." Mama felt embarrassed and kept to herself after that incident, feeling ashamed that this woman laughed at her. Nonetheless, it didn't make Mama doubt the decision to move to Houston in the least. I'm eternally thankful to them for their complete support.

"He was very saddened by the news," Mama told me after the meeting with Jeff. "I could see it in his eyes, but he was a gentleman about it and was very kind to us. He was not mad at us. He understood our reasons. He has good character and has always been very kind to us."

I wasn't at the meeting with Jeff, but I can only imagine that the news must have felt like a dagger through his heart. I felt some of that dagger in my own heart. Jeff had taught me almost everything I knew, and we had built such a special coach-athlete relationship. We were close, and I depended on Jeff for so much. He told my parents he'd really enjoyed working with me and was very sad to see me go. It was startling to me that things could change so quickly, that one day I was picturing myself going to the Olympics with Jeff, and next I was in a new gym with new coaches and new teammates.

In my parents' minds, Bela and Marta had the experience and power to bring their young American gymnasts to the Olympics—they had a history of doing so, and this is why they assumed it would be the best place for me to train. At the time, it was *the* place Elite gymnasts of my generation strived to learn if they dreamed of making it to the Olympics—that is, *if* they could get accepted into the gym and *if* they could survive the training.

It was the summer of 1991 when Mama, Tata, and I piled into our van for trip number two to Houston to see if I was "promising" enough and had the makings of a future Olympian in the eyes of the Karolyis. I was nervous, excited, and still pretty confused. I'd never been to an audition or evaluation of any kind and didn't really know what to expect. I kept asking Mama and Tata what I'd be doing at the audition and hung on every word. Tata described it as a day of training with the highest level in the gym—the Senior Elite gymnasts (those training for a shot at the 1992 Olympic games). The Karolyis would probably watch me and assess my skills, Tata surmised, then they would decide which training group I would be placed in. I could certainly handle that, I thought, and felt a wave of relief as I stared out the car window at the houses and buildings and broken-down cars on the side of the highway. I pictured myself wowing the Karolyis with a big smile on my face.

When we arrived at the Karolyi gym midday, I couldn't wait to get inside. Had I blinked when we pulled into the gym parking lot, I never would have known that we'd arrived. A lone sign reading "Karolyi's Gymnastics" in black letters hung to the left of a long, old warehouse. It didn't look like a gym at all; the sign was the only indication that we were in the right place.

The front door was glass, similar to my old gym, but once I stepped inside, everything was different. The lobby was deserted and all the lights were off, which felt odd to me because at La-Fleur's there was always some combination of gymnasts, family members, or staff in the common areas. Here, the air felt cold and untouched—definitely not the warm, fuzzy atmosphere I was used to. The only light came from an office off to the right. Looking through a viewing window in the lobby, I could see that the main gymnasium was also empty and dark, so I figured everyone was either on their lunch break or at home resting from morning practice. Mama and Tata headed toward the office with the light, but I stayed behind trying to get a closer look at the gym through the darkness. I was dying to see the legendary spot where Olympians trained.

I saw Marta Karolyi walk out of the lighted office, so I quickly ran to catch up to my parents. We followed Marta into her office, where we exchanged brief hellos and were immediately joined by Bela Karolyi. Marta, in black tights and a "Karolyi's Gymnastics" T-shirt with a sweater draped over her shoulders, looked just like I had remembered from television—short, dark hair with blond frosted tips and very, very tanned. Bela, standing beside me, was even bigger than he had appeared on television, and I had to tilt my head all the way back to see his face as he stood in front of me.

Marta looked directly into my eyes.

"Hi, Dominique, how you doing? You ready for workout?" She spoke with a thick Romanian accent. I nodded and smiled.

Bela looked down at me, then gave me a big, welcoming bear hug. I disappeared into his arms. I remember smelling his cologne—a strong European scent that smelled familiar but I couldn't quite place.

"Hello, Dominique. You ready to show us what you can do? All right, then!" He patted my head and turned to talk to my parents, explaining to them, in Romanian, that they should bring me for the "evaluation" workout the next morning at seven sharp.

We arrived early at the gym that next morning. I was able to get situated and tuck my athletic bag into one of the empty cubbies in the Elite's locker room before the other gymnasts arrived. I sat there, taking in my surroundings and waiting for practice to begin. The other gymnasts started to trickle into the surprisingly tiny locker room as it drew closer to seven. They were milling around, exchanging hellos and doing final prep for training. The girls seemed pretty friendly, but it was hard for me to focus on small talk when I was anxious for my evaluation. I didn't say much. The last few minutes seemed like an eternity, sitting there waiting for the clock to hit seven before stepping out of the locker room and onto the floor.

On the hour, and not a second past, I followed the older gymnasts out the locker room door and onto the floor in a single-file line, tallest to smallest. We lined up on the floor exercise mat for the morning running. Almost as soon as I stepped onto the gym floor, the coaches and staff placed me with the "1992 hopeful" group—meaning, I was a hopeful for the 1996 Olympics. That I was working out with this *Elite* group of gymnasts made me smile on the inside. I figured my prospects looked good to be taken under the Karolyis' wing.

The Senior Elite "1992 hopefuls" included Kim Zmeskal, Betty Okino, Hilary Grivich, and Kerri Strug, with Jennie Thompson and me as the "1996 hopefuls." I was still pretty nervous and knew I looked a bit lost next to the other gymnasts in my cluster who already knew the drill and exactly what to expect. I could tell that most of the girls knew one another well, especially Betty, Kim, Kerri, and Hilary, who chatted during our free moments. Jennie was the only one who appeared a bit unsure, like me, and I wanted to talk with her, but I didn't get the chance. The girls were welcoming and kind to me, but I was definitely the newbie, the outsider—something I hadn't felt inside a gym for a very long time.

I was tagging along, following our leader, Kim. I was at the end of the line bouncing nonstop like a little kangaroo and trying to keep up with the extensive running drills, which were difficult for me. I was nervous to let them see me huffing and puffing. I had a growing side cramp that was killing me, but I kept my mouth shut and just kept breathing like everyone else. We ran backward, forward, kicked our knees up as high as they would go, jumped from side to side with legs together, and I tried to give every move my best effort.

I wanted to impress Bela. I'd never done this kind of running for such a long period before, so I tried my best to keep up even though every now and then I'd fall behind slightly. Bela didn't say much to me during the evaluation. He mostly watched both me and Jennie Thompson closely, while barking orders in his deep voice at the group in general. He definitely was serious in the gym, not at all a teddy bear, and that frightened me somewhat because he seemed completely different from the man who gave me the bear hug the day before. I just did my best to follow the other girls like a good little soldier, looking to please and get praise from Bela, so my parents would be proud of me.

After the running and sprinting sessions, which lasted about forty-five minutes, we moved on to conditioning, which lasted another forty-five minutes. All I could think was *When is this going to be over?* The cramp in my side was still aching, and now my legs were starting to cramp and grow tired as well, but I didn't want to let it show on my face that I was struggling. I was terrified of looking bad, so I kept pushing myself to keep up with the older, more experienced girls. I reached deep and, fortunately, my competitive streak carried me through the rest of the conditioning session. I was 100 percent determined to give a solid impression, as if my life depended on it.

I had been looking forward to doing the uneven bars and was happy when Bela finally signaled that we were moving on to that apparatus. I was worried that I was already a bit worn down from all the running, conditioning, floor drills, and vault before I even had a chance to show Bela what I could do on bars.

I remember prepping for bars during the few minutes after the vaulting session—thinking over and over in my mind which dismount I should demonstrate. I originally thought I'd impress Bela with my full-out dismount (two saltos in a tucked position with a 360-degree twist on the second salto), but I hadn't perfected it on a hard landing surface yet. I'd always used a soft landing pit at LaFleur's to cushion my landings in practice. But at Karolyi's there was no pit in sight. I couldn't believe it! I'd never been inside any gym that didn't have a soft pit. I knew from what I'd read and seen on television that the highest-level Elite gymnasts also used soft pits to practice new maneuvers and landings. Where was it?

I took a good look around the gym to see what else was missing. I had been so eager to see where world-class gymnasts trained, yet all I saw was old, worn, beat-up equipment. There wasn't a single item that appeared new or semi-new. With continual hard training, gym equipment takes a beating and needs to be replaced from time to time in order to provide the support and safety for which it was intended. Even the floor beneath my feet felt fuzzy and a little lumpy, but I sure as heck wasn't going to complain. I figured maybe that was what helped the Karolyi gymnasts get tougher.

I decided to nix my hardest element on the bars. I was a bit nervous and didn't feel safe landing without the soft pit, so I didn't even mention it to Bela. I momentarily reconsidered at the last minute while I was over the chalk tray, but I was ultimately too afraid and thought it better to play it safe for now. I had plenty of difficulty in my routines and figured I should just nail the things I knew instead of trying a riskier maneuver.

I remember being taken aback at the fact that Jennie Thompson was right up there with me in terms of level of difficulty in her routines. It was the first time I had seen someone my age who could do some of the same skills as me. Jennie was a rock-solid gymnast and immediately had my attention. With her blond hair, blue eyes, and tiny stature, she looked like the all-American gymnast. She was super light in weight and looked like a feather on the bars, moving from one release to another so gracefully. Her gymnastics skills were much "prettier" and more elegant than mine at the time. I hadn't developed much finesse to my skills at that point, relying primarily on raw talent and the skills I had learned from Jeff. Jennie was also more flexible than I was and had nicer lines. It was a rude awakening to be working out with another "tiny pixie" who could do what I could do—and in some ways, better. She was a reminder of what I needed to work on. From the very beginning, it was clear that Jennie would be my main competition at Karolyi's. She was extremely talented, and I knew I had my work cut out for me if I wanted to keep up with her. I clearly wasn't the best in the group, but I felt that I had the potential to be.

After bars, we moved to the balance beam, and I could feel myself getting nervous, more so than earlier. I had seen Marta arrive toward the end of the bar rotation. I was standing at the chalk bowl and through the glass windows in the lobby, I had a clear shot of her coming. She walked into her office, set down her things, then came out and just stood by the beam—*her* event. I was most nervous about performing on beam to begin with and now, seeing Marta standing there, waiting, made me uneasy as we finished up bars.

I learned later that this was the way Bela and Marta did things. Bela liked to coach solo with the gymnasts during the running drills, conditioning, floor, vault, and bars, and Marta liked to train her event, the balance beam, by herself. They only stayed for each other's events if extra help was needed to work on something specific. It was better for everyone this way, because when they were there at the same time, they'd usually bicker back and forth, which made the sessions more tense.

I had the last pick as to which of the balance beams I would work on. Kim, Betty, and Hilary had chosen the beams closest to where Marta usually stood, Kerri had the next beam, and the two end beams that nobody wanted were left for Jennie and me. I was the weakest link at this point and I felt it. I followed the lead of the older gymnasts and jumped straight up onto the beam. We did a short warm-up, and when the older gymnasts headed into their compulsory exercises, Jennie and I were instructed to work on the skills we already knew.

Marta had high expectations on her event. I saw it in the way she watched the older gymnasts with such intensity and scrutiny. If you weren't strong on beam, she didn't give you much of her time or attention. She liked those gymnasts who were good on her event, so I knew I had to impress her, and I tried my very hardest—really went all out. I made mistakes, falling every now and then, but I'd jump back up quickly and secretly hoped that she missed those turns, but I'm sure she saw everything. About an hour later, I breathed a sigh of relief that I'd made it through the beam rotation, and practice in general, without any major embarrassments or injuries.

On the drive home, my parents didn't really discuss my performance or what they had talked about with the Karolyis. I was exhausted physically and emotionally from the evaluation, and I was just happy to be heading back to Florida.

I remember sitting at the dinner table a few weeks after trip number two when Tata asked me about moving to Houston to train with the Karolyis. We were already following Tata's plan every step of the way, so it was almost silly to even ask what I thought at that point.

"Do you want to go?" Tata asked, but what he really was saying was, *"This is where you want to go."*

All I could say was "Okay."

Tata was ecstatic at the opportunity to have the most famous gymnastics coaches in the world coach *his* daughter. Mama later described how they were "swollen with pride" that the Karolyis had accepted their daughter to train with them. I figured if my parents truly believed it was the right thing to do, then I had to believe it, too. I was a kid who had just turned ten, after all. How much of an opinion could I really offer? I knew they wanted me to be an Olympic champion, and in their minds, they believed Bela and Marta Karolyi had the coaching and political power to help make it happen. They had coached the iconic Nadia Comaneci, also a Romanian, so my parents thought they would be a perfect fit for me. Why wouldn't they? On the surface it appeared to be the perfect move.

It was December 1991, when trip number three came knocking at my door. The call had come from the Karolyis, and before I knew it, my parents packed our things, loaded up the moving truck, and just like that, we were moving—Maia and Papu included. We left in typical Tata style: we never looked back. That's just how he thought; move forward and that's it. Done. No long good-byes.

I don't think Tata ever knew how tough it was on me to leave the one place where I had felt so comfortable and safe. To him, Florida was merely a stepping-stone to bigger things, but to me it had meant so much more. Despite this, I kept quiet as I normally did, never expressing my sadness to anyone. I was dying on the inside having to leave Jeff, Julie, Beth, my teammates, and my friends—the first real friends I had. "Okay" was all I mustered when Tata asked if I wanted to go. I expressed nothing else.

Mama drove the car, and Tata, the large U-Haul van. I don't remember much of this trip except that I slept a lot, and when I wasn't napping, I had a pit in my stomach—a mix of sadness to be leaving Tampa and fear of the unknown of Houston. I wondered . . . Would these amazing gymnasts accept me? Would I be happy there? I knew deep down that the answers to these questions really wouldn't make a difference. I wouldn't have a choice one way or another because my parents already had sacrificed so much to get me into that gym. I knew I couldn't disappoint them.

In Houston, we settled into an itsy-bitsy two-bedroom apartment. It was all we could afford, but it was home to the six of us.

Mama enrolled me in the fourth grade at Ponderosa Elementary School in December 1991, halfway through the school year. Another neighborhood, another school, another gym. I was getting used to it.

I remember one cold morning after we'd arrived in Houston, the windshield of our car had frozen overnight and Mama couldn't see two inches in front of her. Coming from the balmy winters of Tampa, I found this funny that a windshield could "freeze," but then panic set in as I realized that a frozen windshield meant I could possibly be late to the gym for training, which was simply unacceptable to the Karolyis. I remember sitting in the passenger seat of the car while Mama ran into the apartment to boil some water. Tata poured the scalding water over the windshield, and I watched as the frost and ice melted away. Mama and Tata had some peculiar methods of doing things, but somehow they always confidently tackled the problem at hand. The windshield was good as new and Mama got me to the gym on time. The Karolyis did not tolerate anyone arriving late for practice. I had seen Bela kick Hilary out of the gym for practice just for being the last one to walk in the gym even though she wasn't late, just the last one in. From that day forward, I was ready plenty early in case some other crazy Houston roadblock stood in our way.

My official training at the Karolyi gym pretty much took up where I'd left off at my evaluation. I, along with Jennie, jumped into the Senior Elites group with Kim Zmeskal, Betty Okino, Hilary Grivich, and Kerri Strug. It was a very big deal. Very few my age had ever had the privilege, and I wasn't going to waste this opportunity. I was proud to be training in Gym Number 1 with these 1992 Olympic "hopefuls." Gym Number 1 was not only separated by status from Gym Number 2 and Gym Number 3, but was physically partitioned off as well. Gym Number 1 was separated by a glass sliding door, and gymnasts from lower groups were never allowed in Gym Number 1—it was reserved only for the Elites in training. The rules were strict at the Karolyis' and everyone knew them and obeyed them.

Gym Number 3 was pretty much abandoned at the time. Nobody liked going in there because it had the worst of the worst run-down equipment. I specifically remember an old gray Nissen balance beam that was torn up around the edges. I got shivers at the thought of working out and landing on something so hard and torn up under my feet. I was surprised that the Karolyi gym had such old equipment. It seemed strange to me that a gym with the country's highest-level gymnasts didn't have newer equipment for training.

Shortly after I joined the gym, I had my first exhibition with my new teammates at Houston's Salute to Olympic Gymnastics Hopefuls at Rice University. My team at the exhibition consisted of the 1992 Barcelona Olympic hopefuls Kim Zmeskal, Betty Okino, Hilary Grivich, Kerri Strug, along with 1996 hopefuls Jennie Thompson, myself, and other Karolyi gymnasts from various levels.

I was floored when I saw that *the* Nadia Comaneci and her soon-to-be husband, Bart Conner, were television commentators for the event. Nadia Comaneci was the gold standard for gymnastics, and as a Romanian, she was not only my family's hero, she was a hero to her entire country. I couldn't believe I was actually in the same room with her.

When Bela called me and my teammates over to meet Nadia and Bart behind a blue curtain, I did everything I could to appear calm, because on the inside I was exploding. We locked eyes, and I felt an instant connection with her. I wasn't sure if it was because we shared the same heritage or because we were both selected by the Karolyis to train at such a young age, but I felt like she somehow understood me and what I was going through as a ten-year-old Elite gymnast better than anyone else in that room. I felt as if we had this unspoken understanding of each other. I had dreams, but standing there that day meeting her, who would have guessed that

I'd one day follow in her footsteps to win gold for my country at the age of fourteen, just like she had done for her country.

I was timid and quiet when she spoke to me, but I couldn't stop smiling and staring at her. It was hard to not be mesmerized—besides being a legend in my sport, Nadia was so beautiful. She had strong European features: big brown eyes, shoulder-length dark hair, and an hourglass figure that left little doubt she was still in great athletic shape.

At the time, I secretly wondered how she'd endured all that she'd gone through in her life to get to the very top of her sport—and to stay at the top. From my parents, I knew that during her era of competition, gymnastics was different and that she trained under a dictatorship in Romania. I wondered how that must have affected her on the inside because she always looked so stoic and calm and carried herself with class and dignity.

Blond-haired, blue-eyed, and still in prime physical shape nearly eight years after he'd won his two gold medals at the 1984 Los Angeles Olympics, Bart Conner was the happiest and sweetest gentleman I'd ever met. Being around Bart put a smile on my face. I couldn't believe he took the time to ask me, a little pipsqueak, about my gymnastics, and I could tell he sincerely listened to what I was saying and that he wanted me to do well. With the exception of my first coach, Jeff, most of the men I knew in my life up to that point were not as well mannered or polite, especially not with kids. The two most prominent male role models in my life, Tata and Bela, in fact, both terrified me. Then here was Bart—an Olympic warrior who was genuine, kind, and positive. This stranger was a ray of sunlight that day, and he and Nadia have remained friends ever since, even serving as godparents at my wedding in 2006.

It was at this exhibition that I got my first taste of interacting with the public and the media. After the event, a fan was working his way through the exhibition floor collecting autographs on his white T-shirt with a black Sharpie pen. He approached me and

Jennie and asked us to write "1996 for sure" because he was so sure we'd make it to the 1996 Olympics. I was overwhelmed by the attention and also by this stranger's confidence in me. In my experience, only Mama and Tata had been so certain about my future. I hesitated to sign the shirt, thinking that it might somehow be against the Karolyis' rules and also, I was only ten years old. There was a long road ahead of me before the Olympics, and I didn't want to jinx it by signing this guy's shirt. I wasn't sure what to do. I froze. The fan persisted, so I relented and wrote "1996 for sure!" and Jennie and I signed our names. I had butterflies in my tummy because I was afraid of what Bela might say when he saw it, which I knew he eventually would because his signature hadn't made it onto the man's shirt yet and I knew this persistent fan wasn't leaving that exhibition without Bela Karolyi's signature.

In later years, Bela would tell and retell the story to poke fun at me. By the time he recounted the story in a 1995 segment on NBC, it was so exaggerated, it went something like this:

". . . And in an interview she wrote, 'Dominique Moceanu 1996 Olympic All-Around Champion for sure!'"

Bela laughed and made big hand gestures mimicking how I'd signed the shirt. Bela, like Tata, had a knack for telling stories, and if there was a camera crew or media in the vicinity, watch out! It was always a love fest because reporters and camera people all marveled at Bela's effortless charm and charisma, and Bela loved having an audience.

"I never said that! I would never sign my signature as the 'All-Around Champion for sure,'" I cried to Mama after the NBC interview aired. I was so ashamed and embarrassed that Bela had painted me as an overconfident brat. The one thing I was certain of, even very young, was that nothing was ever 100 percent certain in sports. I was raised in a superstitious household where saying things like I'd be the "All-Around Champion for sure" was definitely tempting fate. Later, by the time I'd heard the story a few more times from Bela on television, I'd grown a thicker skin and it bothered me less and less, even though Bela exaggerated the details more and more.

As I had only been training with the Karolyis for a short time prior to this exhibition, I'd had little time to prepare. Bela and Marta didn't like the floor routine I had prepared at LaFleur's gym, so they told me I needed to learn a new routine in time for the exhibition. Team choreographer and fellow Romanian Geza Poszar was to work with me. Geza had been with Marta and Bela since the early days in Romania when they were training Nadia and her teammates. Marta, Bela, and Geza continued to work together after all three fled Romania for the United States in the early 1980s.

Expectations were higher than ever, and I wasn't yet used to the energy of the gym, which was very tense and so different than I'd ever felt before. I was nervous to start on this routine—and the music selected by the Karolyis didn't make it any easier. The foundation for any floor routine is the music, and the Hungarian folk piece Bela and Marta selected for me sounded strange and foreign, even to me. I felt completely detached from it. But I also knew that it didn't matter whether I felt it suited me, or whether I liked it. I was to dance to it, period.

I remember the first day Geza and I started working on my routine. After my morning conditioning, circuit training, and regular team practice with Kim, Kerri, Betty, Hilary, and Jennie, I stood in the center of the gym with Geza while everyone looked on. Usually, these sessions were done in private, one-on-one between the gymnast and choreographer. For some reason, it was decided that it would be a good idea to have my first floor routine session in front of the rest of the team.

The gym floor was old and worn under my feet and had very little bounce. It didn't have that familiar feel of the floors at the competitions or at my old gym. I also felt awkward and self-conscious standing there with everyone staring. Geza played the Hungarian folk music a few times to get in touch with it and get his creative juices flowing. He had dark black hair with streaks of gray, a salt-and-pepper mustache, and wore a beret and satchel. He looked like a European artist and I liked that. I never knew any other man to carry a satchel, and I have to say that it looked good on Geza. During our private lesson sessions later, he would remove his satchel and beret, but, here with our audience, he stood in full garb. He had a friendlier vibe than the others I'd met at the gym, and I felt comfortable with him. I loved that he had a sense of humor.

Geza started working on the opening pose and initial dance sequence. This first section is typically short and sweet as most gymnasts want to limit the dancing at the beginning in order to be fresh going into the first, and usually most difficult, tumbling pass of the routine. I had always liked the intro dance sequence and had fun with the moves, but that day, as I stood in the far corner of the floor, I wasn't connecting at all. I had to strain to hear the music, but all I could hear was Bela talking to my teammates. I tried to focus on Geza as he instructed me to do eight long leaps in a circle to the beat of the music, but the music was drowned out by Bela, who was commanding my teammates to do running drills in a large circle around the mat where Geza and I were working. Why the heck did he have to make them run around me?

For the life of me, I couldn't do the eight elongated steps on beat and the more I tried, the less I could hear the music, the more I got distracted, and the worse it got. I wanted to crawl under the rug and hide. All eyes were on me and felt like they were burning through my skin.

"1 . . . 2 . . . 3 . . . 4 . . . 5 . . . 6 . . . 7 . . . 8 . . . JUMP!" Geza began counting out loud in an effort to help. Still, I struggled. He raised his voice and started counting again and demonstrating how I was supposed to jump on the last count and land with legs glued together, slightly bent, with arms extended in front and behind in a diagonal. I tried it over and over again, but I couldn't get on beat. Kim and Betty even chimed in with Geza's counting to help me get on beat, but it didn't work. It was my first solo display for my new teammates, and I was humiliated and flustered. My eyes welled up as I tried my hardest to fight back the tears.

I couldn't understand why it was so difficult for me. I'd performed these types of moves countless times and had performed far more challenging sequences in front of crowds and judges for years.

Bela had turned his attention from my running teammates to my mediocre performance. It was the first time he really got frustrated and lost his patience with me. It stung like needles when he shot a look at Geza, snickered, and laughed disdainfully while shaking his head. I felt stupid. I was disappointed with myself and felt horrible for letting people down. I tried to hide my watery eyes from Bela.

Geza ended up changing the first steps of the routine to make it simpler for me, and although I was humiliated, I was also relieved just to be able to move on to the next sequence. I tried to hide my disappointment, but it was all over my face.

"Stop making faces. Stop playing the fool!" Bela barked.

As a ten-year-old, I had no idea what "Stop playing the fool" even meant, but he used that line often in the gym with me and the other girls when he was mad, so I knew it wasn't good. At first, I never realized I was actually making a "face" when he would yell this at me. I became very self-conscious and tried extra hard not to make any facial expressions at all, happy or sad. I eventually perfected my "gym face," which showed zero emotion. I'd challenge anyone, even Mama or Tata, to know what I was thinking or feeling when I donned my gym face.

By this time, I had been at Karolyi's gym for only a couple of months. I felt worse about my skills as a gymnast than ever before.

As the weeks passed, I began to feel more inadequate and less confident in my own abilities and capabilities. Self-doubt was taking hold, and it confused me because up until then, the gym was where I had always felt my strongest, my best. I began to dread each new day with the Karolyis more and more. I could never tell anyone this, of course. I didn't want anyone to think anything less of me, especially Mama and Tata, who had made so many sacrifices for me and had worked their entire lives to get me here. I kept it inside, to myself. I had to endure.

Chapter 6

THE KAROLYIS

Throughout my competitive career I've seen my share of coaches, twenty-three last I counted. Each helped me grow as an athlete and as an individual, and I am grateful in one way or another for all of them. Looking over the long list, however, my first coach, Jeff LaFleur, made one of the biggest impressions on me. His coaching style, expertise, and positive attitude helped me flourish as a gymnast at a very young age and led me to believe that I could achieve anything I set my mind to in the gym. He taught me the fundamentals of my sport and developed me into a national contender. Basically, he developed and nurtured me into a legitimate Olympic hopeful and then, per Tata's grand plan, handed me over to the Karolyis. Even at the end of my career, Jeff remained one of my greatest inspirations.

Most gymnastics fans I meet think the Karolyis coached me for the bulk of my career and are surprised when I tell them that the Karolyis were more like "handlers" or "managers" than gymnastics coaches. During the time I trained with Karolyi's Gymnastics, from the ages of ten to fourteen, I was actually "coached" by the Karolyis for only very short spurts of time, here and there. I had a string of many different coaches hired and fired by the Karolyis several times each year. I can name ten coaches that I had in that four-year period alone, but I'm sure there were more I'm forgetting. Ten coaches in four years would be more forgivable if I had bounced from gym to gym, but I was at the same gym, Karolyi's gym, for those years. For a young gymnast in her prime, that revolving door of coaching staff and lack of consistency was very stressful and made life more challenging for me overall. With each new coach came a learning curve—getting to know his or her coaching method and style and getting to know and trust that coach as a partner in my training—however briefly.

I had heard different rumors as to why so many coaches came and went so quickly from Karolyi's gym. It was said that some left over compensation issues or they didn't want to put up with the micromanaging Karolyis while others were said to have been fired by either Bela or Marta without explanation. These, of course, were just rumors that rumbled through our locker room. I was never involved or included in any discussions regarding my training, so no one ever explained or gave me a heads up as to when, how, or why one of my coaches would be coming or going. I just knew that it seemed like every time I blinked, there was a new coach to adjust to.

The Karolyis often brought in "experts" to help the gymnasts, most of whom were of Russian descent. For the time I was training at Karolyi's gym, I feel I really learned the most from my Russian coaches—especially legendary coach Alexander Alexandrov. Second to Jeff LaFleur, Alexander was the biggest influence on my gymnastics. He utilized traditional Soviet philosophies and techniques, and I credit Alexander's method, in large part, for my win at the Junior National All-Around Championship in 1994 when I was twelve years old, as well as my win the following year at the Senior National Championships in 1995. At thirteen years old, I became the youngest ever to hold the Senior National All-Around title, and it was Alexander's patient and measured teaching that led me to achieve those goals.

Amidst all the instability, Alexander was a godsend and, in retrospect, the best move the Karolyis ever made for my development and career. Alexander worked tirelessly with me one-on-one, trying to help me perfect my form and upgrade my difficulty. His results could not be denied, and I actually got to work with him from the age of twelve to almost fourteen—a relative lifetime compared to the revolving door of short-term coaches I had at Karolyi's gym prior to Alexander's arrival. I had grown accustomed to not ever knowing who my coach would be when I arrived each morning, so each new day that I saw Alexander, I was grateful for the stability, the continuity, and to be working with a methodical, knowledgeable coach.

Shortly before I turned fourteen and just prior to the 1995 Senior National Championships, Bela let Alexander go. Apparently, he wasn't needed anymore. This hit me hard. I felt abandoned by his sudden departure and uneasy about going back to the "revolving door" style of coaching.

Leading up to Alexander's untimely dismissal, I had been training primarily alongside American World Champion Kim Zmeskal and three-time Olympic gold medalist Svetlana Boguinskaia (the "Belarusian Swan"). The three of us trained and worked hard together every day under Alexander's watchful eye. It had far and away been my most solid, stable training period since I had joined Karolyi's gym—great coach, great training partners, and a stable daily routine the four of us muscled through together. As we were leading up the Senior Nationals, sometimes Alexander and I would work one-on-one for three-a-day trainings. I was growing, developing, and improving quickly, and Alexander was helping me focus. Momentum was building. I went to sleep each night believing I was getting better and better. Then the rug was pulled out from under me.

I felt cheated that he was taken away without warning. This was someone who was personally guiding my progress for several hours each day, and then one day he was just gone. He taught me many skills that I'd later compete at the Olympic Games, including a double layout dismount and a double layout full-out dismount off the bars (two flips in a layout position with a 360-degree twist on the second flip). I often joked that the last summer working with Alexander was my "Rocky Balboa" period of training—very focused and serious, working out three times a day, five to six days a week. I can only imagine what could have been had we kept moving down that road.

Bela hadn't spent a lot of time with me in the gym for most of that year, but in the weeks immediately leading up to Alexander's surprise firing, Bela started transitioning back into the gym, helping with training a bit more here and there. It was almost as if he was getting his feet wet again after being away from hands-on training for some time.

The day Alexander was fired, Bela walked into the gym for 7:00 a.m. practice as if nothing had happened. He entered alone and walked past us as we stood in our standard lineup for our morning run. No Alexander. I was confused and knew my teammates were, too, but no one dared ask or say anything for fear of getting in trouble by questioning Bela. We had our entire practice without Bela mentioning Alexander once. My coach, who had never missed a day of training, was gone, just like that. I knew it must have come as a surprise to Alexander, too, because the previous evening we had ended our day just as we always did—talking about what we'd do the next morning. It wasn't just me. My fellow gymnasts were also shocked and sad once we realized that Alexander was never coming back. We didn't even get to say good-bye.

I was a naïve thirteen-year-old and it took me a while to process why Alexander had been fired when everything had been going so well. I had made tremendous progress with Alexander; it just didn't make sense for him to be dismissed out of the blue. Later, however, the reason he was removed from the equation started to crystallize in my mind. I believe that Bela saw I was in top form and my confidence was high. Alexander had trained, instructed, and readied me for the Senior National Championships, and it seemed that Bela was going to capitalize on the moment. Having Alexander at Senior National Championships would only take the spotlight away from Bela. Only one coach was necessary at the big events, and since Alexander had already fully prepared me, he was no longer needed.

Alexander deserves the credit for much of my success in 1994 and 1995 and is responsible for teaching me nearly all of the up-graded elements that I'd compete with at the Olympic Games in 1996. I will forever be grateful to him.

In my adult years, I'd reminisce about our training time with Alexander with my dear friend Svetlana, who was also very close to him. Years later, she told me that after that first day of practice without Alexander, she'd managed to call him to ask what had happened. Alexander said the Karolyis simply told him to leave and never return.

Marta also started coming into the gym on a more regular basis to coach balance beam, alongside our other beam coach, Jackie McCarter. Jackie was brought in to help coach beam at the same time future hopefuls Brittany Smith and April Burkholder joined our group. Jackie was assigned to work with Kim Zmeskal and

these new hopefuls, while Marta focused her attention on Svetlana and me. Marta loved a good beam worker and, at the time,
I was a force to be reckoned with on balance beam as well as the
all-around. Balance beam was the key to being in Marta's good
graces—something I learned immediately. I worked hard to im-
prove on beam from the moment I started at Karolyi's gym. I had
earned her attention and now, as a thirteen-year-old, I was the
gymnast with the highest expectations to perform on beam.

The air always seemed different when Marta and Bela were
in the gym—colder and more tense. The change from Alexander's
coaching style to Bela's was sharp, and that feeling of instability
returned with a vengeance. I knew I had to keep moving forward
even though I felt so unhappy and stressed out. Alexander's name
was never mentioned in that gym again. The skills we had learned
from him were "what *we* taught you," as if the coach who had actually taught us had never existed. This was so hard for me because I
felt like I was unwillingly participating in the betrayal of someone
I cared about and who had been so good to me. I had grown to
trust and rely on Alexander so much. But I didn't dare show that
I missed him in the presence of Bela or Marta. That would have
been the kiss of death for me. Weakness was simply intolerable
in the gym, even for a thirteen-year-old. It was never important to
Bela how I was mentally or emotionally, as long as I performed on
the mat. I was expected to be a warrior. I stuffed my anxiety and
sadness way down until I could barely feel anything at all and focused on the Senior National Championships.

Soon after the Karolyis stepped in, my body began to break
down. Alexander had a particular style that was very calculated. He
was knowledgeable about physiology and in tune with his athletes;
he knew how to protect our bodies when we were exhausted. Alexander was no softie—he knew how to push me to my limits when
he knew my body could take it. But he didn't treat me like a little
machine; he treated me like a human being with human parts.

Through his methods, he got more out of me physically than I ever thought possible and more than any other coach I had, yet he was very mindful of keeping my body healthy and strong and not over-taxed. I never once had a major injury throughout my time with Alexander. Conversely, I had many injuries during the time Marta and Bela served as my coaches.

I can't count the number of times I watched other gymnasts push through unreasonable and dangerous pain just so they wouldn't have to admit to the Karolyis they were hurting in the gym. It happened to others time and time again and, for me, it ultimately led to my body breaking down right before the biggest competition of my life, the 1996 Olympic Games, with a stress fracture in my right tibia. The Karolyis knew when I was injured—it was obvious to everyone in the gym—but they also knew I didn't dare complain about my pain. If I had ever started to talk about my pain or injury, they would immediately cut me off, dismissing it and making comments or gestures that I was becoming weak, faking, or exaggerating injury out of laziness.

These negative mind games were a regular part of their coaching style and confused my psyche. I actually started to buy in to their psychology and believe that, perhaps, I didn't hurt *that* much and that the sharp drilling pain in my leg was coming from my head. I remember thinking, *Is it my fault that I am in so much pain?* After a time, it was difficult to know exactly how I felt because I was constantly working to deny my pain.

Shortly after Alexander was fired, I set out for the 1995 Senior Nationals. I made a splash at my first competition in the Senior division, winning the All-Around title at the age of thirteen. It was a dream competition, and I was hitting everything just perfectly on that summer evening. The meet couldn't have gone better, closing out the competition with one of my favorite events, the floor exercise to the music "Let's Twist Again" in my fire-engine red, long-sleeved leotard. I felt unstoppable as everything went right.

The crowd roared for me. The final performer of the evening, I nailed my routine to win the title. As I jumped off the podium, Bela gave me a big bear hug, and Marta, too—both all smiles. Excited to win, feeling the energy of the crowd cheering and relieved to see the Karolyis so happy with me, I bought in to their excitement, but inside, I was thanking Alexander, knowing he deserved all of the success in front of the cameras. He was the one behind the scenes who had coached me and worked on my routines right up to that point, and I was sad that he wasn't there to share any of the glory. In contrast, Bela somehow always managed to plant himself perfectly for those camera-friendly moments—at times forcibly grabbing the spotlight whenever the opportunity beckoned. It was no surprise to me that Bela often would be a bigger star than his gymnasts, and he always charismatically put on a show for the television, acting like he "loved" his gymnasts. Bela exaggerated his affections for us in public, which was perversely rewarding at competitions because we feared him so much and were so desperate for his praise. He was a different person altogether when the cameras weren't rolling.

Upon our return from Senior Nationals, we immediately began training for the 1995 World Championships. Winning the National title was not really mentioned after that first night, and it seemed forgotten altogether once we got back to Texas. I learned later from Mama and Tata that the Karolyis had instructed my parents not to celebrate or give me too much praise for winning the All-Around title.

"Don't tell her she's doing well, because she'll get a big head and won't want to work anymore," Bela apparently told Tata and Mama.

I know now that my parents were so very proud of my achievements (they told me so years later), and they did show their joy when I saw them briefly after the competition, but they followed Bela's instruction at the time and we never celebrated. I had to compete the following morning, so I couldn't stay up later than normal to bask in the win. I had assumed we'd get to celebrate together as a family once we returned to Texas, but I was wrong. I was the youngest in history to take the title, and with the second-highest score recorded up to that point. The newspapers and media made a bigger deal of it than my own coaches and family did. We can never recapture those moments, and that's something my family and I regret. I completely understood the need to refocus my attention on the next goal but would have benefited tremendously from some acknowledgment of my success for such an enormous and monumental win. I was sad and disappointed that my own parents didn't appear to share my excitement or tell me how proud they were at the time.

Years later, I'd talk about this with Tata, asking why he didn't tell me he was proud of me.

"How could you *not* know we were proud of you?" he'd say.

"Well, Tata, a child has to hear it sometimes, you know?" I'd reply while promising to myself that I'd never make that mistake with my own kids. No matter how much *more* I knew they could achieve or how much *more* they were capable of, I would always remember to acknowledge their hard work and celebrate their milestones along the way.

Matters only got worse when I went to the 1995 World Championships in Sabae, Japan. It was my first competition out of the country with the Karolyis, and it was a big deal to be named to my first World Championship team. I had my fourteenth birthday just before leaving for Japan. It was a big step to compete internationally, and I was anxious and excited.

It was not Marta's or Bela's style to do any mental preparation regarding what to expect, and once we arrived, I quickly realized I had to figure things out for myself.

I will never forget opening day of compulsories at Worlds in Japan when Bela made me do my compulsory bar routine over and over and over again during morning warm-ups. It is typical for most gymnasts to do a few run-throughs during morning warm-ups, then stretch and rest to preserve their body and energy for the official meet. After the sixth, then seventh time he instructed me to complete my routine, I was sure he'd say I was done.

Again, he'd gesture.

After the tenth and eleventh time, I started to wonder if there was an end in sight, or if he was trying to get me to break down and beg him to stop. I didn't. I focused on the task at hand and plowed through it, pushing down and ignoring any pain or exhaustion. It never seemed perfect enough for Bela. In all, he made me do my entire routine *sixteen* complete times. By then, I was the only gymnast in morning session still working out. All of the other members of the World team were sitting around the gym, stretching and just watching, waiting for Bela to say I was finished. I didn't understand. I thought maybe Bela wanted to humiliate me in front of the other gymnasts to make sure I didn't get a big head, having won US Nationals. With almost no rest in between, my hands were on fire, and by the eighth or ninth run-through the physical and mental drain started to accumulate no matter how much I suppressed it, and I began to make silly, uncharacteristic errors on my bar routine, which seemed to infuriate Bela.

Frustrated that I was getting tired and not executing perfectly, Bela loudly accused me of eating too much and suggested that I was starting to make mistakes because I had gained weight during my visit to Japan. He ordered me to get on the scale, so he could weigh me right there for everyone to see. Looking back, I'm sure he knew perfectly well that I was making mistakes because I had just done my compulsory routine *sixteen* times in a row, not because I had eaten too much.

This was typical Bela. It seemed to me that any time practice wasn't going well at the gym, he'd try to blame it on my weight and threaten to call my parents (which really meant Tata), so Tata would then punish me for having eaten too much. I resented that

Bela's style was not to deal with me as an athlete and, like other coaches, help me work though the particular apparatus, maneuver, or routine that was giving me trouble at the time. Instead, if ever I struggled with something, it seemed that his quick solution was to tell me I had eaten too much and then proceed to rile up Tata, who he knew ruled our family with an iron fist. It didn't take much to ignite Tata's temper, and when Bela told him that I was slacking off, eating too much, or not doing as I was told in the gym, I would pay the price with a fierce thrashing or interrogation from Tata when I got home. Sometimes Bela looked almost giddy with anticipation when he was threatening to call Tata. I'd heard other athletes tell stories of how Bela would be abusive to young gymnasts back when he was coaching in Romania. This, obviously, was not something he could get away with as easily in America, but with me he had a connection to the old world. I sensed that Bela was aware that he could easily have me beaten with one phone call to my father, and I perceived that threat on many occasions. The unfairness of it all added to my anxiety and unhappiness—especially since Bela never shared my accomplishments with Tata. I can honestly say that the entire time I was at Karolyi's gym, I gave gymnastics everything I had every day, never taking shortcuts, never slacking off, even when Bela wasn't watching. His way of erasing human error was to tell Tata I was "being lazy again." I wasn't sure which was worse: Bela describing me as "lazy" or Tata believing that it was true.

I imagine Bela's threats to call the parents of the other gymnasts weren't as effective because the more American and Americanized parents weren't as likely to participate in fear and humiliation tactics victimizing their own children. Bela was, however, a threatening and intimidating force in the gym to *all* of the gymnasts. The difference was that he seemed to know to draw the line at the gym doors for most everyone else. My family, however, was easily manipulated. I could never stand up for myself at home or in the gym in these situations because no matter what I said, it seemed I was always wrong and "they" (Marta and Bela) were always right. There was no room for discussion or even an opinion on my part, and I discovered that the best way to limit trouble was to say nothing at all. As time went by, I feared Bela calling Tata to punish me at home. It got to the point that I began to worry more about the whole punishment cycle than about my gymnastics.

When Bela weighed me in front of all my US teammates and coaches at Worlds after making me do my compulsory bar routine sixteen times, it was one of the most humiliating moments of my life. I couldn't even look the other gymnasts, who were watching and waiting to see what Bela had in mind for me. I didn't want to see their reactions as I stepped on the scale. I closed my eyes, waiting and praying that I hadn't gained any weight. I knew that if I had gained even a fraction of a pound, Bela would explode with a barrage of insulting names and threats of calling my father.

"Thirty-one kilos," Bela called out loudly for the world to hear, or so it felt.

Thirty-one kilos? What the heck does that mean? I thought to myself. I wasn't familiar with the metric system, and I held my breath waiting for Bela's reaction to see if 31 was good or bad. Bela didn't explode and just sort of walked away, leaving me standing on the scale, so I figured 31 kilos was a good number. Once back in my hotel room, I got out a pen and paper to do the conversion and discovered that 31 kilograms is equivalent to 68.2 pounds.

Ironically, this meant that I'd actually lost weight since Bela weighed me last. I had consistently weighed in at 70 pounds, and I was relieved that he couldn't use my weight against me. I'd been sure to pack healthy snacks such as crackers and canned tuna in my suitcase because I knew that low-calorie food might be an issue in Japan considering the difference in language and limited access to foods. I ate almost all of my meals with the Karolyis, and sitting alone with them for breakfast, lunch, and dinner was always tough, especially because I was their only individual athlete competing for Team USA at the time. They watched my every bite, monitoring even the smallest of meals—while they ate whatever they wanted right in front of me. I remember drooling over the warm breads they would eat at lunch and dinner, but they made it clear that I was never allowed to even touch the bread basket. I never ate a single crumb of bread in front of them for the entire time I trained with them. That's just the way it was. I wasn't alone in this. I don't remember seeing any other gymnast reach for the bread basket, either, but we'd all salivate for bread while Bela and Marta ate it. I loved food, and it only became more of an obsession when I wasn't allowed to have it.

By the time Worlds opened later that day, I felt worn out, both physically and emotionally. Instead of being warmed up and mo-tivated, I felt exhausted and beaten down. I couldn't understand why Bela made me work so hard prior to the competition. I was especially nervous for the compulsory bars, which included a chal-lenging element—a handstand half pirouette to free hip and half pirouette in one connection attempt. I ended up making an error on this skill in the competition, causing me to lose critical points that I needed to medal in the All-Around. I was frustrated because I knew I was more than capable and ready to medal at this competition. I felt afraid the entire time I was in Japan, and I couldn't go to my coaches for support because it was Marta and Bela I feared most.

What little I saw of Japan was beautiful. Of course, we spent most of our time in the gym and hotel room, and my every move was monitored by the Karolyis, more than any other gymnast. They treated me differently, and by differently, I don't mean special— though it may have seemed like preferential treatment to some of the other gymnasts. I wasn't allowed to sit with the rest of my teammates, even on the bus, as Marta always reserved a seat for me in the front row, next to her, for every trip to and from the gym and competition arena. On those trips she barely spoke to me. It was a sad and lonely experience to sit there with Marta as all of the other Team USA gymnasts passed by and worked their way to sit together in the back of the bus and chat like normal teenagers.

My parents thought the Karolyis knew what was best for me as a world-class gymnast and put all of their trust in them. This left no room at home to voice my concerns about what happened during training. Mama and Tata had given everything to get me to this point to train with the Karolyis, and I just couldn't dash their dreams by telling them how miserable I was. I still wanted to be a champion of the sport I treasured—that never changed—but I didn't know how to cope with the fear and anxiety I felt during my training with the Karolyis.

At night, as I went to bed, I prayed to have a good attitude and to not let my fear show on my face before I entered the gym daily. I prayed to have near-perfect routines every day, so I wouldn't get into trouble for being "lazy."

During this time, Mama became more involved with the Karolyis and the gym in general. She offered her help any chance she could. She figured that if she was helpful to the Karolyis, they would treat me well. If Mama had been right, I should've been treated like a queen for the amount of work she did for them. Running errands, picking up groceries, helping clean—Mama bent over backward to please them in any way she could, almost behaving like a servant at times, which I hated. Mama even spent time helping at the Karolyis' ranch house in New Waverly, Texas, from time to time. Mama made herself available to help with chores, errands, anything they needed.

The Karolyi ranch actually holds some of my darkest memories. Every so often, Bela held mandatory training sessions at the ranch. (It is where the current US National Team Training Center is located.) The older gymnasts dreaded going to the ranch, which was about an hour outside of Houston in New Waverly, the middle of nowhere. They had warned me about the terrible equipment, especially the vault runway and the floor exercise mat. Considering the run-down equipment we had at the regular gym, it was hard to imagine anything worse. They also told me about the extra-long workout sessions and Bela's refusal to turn on the air-conditioning during the unbearable hot and humid Texas summers.

What they didn't warn me about was the food, or should I say lack of food, which I learned the hard way during my first "ranch" experience in 1991, shortly after I joined Karolyi's gym. I knew it was going to be a very long weekend as soon as I saw the other gymnasts carrying bags of food alongside their luggage. Bags of food? No one told me that we had to bring our own food. No one ever told me or Mama that they didn't serve food at the ranch. I was ten years old, for crying out loud! If Mama had known, I'm sure she would have cooked up a batch of Romanian favorites for me to bring. Instead I showed up with my lime green school lunch box and the one sandwich Mama made as an emergency snack in case I got hungry before our first meal. Mama was floored to later learn that, as a rule, the Karolyis did not provide food to their gymnasts, even when we'd be at the ranch for days. I was too embarrassed to ask the Karolyis for food, so I figured I would divide my sandwich into four pieces and try to hold out as long as I could.

Luckily, I was rescued by my teammate Betty Okino, who noticed my little lunch box. She and my other teammates saved my life that weekend by all pitching in and sharing pieces of their food with me.

Leading up to the Olympics in 1996, Kerri Strug and I spent the entire summer living and training at the Karolyi ranch. I learned my lesson from previous years about bringing food, so I was prepared heavily for this long summer stay. Bela and Marta ran their annual gymnastics summer camps and trained us at the same time. The campers would come in to watch our training every now and then. On Saturday evenings, Bela and Marta would have Kerri and me demonstrate routines and conduct mock meets for their campers. It was fun at first, but became draining week after week because the performances took place during what were supposed to be our "rest" periods, and I began to feel fatigued. I also missed my home, but I was focused on this final push to the Olympic Games later that summer.

My dearest friend and my most trusted confidante to this day is Janice Ward. Janice came into my life like an angel when I was ten years old. I call her my "adopted aunt." When I met her, I needed her more than I realized. She worked as a masseuse and physical therapist at the chiropractor's office less than half a mile from Karolyi's gym near highways FM 1960 and I-45. I had regular appointments with Janice to keep my aches and pains to a minimum, but what she provided me with was infinitely more valuable than my physical therapy sessions. She was one of the few outsiders my parents trusted, and she quickly became part of my family. She was our slice of American pie, introducing and explaining to my family aspects of American culture and traditions that we never understood or even knew about. Janice was also the only adult in my life at the time who seemed to recognize that, despite my serious training and Olympic goals, I was still a small child. She tells me now that it broke her heart to see a young girl not experiencing any of the joys of childhood. As her relationship grew with me and my family, she did everything she could to bring me some aspects of normalcy. She would talk to me about things other than gymnastics, do arts and crafts with me and my sister Christina, and she would take us to Chuck E. Cheese's every once in a while.

During that summer before the Olympics when I was living on the ranch, Janice decided to make me a life-size patriotic teddy bear. She nicknamed it "Georgia," referencing the upcoming Olympics in Atlanta, Georgia. Janice was very creative . . . she cut a hole in the bottom of the teddy bear and used it as a secret place to stash little sweets for me to enjoy while at the ranch. She had added a Velcro trapdoor to keep the goodies tucked into the teddy bear and out of sight so Marta or Bela wouldn't find out. She sent me off to the ranch with this cute teddy stuffed with chewing gum, flavored Mentos, and a few Twizzlers (my favorite!). The gum was a life saver and would help me pass time when I was hungry. I wasn't allowed to eat the foods I craved, so the gum (and Mentos or Twizzler every once in a while) helped satisfy my cravings. I would go through several packs of gum a week—and Janice always smuggled in more for me in the secret teddy chamber or my gym bag when I ran out!

I loved that Janice understood my need to be a kid even when I was stressed to the limit and training for the biggest competition of my life, the Olympics. She knew how much I wanted to be an Olympic champion and was always supportive. I also admire her for not allowing herself to be bullied by the Karolyis and even standing up to Marta a few times when she disagreed with the way Marta was treating me. It was no surprise that Marta and Bela did not like Janice. I don't think they knew how to deal with a strong woman who didn't take their word as gospel. They did not want her around me, but by the time they realized this, it was too late—we had already become friends for life.

I will always be grateful to Janice for providing me the unconditional love I desperately needed when I hit some low points and doubted myself. She has always been there for me for more than twenty years. I don't think I could have made it through the brutal summer leading up to the Olympics without her support.

My low point during that summer came one afternoon during nap time when Tata burst through the door of the cabin I shared with Kerri. I was shocked to even see Tata at the ranch, especially in the middle of the day. I was frozen because I recognized that anger and rage in his face. Kerri sat up in her bunk, surprised and frightened.

What did I do? What did I do?! I kept asking myself. I was frightened and stunned and could barely react as he lunged forward, face bright red with fury, grabbed my ear, and literally pulled me out of bed with one powerful tug. My mind was racing. I was mute and in shock.

"Why aren't you working hard, Dominique? I'll show you" was the first thing I remember Tata saying in his stern Romanian. I still didn't know why this was happening. Tata shoved me out the cabin door and said we had to go to Marta and Bela's main house. Tata grabbed my ear again and dragged me a couple hundred yards across the compound toward the Karolyi house. It was close to three in the afternoon, an hour before training at four. I wondered where Mama was, hoping she was nearby so maybe she could save me. I hustled to keep up with Tata, and the mystery of what I had done wrong eclipsed the sharp pain on the side of my head where Tata had an iron grip of my ear.

"What did I do?" I cried out to Tata in Romanian. No answer.

The next thing I knew, we were at the front of the Karolyi house. I remember looking over at Bela's huge guard dog that he kept on a chain. I was always scared when I walked by because he would growl and bark at me. I would try to stay to the far left of the driveway as far away from the dog as possible, but today, I was hoping that Tata would walk toward the doghouse so the dog might bite Tata's leg and I could escape. It was a terrible thought, but I was scared and desperate to get away. How was I going to handle both Bela and Tata?

As I entered the Karolyi house, my heart sank. Mama, staring mournfully at the floor, was waiting quietly with Marta and Bela in Bela's den. It was clear Mama wasn't going to be saving me. The room was musty and still. I had been in Bela's den before, and I called it the Room of Death. The walls were covered with the heads of all sorts of animals Bela had hunted and then had stuffed. Lots of deer heads and the scariest wildcat I'd ever seen with his mouth agape and sharp teeth snarling. I looked down at the green carpet to avoid eye contact with the dead animals and awaited my fate.

Everything felt as if it were moving in slow motion and then Tata's booming voice trumped everything.

"Why do you have food!?!?" Tata snapped in Romanian.

Then he started saying that the Karolyis had called him up to the ranch because I was not "working hard." I just stood there completely frozen. I felt like I was in a dream and I thought if I didn't move, maybe they wouldn't see me. I was scared to death. I feared that this was all because of the Mentos and gum.

The Karolyis were standing directly behind Tata, smugly shaking their heads. I hated the look of satisfaction on their faces as Tata scolded me. I looked to Mama, who was standing to Tata's right. She looked sad and powerless.

"Why are you here if you're not going to work hard?" he continued before I could even process his first question.

"Why are you eating what you're not supposed to eat?" And with that, I figured out what this was all about.

Oh, I said to myself, *the candy.* I suspected this meeting had been motivated by the food found in my teddy bear or my gym bag. Other gymnasts had suspected that the Karolyis would search luggage, the rooms, and the fridge in the cabin house where gymnasts stayed, looking for hidden food or other things they considered a distraction. I never found out how they knew about the teddy bear, but I didn't answer Tata as he kept getting angrier and angrier. Mama's eyes were sad, which only made me feel worse.

"Why are you eating what you are not supposed to?" Tata blurted one last time before hitting me across my right cheek so hard that it made my whole body jerk back. The blow made a loud noise and I grabbed my cheek with my right hand to try to stop the stinging. It didn't help.

At that moment I despised the Karolyis for calling Tata and

hated Tata for humiliating me in this way for eating a handful of Mentos and a few Twizzlers. I rarely had chocolate or high-fat food, only a few low-fat treats that I ate sparingly.

I remember refusing to give them the satisfaction of seeing me cry, but somehow I still felt tears flooding down my face.

I lost all respect for Marta and Bela at that moment as the two of them stood there seeming to gloat and nodding as if their mission were complete. I couldn't bear to look at them anymore. Nobody, including Mama, reacted to the wallop across my face. I figured they all knew it was coming—God knows, Mama was expecting it since she'd seen Tata lose control and get physical countless times before.

I just stood there before them, staring down at the green carpet beneath my feet. Tata could've beaten my seventy-pound body to a pulp. I would never have told them it was Janice who smuggled in my treats. They didn't deserve to speak her name. I didn't even want to look at any of them. Marta spoke next.

"Okay, get ready for practice."

Time had frozen for me during this incident. Marta breaking the heavy silence served to remind me that I had been in the den for about half an hour receiving verbal and physical abuse.

I ran out of the house. As soon as I passed the guard dog, I started sobbing. I sprinted back to the cabin even though I really wanted to run deep into the forest outside the ranch and never be found again. Horrible thoughts ran through my head. I wanted to get as far away from that place, the Karolyis, and my father as I could and never come back, but somehow I kept heading toward the cabin. I prayed for God to help me get through practice and the next few months before the Olympics. I had made way too many sacrifices to get to where I was, and I wasn't going to let these cowards take my opportunity from me. *After the Olympics,* I thought to myself, *I will be finished with this goal and I don't have to see the Karolyis again.*

When I opened to the door to our cabin, I saw Kerri in the bathroom getting ready for practice.

"What happened?" She looked scared and worried, her eyes as big as saucers. I know she probably thought she saw a monster barge through our door when Tata came to grab me. I didn't have the heart or energy to tell her the details, both for her sake and for mine. I was drained. I moved in slow motion, putting on my leotard and putting my hair in a ponytail for practice. I still don't know how I mustered up the strength to get through that afternoon session, but somehow I did it.

Chapter 7

JENNIFER

I still wake up sometimes and wonder if it was all a dream—do I really have a "secret sister"? I sometimes literally shake my head in disbelief at what a whirlwind these past few years have been for me and my family: the birth of my children, the death of my father, and, after twenty years of being kept in the dark, the discovery of my sister Jennifer. Since Jennifer came into our lives in December 2007, I've spent countless hours daydreaming and reliving my childhood, picturing how different my life would have been had Jennifer been a part of our family growing up. I find myself imagining "what if" and "what could have been" over and over again. Sometimes I get so angry at my parents for knowingly separating us, and I can't stop dwelling on what *should* have been. Other times, I am more sympathetic and understanding, and I can see that Mama and Tata actually believed they were doing the right thing for everyone concerned. The one certainty is that my sister Christina and I are grateful that Jennifer is finally in our lives today.

We have been trying to catch up for lost time and learn as much as possible about Jennifer, but how do you cram twenty-plus years of life that's been lived into the here and now? Every day, we uncover something new or surprising about Jen, who is truly an incredible and inspiring person.

Jennifer was born in Salem, Illinois, on October 1, 1987. She grew up in Hardinville, Illinois, a town near the Indiana border that is so small I couldn't even find it on the map. As Jennifer describes it, Hardinville had one four-way intersection with stop signs at the center of town and no stoplights. Quite a contrast to my childhood neighborhoods in Hollywood, Chicago, Tampa, and ultimately Houston, which has over 2.3 million people and lives by the motto "Everything is bigger in Texas!"

Jennifer was adopted within the first few months of birth by Sharon and Gerald Bricker. Having now had the pleasure of knowing the Brickers, I understand how and why Jennifer has grown to be such a strong, confident woman. The Brickers are some of the most kind-hearted, down-to-earth people I have ever met. Sharon and Gerald had three sons: Brad, Brian ("Bubba"), and Greg, and had always longed for a fourth child, a daughter. Sharon wasn't able to have more children, so they decided they would adopt a baby girl, and that's how Jennifer entered their lives.

The Bricker boys were fourteen, twelve, and ten years old when Jennifer came into the family. The brothers were excited and enthusiastic about adding a little sister. Brad, Bubba, and Greg absolutely adored Jennifer and doted on her. She was the princess of the family in the sense of being the only girl, and the boys were extremely protective of her, but they certainly didn't treat her like a delicate little flower. They taught her to be tough, rowdy, and bold. That she had been born without legs was never considered a handicap to any of the Brickers, and from a very early age, Jennifer participated in every sport, game, or adventure that got in front of her. Alongside her three big brothers and neighborhood friends, she would jump off of things, climb trees, do handstands and flips, get dirty, and fling herself into any stunt or physical feat you can imagine that the most rambunctious young boy might do. Jennifer credits her brothers for teaching her to be fearless, and they are all still very close today.

By the time of baby Jennifer's arrival, Sharon had retired from the bakery where she'd worked when the boys were young and where she'd become known for baking the "best cakes in town." Sharon was now a stay-at-home mom available to care for and nurture baby Jennifer full-time. Over the years, Gerald worked as a carpenter and also at oil refineries, which required heavy physical labor. The Brickers are a hardworking, loving family who stressed strong morals and family values. As Jennifer describes it, her home life was stable and full of love and support. She says her parents had minor arguments and bickered here and there like any other family, but they always "talked out" their problems, so there was never lingering tension in their home.

Jennifer's words, "talked out," stuck in my mind. How I had wished my parents did more talking when I was young. I mostly remember Mama and Tata either arguing when they disagreed or not talking at all. And the tense moments in our home were far more common than the peaceful ones. Many of Christina's and my childhood memories were plagued with fear, sadness, and occasional threats of violence. When I think about these painful times, I am happy for Jennifer that she had such a positive home life— and I can't help but think that the Bricker home was a better place for Jennifer to grow up than mine was.

Jennifer easily recites her mom's daily routine from when Jennifer was a child: Sharon would wake early, around five or six in the morning, fix breakfast (usually bacon, eggs, and toast for Gerald), get the boys off to school, then spend the day with Jennifer. Her mom was an even-tempered, happy woman who cherished being a mother to Jennifer and her brothers and taking care of the house and family business while Gerald worked.

Jennifer describes her father Gerald as "a strong man's man, with a sensitive side." Jennifer says that she and her father are similar in a lot of ways—hardheaded and strong-willed, but compassionate, too. Whenever Jennifer had an argument with her parents and stormed off to her room, especially during her teen years, her dad would always wind up coming to her room to talk to her.

"Can we be friends?" her dad would say, to kick off the conversation, and they'd end up talking and working things out.

What I wouldn't have given for Tata to have said, "Can we be friends?" or anything even remotely similar to me, Christina, or Mama after one of our family blowups. Of course, in Tata's defense, his "rule the house with an iron fist" mentality was clearly a rehash of what he had witnessed in his own home when he was a child. He grew up watching his father explode and become physically abusive to his mother; he rarely saw any love or kindness expressed between them. I know his history doesn't justify or make it okay that he was abusive to us, but it does give me a better understanding of Tata and the world he came from. It's very difficult to break free from that pattern of abuse, especially when you've been surrounded by it your entire life and haven't had positive role models. I just wish things had been different in our home, for all of our sakes.

When Jennifer reminisces and relives her childhood anecdotes with me now, she often chuckles and smiles. She has so many joyful memories that I'm actually in awe at times. Right before I met Jen, I had a million questions and a million concerns, too. I wondered if she was lonely, growing up away from her two sisters, if she had felt abandoned by her birth family, or if she had had a difficult life of struggle because she was born with no legs. To know Jennifer now and see her as part of this tight-knit Bricker family, I realize how off-base my initial concerns were. Her life is almost the exact opposite of what I had imagined when I first heard from her. During our first conversation, I found myself thinking, *Thank God someone was watching over her, so she didn't have to suffer like Christina and I did.*

Jennifer attended public school ten miles from her home—in Oblong, another small town with a population of approximately two thousand. When she started kindergarten at Oblong Elementary School, the other children obviously noticed that Jennifer was different. Moving around in a wheelchair naturally drew attention.

"This is the way God made me," Jennifer would always respond matter-of-factly when other kids stared or asked what happened to her legs. That's what her parents had always told her and that's what she believed. No one treated Jennifer differently at home—she participated in every activity just like her brothers and was expected to contribute to the household chores and responsibilities just as her brothers did. She certainly didn't expect anyone to treat her as "handicapped" at school, either. Jennifer recalls that within a very short time the other students were completely used to her. So much so that they'd often forget that she didn't have legs. Growing up, Jennifer sometimes wore prosthetic legs that had been specially designed for her, but ultimately she felt that they slowed her down and stifled her, so she wore them only once in a while. I was shocked when Jennifer told me that her public high school was in a four-story building with no elevator. She climbed the stairs between classes just like everyone else and had a wheelchair stashed on each floor in case she needed it.

To Jennifer, having no legs simply means that she may have to go about doing what everyone else does a bit differently, but it has never dawned on her to not do these things at all. Gerald and Sharon always taught Jennifer that "I can't" is not part of their vocabulary, and it wouldn't be part of Jennifer's, either. Her parents instilled great confidence in her and nurtured her self-esteem from the start. Jennifer grew up believing she could do whatever she set her mind to.

Sports was one of those things Jennifer gravitated to with gusto. Like Mama, Jennifer is a natural athlete, and since childhood she has demonstrated a high level of coordination and skill with almost anything she attempts. Jennifer loved sports and participated in almost every athletic activity offered from the time she was very young through high school. She did softball, basketball, volleyball, gymnastics, and tumbling, among others. Sometimes her parents would have to alter her equipment in order for her to play a particular sport, but they always seemed to figure it out. I've actually seen some of the Brickers' home videos of Jen rounding the bases in softball and diving for a volley in volleyball. She's always been a competitor. There wasn't anything her parents ever discouraged her from doing, or at least trying. Even when Jennifer decided she wanted to roller skate with the other kids, her parents crafted makeshift skates that could attach to her hands and voilà, she was off!

"If I had wanted to be a soccer player, I know my parents would've figured some way to help make it happen," Jennifer has said.

Jennifer says she was also very lucky to have had wonderful teachers who encouraged and supported her throughout her school years. All of her teachers had a positive impact on her in some way or another, but in particular, her fifth-grade teacher, Mrs. Sweat, stands out. Mrs. Sweat, an eccentric woman with big, wild curly hair and long fingernails, reinforced what Jennifer's family had taught her about standing up for yourself even when it feels like the world is against you.

Like it was yesterday, Jennifer shared with me a story about spending the day with her family at Holiday World amusement park in Indiana when she was about eleven years old. After waiting for hours to ride a roller coaster, she was immediately turned away once she reached the front of the line because she didn't meet the height requirement. She felt this was unfair because she was tall and large enough to sit in the seat to be properly secured by the harness and seat belts the same as everyone else. Her body was actually bigger than those of many of the children on the ride. Jennifer would've understood if there was a safety concern, but she had previously been allowed on other roller coasters, some bigger and faster than this one. Her parents never would have allowed her to get on a ride where there was any doubt regarding safety. Had she been wearing prosthetic legs, she would have met the height requirement, but having them hang below her belted body in the roller coaster seat would not have made her any safer, just taller. The people operating the ride didn't want to consider any of these particular facts. They took one look at Jennifer and told her she couldn't ride. Period. She was never going to be able to reach the height requirement for this ride, even when she was an adult.

The next day at school after Jennifer shared what had happened at the amusement park, Mrs. Sweat devoted a good part of the day to discussing discrimination and teaching the class why it's wrong to judge or deny people rights simply because they "look" different. Jennifer was taken aback and deeply thankful for this lesson by her teacher. Moments like this reinforced Jennifer's confidence and her belief that she should have the same rights as others even though she was born different. She decided that her adventures in life were not going to be decided by what other people perceived she could or could not do.

Growing up with three older brothers, Jennifer was not only adventurous, she was a complete daredevil. Besides riding four-wheelers and rough-housing with her brothers, she'd scare her parents half to death by jumping off their second-story spiral staircase onto the living room couch below time and time again. She was also a skilled and agile climber and, with book in hand, she'd easily make her way up a big backyard tree to wedge herself between the branches and read for hours.

As long as Jennifer can remember, she was a fan of gymnastics and would watch the US and international competitions and exhibitions whenever they were televised. She was drawn, in particular, to me, the littlest gymnast on the floor, and found herself cheering "little Dominique" on from the beginning. I reminded Jennifer of herself—we were both petite, with dark hair and eyes, and strikingly similar facial features. Jennifer knew she was of Romanian descent, like me, so she felt an even greater connection. She tells me she used to ask her parents if they thought she and I looked alike. I get goose bumps when she shares how she used to tell her parents that we looked "like sisters."

Jennifer watched all my televised meets, read books and articles about me, and declared to her family that she was going to meet me one day. It's mind-boggling how our lives crossed as kids and have come full circle as adults.

"I want to be a gymnast," Jennifer announced to her parents when she was in second grade. With that, they enrolled her in gymnastics classes, which then led to tumbling classes.

Jennifer's entry into gymnastics coincided with the 1996 Olympics in Atlanta, where I reached my own goal of winning the gold medal alongside the other members of the Magnificent Seven. Jennifer tells me that watching me compete and succeed, even though I was so young and tiny compared to my peers in the sport, inspired her to start competing in gymnastics and tumbling. With her strength, coordination, and focus, Jennifer quickly excelled in tumbling, eventually competing over the next four years and winning various competitions in her age division.

By the time she was twelve, Jennifer had become a small-town hero through her tumbling feats, having participated in four state meets, one in which she took the title of State Champion, as well as competing in three national meets and one Junior Olympic meet. Upon entering high school, Jennifer felt she had accomplished all she had set out to do in the sport of tumbling and was ready to tackle new challenges. She also looked forward to having more free time to hang out with her friends, do girly things like experiment with makeup, and just be a teenager.

Jennifer's positive outlook has served as an inspiration for me, even in the short time I've known her. She looks at life not as an obstacle, but as an opportunity. Clearly, because of her physical challenges, she has had to conquer a number of things on a daily basis that the rest of us don't even think twice about, but she nonetheless moves forward with her trademark "no excuses" attitude, which I absolutely love!

Chapter 8

OLYMPIAN

The time leading up to the 1996 Olympics was the most demanding and stressful of my career. The sport I had loved so much was slowly becoming a nightmare as I trained with Bela and Marta Karolyi the summer before the Olympics. I pushed myself as hard as I could, but I always felt like I couldn't please them. I kept telling myself that they were just trying to get 100 percent out of me, like any decent coaches, but they were so out of tune with where I was mentally, emotionally, and physically that their tactics were having the opposite effect. I was already fiercely competitive and sharply focused on the goal of Olympic gold. I'd been in love with gymnastics forever, it seemed, and since my very first media interview at the age of nine, I had envisioned nothing more vividly than standing on the Olympic podium receiving my medal. That dream was *almost* a reality. After years of work and total dedication, it was so close I could taste it. Deep down, I loved gymnastics with all my heart, so I was devastated and confused when I began feeling apprehensive about walking into the gym each morning. Leading up to the most important competition of my career, I felt unprotected and vulnerable in training.

I was so afraid to make mistakes and get reprimanded by my coaches that the joy of the sport started slipping away. Bela would threaten to call Tata whenever I'd make mistakes. Bela knew he had total control over me, and he used this power to intimidate me, not to motivate or empower me, and I hated that. Just like he'd done when he found the Mentos in my Georgia bear, Bela knew one phone call would have Tata carrying out the physical punishment Bela thought I'd deserved. I was mad and disappointed with all of them for stealing my joy and happiness from gymnastics.

Performing my routines—both compulsory and optionals—was packed with difficulty, yet executing them was the least of my worries. The real anxiety in the pit of my stomach was fear of Bela and Marta berating me for any error. For most gymnasts, practice is supposed to be the place to get all the mistakes and kinks worked out as the routines are mastered. My routines were nearly perfect already, and we were just putting the final touches on them. I typically did six compulsory beam routines in the morning and six optionals in the afternoon session, and there were weeks when I wouldn't miss a single routine. I'd challenge myself to see how long I could go without a fall—on beam, I once went three weeks. I'd go weeks without a fall on my bar routines, but I still felt the pressure every day, every minute, to make zero mistakes because I knew one fall, one slip-up, could set off Bela and Marta and erase all the good

I'd done up to that point. Maybe, for some gymnasts, the Karolyis' style of coaching made them stronger, better athletes, but, for me, the fear tactics and scrutinized training methods kept my nerves unsettled, made me feel tight, and sapped joy from my sport.

There were times I felt strapped into a straitjacket, trapped living and training at the Karolyi ranch that summer. My every move was monitored by Bela and/or Marta around the clock, 24/7. Spending day in and day out with them, you'd think a personal bond would form, and a certain level of trust would be established, but I could never fully trust either of the Karolyis even though I desperately wanted to. Bela and Marta made no effort to create a real connection with me. I was terrified of them and found myself counting the days until I could break away. Of course, this meant that I was counting the days until the Olympics were over and done, and *that* was the most confusing thought of all. I had waited my whole life for this, and now I couldn't wait to be done with the Olympics, so that I could be done with the Karolyis? This was not at all how I'd envisioned the summer before the biggest competition of my life.

Thank God for Kerri Strug. Earlier that summer, Kerri moved in with me to the log cabin house next door to the Karolyis' main house at the ranch. It was just the two of us training with the Karolyis at that time. Had I been there by myself, I think I would have gone crazy. We were good training partners, both with an unwavering work ethic. We pushed the best out of each other. Our training was focused, intense, and left no time for fun or socializing. Kerri was eighteen years old, four years older than me, so, aside from gymnastics, we didn't really have much in common then, but our time together built a foundation for a strong friendship years later as adults.

Like me, Kerri was relatively shy and quiet, and respected the rules. From what I remember, she had trained with Bela and Marta leading up to and throughout the 1992 Olympics and then returned to train with them in 1996 in preparation for the Atlanta Olympics. I can't speak for Kerri's experiences because they were certainly different than mine, but I noticed right away that Kerri was treated differently by the Karolyis. They dealt with her in a softer tone and with a basic level of respect. If we were both doing routines on bars, for example, it didn't matter if mine was nearly flawless, Bela or Marta would criticize me sharply and make disgusted faces when I made even the slightest mistake. I often wondered at the time why they were so much harsher on me and figured that they just liked Kerri more as a person—she *was* very sweet and respectful. That's not to say that Bela and Marta didn't ride Kerri. There were many times at the chalk tray when we'd share a quiet look, both rolling our eyes about something the Karolyis had said or done. I admired how Kerri handled herself and was so grateful to have her there.

Years later, Kerri explained that her parents had talked to Bela and Marta prior to her return to the ranch in 1996, telling them that they wouldn't be able to treat Kerri "the way you used to" if she was going to come back to their gym.

Geez, I thought, *was that all my parents needed to say to get the Karolyis to treat me like a human being?*

Often after particularly hard training sessions and demoralizing chastisements from one or both of the Karolyis, I would feel let down by them, by Tata, and even by Mama. Tata and Mama repeatedly made it clear that they were taking their marching orders from the coaches. My parents were prideful, hardworking people, but they put all of their trust in the legendary Karolyis, leaving me little room at home to voice any difficulties at the gym. Our family already had enough stress and conflict with Tata's mood swings and financial strains. I didn't want my parents arguing over my gymnastics, the one thing they both seemed to agree on.

I don't think the Karolyis ever thought much of me, Mama, or Tata anyway. To them, we were just a poor Romanian immigrant

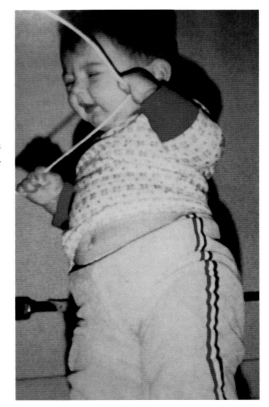

Me at six months old on a clothesline. (*Courtesy of the author*)

Tata, Mama, and me in Hollywood, 1981. (*Courtesy of the author*)

With my sister, Christina, at the Olympics in Atlanta, 1996. (*Courtesy of the author*)

Tata, Mama, and me receiving my official congratulatory certificate from the Olympic Games in Houston, 1996. (*Courtesy of Janice Ward*)

Tata, Mama, and me at the Planet Hollywood after-party following our Team Finals victory in Atlanta, 1996. (*Courtesy of Janice Ward*)

With Aunt Janice at my home in Cleveland, Ohio. (*Courtesy of Janice Ward*)

Pregnant Mama and Tata at the beach in California, 1981. (*Courtesy of the author*)

Me with Bela Karolyi. (*Courtesy of Dave Black*/International Gymnast Magazine)

Performing one of my favorite floor routines at the Goodwill Games, July 1998. (*Courtesy of Eileen Langsley*/International Gymnast Magazine)

A pose in my beam routine at the World Championships in Sabae, Japan, 1995. (*Courtesy of Eileen Langsley*/International Gymnast Magazine)

My floor exercise at the World Championships in Lausanne, Switzerland, 1997. (*Courtesy of Eileen Langsley*/International Gymnast Magazine)

On the podium at the Goodwill Games in Long Island, NY, 1998. (*Courtesy of Eileen Langsley*/International Gymnast Magazine)

On beam (one of my favorite events) during the World Championships in Sabae, Japan, 1995. (*Courtesy of Eileen Langsley*/International Gymnast Magazine)

A pose in my floor exercise at the U.S. National Championships in New Orleans, 1995. (*Courtesy of Dave Black*/International Gymnast Magazine)

Mike and I cool down with a stretching session while training for my comeback at Gymnastics World in Cleveland, Ohio, 2005. (*Courtesy of the author*)

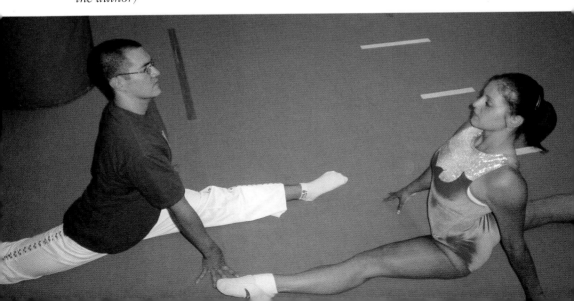

With my 1996 Olympics gold medal at a photo shoot in 2006. (*Courtesy of Achille Bigliardi*)

With other gymnasts at the National Team Training Camp at the Karolyi ranch during my comeback, July 2006. Pictured left to right: Dominique, Brittney Noble, Shayla Worley, Nastia Liukin, Amanda Castillo, and Shawn Johnson. (*Courtesy of the author*)

With most of my Magnificent Seven teammates at the White House, 1996. Pictured left to right: Jaycie Phelps, Dominique Dawes, Amanda Borden, Dominique, Amy Chow, and Kerri Strug. (*Courtesy of the author*)

The Magnificent Seven reunion in Atlanta, 2007. Pictured left to right: Amanda Borden, Amy Chow, Jaycie Phelps, Dominique, Kerri Strug, Dominique Dawes, and Shannon Miller. (*Courtesy of the author*)

With Jennifer backstage at the Britney Spears Circus Tour in Detroit, 2009. (*Courtesy of the author*)

Jennifer doing a handstand in front of the Statue of Liberty. (*Courtesy of the author*)

Jennifer climbing her favorite backyard apple tree at four years old. *(Courtesy of the Bricker family)*

Jennifer in a white dress at twelve years old. *(Courtesy of the Bricker family)*

Jennifer with Carmen, Mike, Christina, and special pup Princess at our first meeting in Ohio, May 2008. (*Courtesy of the author*)

Christina, Jennifer, and me in Houston, 2010. (*Courtesy of the author*)

Graduating from John Carroll University, May 2009. (*Courtesy of the author*)

With my beautiful children, Vincent and Carmen, 2011. (*Courtesy of the author*)

Me, Mike, Carmen, and newborn Vincent at home in Ohio, March 2009. (*Courtesy of the author*)

Mike and me at St. John Arena on the John Hancock Tour of World Gymnastics Champions in Ohio, 1997. (*Courtesy of the author*)

Me and Mike at our wedding on November 4, 2006. (*Courtesy of J. Christopher Chisum*)

Me and Nadia Comaneci at the wedding. Consistent with Romanian tradition, Nadia served as the "honorary godparent" for me and Mike at our wedding. (*Courtesy of J. Christopher Chisum*)

Tata, Mama, and me at the reception on my wedding day. *(Courtesy of J. Christopher Chisum)*

Carmen doing a one-armed handstand at age one, December 2008. *(Courtesy of the author)*

family who hung on these world-famous coaches' every word. And we certainly did our share of ass kissing. Mama, the people pleaser she was, always made herself available to help the Karolyis. Whether it was picking up choreographer Geza or some other Russian coach from the airport, baking homemade breads and food for the Karolyis, or running their personal errands for them, she did everything she could to help get me in their good graces. She went above and beyond because in her culture, parents did such things to help their children. By American standards, it may appear like bribery, but for Mama it was typical, expected behavior. It was the only thing she felt she could do to help me.

In his way, Tata did his part as well. I remember when Tata was a salesman at the Ford dealership, he pulled some strings and arranged for Bela to drive a Ford-sponsored vehicle at no cost. Tata was a proud man, and I know he felt taken advantage of by the Karolyis at times, too. I'd sometimes catch a small earful here and there when Tata would vent to Mama about "being used" by the Karolyis, but he'd immediately stop when he'd see me listening. Mama would later tell me that they knew if they had questioned the Karolyis' rules or methods, Bela would have told them, "Take Dominique somewhere else. We don't need her." Tata believed that the Karolyis had the political power to put gymnasts of their choice on the Olympic team. It was far too late in my career to transfer anywhere else. They had already uprooted our family when we moved to Texas. My parents stayed loyal to the Karolyis even as other gymnasts came, went, and came back again. That summer our family avoided talking about how I was treated at the ranch and instead just kept plugging forward knowing the Olympics were almost here.

I was only fourteen years old, but I knew from deep within that it was urgently important that I figure out how to hold on to my passion and keep it burning throughout that summer. I'd daydream about Alexander walking through the gym doors and taking over my training. I cried myself to sleep countless nights wishing I could train with him. Of course, this was just fantasy, but I continued to think about him, replaying the things he'd say and do, especially when I was struggling. I used what he had taught me to work through that difficult summer. I kept reminding myself that it was an honor to train so hard toward such a goal and no one—not even my own coaches—was going to stand in my way to Olympic gold.

For some reason, as much as I felt that Bela and Marta treated me with disdain and lack of respect, I kept trying to gain their approval. I would look at Bela when he was enraged or disgusted with me and I couldn't help but think of Tata. They were so similar in some ways, how their tempers would flare over simple things. I feared Bela like I feared Tata, yet I still tried to please both of them, even when I knew deep down they'd rarely be satisfied with what I'd done or if they were, they'd rarely give any praise. I can't remember a single time that the Karolyis or Tata ever uttered the simple words "I'm proud of you." Later, of course, I'd learn from Mama that the Karolyis had told them that words of praise would limit my progress. They once even asked Janice to remove herself from the gym for complimenting one of the other gymnasts on a job well done. In so many ways, this captures their philosophy—a philosophy that almost destroyed me.

I resented that added pressure of walking on eggshells at the gym, trying not to upset Bela. At times, I envied the relationships I saw between other gymnasts with their coaches at competitions. I remembered what it was like to have someone who demanded everything from me but who also believed in me and made me feel good about myself. I wanted that security and support back in my corner. Here I was, heading into the Olympic Games, feeling less confident than ever before with coaches making sure I knew I wasn't *that* good.

To make matters worse, I was starting to suffer from chronic sharp leg pains stemming from my right shin. It had been an issue for months and worsened leading up to the US National Championships in Knoxville in June. It was obvious that my leg wasn't right, and it was affecting my performances, but the Karolyis did not alter my training in response to my injury. I had seen them push other hurt gymnasts. I worked up the nerve to tell Bela and Marta a few separate times that I was really hurting and that I knew something was wrong with my leg. They seemed to dismiss me each time, muttering under their breath and making sour faces, making me feel like I was faking my injury. They told me there wasn't anything *"really"* wrong with me. By then, my self-esteem had been chipped away significantly, and I actually started thinking that they knew me better than I knew myself, even though, in truth, they barely knew me at all.

During US Nationals podium training (the "official" practice before the competition begins) my leg was hurting so badly I had to literally grit my teeth to stop from crying out at each turn, especially on vault, beam, and floor. I did everything I could to fight back tears. I didn't want to show weakness to Bela and Marta. A few times I winced in pain, which I knew would get me into trouble. "Stop making faces," they would call out, coldly. During floor warm-ups, I fell, landing facefirst onto the mat on my first and fairly easy pass. My leg completely lacked the stability it normally had, and I felt it could give out on me at any time. *How on earth am I going to run down the vault runway?* was all I kept thinking. I could barely put pressure on my right leg in a turn, how was I going to sprint down the vault runway, much less stick a landing?

An hour before I was to leave for the competitive arena, Bela and Marta called my parents and me into their hotel room for an impromptu "parent-coach meeting." I couldn't remember them holding such a meeting before, and they certainly never included me in any discussion about my training, so I had no idea what this would be all about. Based on past experiences with other kinds of "parent-coach meetings," I was terrified.

"Do you *want* to compete?" Bela asked me, with Marta, Tata, and Mama standing behind him staring quietly, awaiting my response.

I just stared back at Bela. He rarely asked my input or opinion on anything and now, an hour before the US Nationals, he was asking me if I wanted to compete. Fourteen-year-old me did not recognize the malicious sarcasm, either. I thought it was some kind of trick question, and I didn't know how to answer. I wanted to say what he wanted to hear, but I was so confused that I just looked at him and then at my parents and back at Bela again. I finally nodded my head yes. In retrospect, I saw that it was a rhetorical question. Bela's way of saying, "Don't complain. You're not really that injured, so suck it up and compete." Of course, Bela knew I had every intention of competing and that I hadn't complained about my injury to anyone else. As we made our way to the arena, I was so frightened—scared of the pain, scared that no one believed me about my leg, scared of falling in front of the public during the competition with the Olympics right around the corner, and scared because I knew I was trapped in a situation where I could never tell my coaches how I truly felt. I felt hopeless and alone. I prayed that the rush of adrenaline I normally got in competition would help me through the pain.

The actual event is something of a blur to me now. The pain was there, but that adrenaline kicked in and I was able to muscle through it for the most part. I ended up placing third in the All-Around. I made uncharacteristic minor mistakes on vault and uneven bars that most likely cost me the gold medal. I was disappointed, of course, yet I still felt total confidence that I would have done even better had I been healthy, and I couldn't understand why Bela didn't see that, too.

"That was NO GOOD, Domi. That was NO GOOD," Bela barked at me after my uneven bars routine.

Bela's comments, seeping with disgust, cut like a knife and

made me feel like a failure. Considering it was difficult to put my weight on my leg, I expected he'd see at least some honor in the fact that I finished my routines without any major falls and that I pushed through the injury to place third despite having to sit out the final day because my leg became unbearable.

I remember how Bela conveniently acted like he was concerned about my injury during the few fleeting moments that the television cameras were filming him on the sidelines. In truth, he was disappointed in me for my errors. It confused me at first, but I soon caught on to the game—with the cameras present, Bela did a 180 and became the animated, entertaining, and caring "you can do it" coach that everyone knew and loved.

My injury was not properly addressed even after we returned to the ranch. We were given one day's rest after Nationals, and that Monday we were back in the gym picking up where we had left off. Kerri and I were training as usual on our compulsory floor routines that morning, and my leg pain was now severe. One day off with no treatment was clearly insufficient. The hard gray floor beneath my feet looked and felt a hundred years old, especially in contrast to the equipment at Nationals. The Karolyi floor was hard as a rock with what felt like no springs at all, which only worsened my leg pain. I didn't know how to train through it. I felt demoralized, and Bela and Marta barely spoke to me—instead shooting me looks of disgust when I was struggling on compulsory floor that morning.

I remember Bela opened the warehouse doors of the gym that morning to try to get some fresh air to circulate. It was another sweltering hot day in New Waverly and I was sweating profusely from the workout. Bela and Marta rarely turned on the air-conditioning for our training even though it was often more than one hundred degrees with strangling humidity. My leotard was soaked through within the first few minutes of our conditioning training. I'd stand in front of the huge dusty fans to try to dry my sweat between runs on vault or floor. My face would turn beet red and I could feel my cheeks flushed and burning. I'm not sure how we managed to not pass out from heat exhaustion.

I tried my best to make it through the workout that day, but my leg literally gave out and I collapsed. I had made it through my tumbling pass okay, but when I went on to my switch straddle dance element, I collapsed right in front of Marta, Bela, and Kerri. I realized my leg had given out during my jump—my leg was so weak that I wasn't able to push off. Crumpled up on the ground, with streaks of pain radiating from my leg, my primary focus was fear—I was afraid of being yelled at by Bela, so I forced myself up quickly. The gym was silent. I attempted the same element and, again, I couldn't push off of my leg properly and collapsed once more. I was afraid to make eye contact with the Karolyis, but with only one training buddy in the gym with you, it's unavoidable.

Marta made a disgusted face and mumbled some words I couldn't make out. I was frozen with fear, so I got up and just stood before them, staring down at the tattered gray floor. I was waiting for them to either yell at me or, worse, threaten to call Tata.

"What you doing? You playing the fool?" I remember Bela saying.

I didn't answer. I just knew they were going to call Tata and could feel my body begin to tremble. I tried to stand perfectly still, but the trembling only got worse—especially my leg—and it was almost like it was no longer a part of my body.

Marta purposefully walked toward me and silently squeezed the back of my neck, digging her fingers in tightly, as she had often done when she was upset with me, and began pushing me toward her office door. She was talking as we made our way to her office, but my head was spinning and I couldn't concentrate on what she was saying. I was trying to read Bela's expression to see if he was going to call Tata.

"Let's call your parents. Maybe your leg is broken!" Marta announced loudly.

I think back now at this whole scene and I can't believe how frightened I was of those five words, *"I'm gonna call your parents."* The Karolyis always threatened me with it, and it never failed to scare the crap out of me. I really wasn't sure who I feared more, Tata or Bela, but I knew that having the *two* of them mad at me at the same time was lethal. By then, I was slightly less afraid of Marta. I had become one of her favorite beam workers, so, at times, she gave me the benefit of the doubt and was a little softer on me than she had been before.

The X-ray and MRI revealed a four-centimeter stress fracture in my right tibia—five weeks before the Olympic Games. Even though I knew it had been getting progressively worse, my heart sank with the news of a fracture. It's the kind of news that smashes Olympic dreams. I was horrified and I panicked, afraid that I wouldn't be healed in time to compete at the Olympics. I was relieved to finally get treatment for my leg, but as I sat out conditioning on the sidelines, I was going crazy seeing the days tick away and the Games inching closer. I eventually trained on bars, skipping my dismounts to limit the pounding on my leg, and I had to stop vaulting and floor exercise altogether for a couple of weeks. I rode the stationary bike for endurance training.

At first, I bought in to Bela's blame game and blamed myself for being injured, as if *I* had done something to cause the fracture. But once I really thought about it, I realized I had done *exactly* what my coaches had told me to do from the moment I woke each morning to the moment I went to bed. I was mad at myself for not being more persistent and insisting that they examine and treat my leg when I first told them something was wrong. I know from years in my sport that next to prevention, quick treatment is key to staying healthy. If you pay attention to the warning signs, you can usually avoid subsequent, more serious injuries from overtraining and overuse. But open communication, and especially talk of injury, was never permitted at the Karolyi gym.

I was still injured and unable to compete at Olympic Trials in

Boston in mid-June. Fortunately, I was able to petition and earn a spot on the 1996 Olympic team based on my scores from Nationals. I was eager to learn more about the other five gymnasts who would be joining me and Kerri on the 1996 Olympic team, which would eventually be dubbed "the Magnificent Seven."

Shannon Miller, the most decorated gymnast in US history, ended up winning the All-Around at US Nationals that year. Like me, she was injured for Olympic Trials and also used those scores to petition onto the Olympic team. I didn't know Shannon well at the time. She was nineteen years old, five years older than me, and had world titles, Olympic medals, and years of experience under her belt. She had been my main competition at Nationals and the media immediately ran with the "rivalry" angle that would continue to pit us against each other for years to come. I remember being taken aback by Shannon's tendency to openly cry during her practices. She was such a fierce and steely competitor at meets that it caught me by surprise. I was mesmerized, watching her tears flow freely while her personal coach continued working with her. I admired that she didn't feel the need to hide her emotion during practices. I knew exactly how she felt, wanting to cry during practice at times, but I remember thinking, *If I ever did that, I'd be in big trouble!* Shannon was living proof that showing emotion didn't mean you were weak or less of an athlete—she has won more Olympic and World gymnastics medals combined than any other US male or female gymnast *ever*.

Jaycie Phelps, who placed second in the All-Around at the National Championships, was immediately thrown into the mix with the rest of us vying for one of the seven spots on the US Olympic team. Her blue eyes, bouncy blond ponytail, brick abs, and gorgeous toe-point on the uneven bars made her presence hard to miss on the floor. Out of superstition, I would not watch any of my competitors at meets until I completed my own events, so I didn't get to see Jaycie's routines, but she was already a consistent force, and I had a feeling she'd be named to the Olympic team. While she clearly possessed a warm and generous spirit for such a competitor, I didn't get to know Jaycie well until after the Olympics when we were participating in the post-Olympic tour. Even though we never said much during our time competing against each other, she was always friendly and kind in passing, and I knew I would like her more as I got to know her.

Believe it or not, aside from Kerri, I rarely had a chance to talk with the other Magnificent Seven gymnasts leading up to and during the Olympics because we were all spread out training in different gyms and saw one another only at the actual competitions. I was given very strict rules by the Karolyis and was allowed to leave my hotel room only for practice, competition, physical therapy, and meals, so there wasn't much opportunity to get to know them at the Olympics. Kerri and I had to sit with the Karolyis for all of our meals, while the other five teammates (Amanda Borden, Amy Chow, Dominique Dawes, Jaycie Phelps, and Shannon Miller) would sit together during the Games. I'd always look over at them as they laughed and talked, and wish I could join them. I'm sure they wondered why the heck Kerri and I never sat with them. I felt badly because it alienated us from the rest of the team to some extent, but deep down I hoped they understood that it was our coaches who didn't permit it.

I'd see our team captain, Amanda Borden, smiling and telling stories at their table. Amanda was outgoing and friendly—a nurturing soul who was kind to everyone. She was so genuine and beautiful, too, with short blond hair, crystal blue eyes, and an inviting, warm smile. Every gymnast on our team worked hard, but I remember thinking at one point that Amanda perhaps wanted the Olympic dream more than anyone. She stayed committed to the sport and continued to work just as hard after barely missing the 1992 Olympic team. Her determination was admirable, and I was happy that she was the captain of our Magnificent Seven team. I felt she truly deserved it, and her experience was helpful to all of us.

Off Balance

I often wondered what Amanda and the others thought of me. I wanted to be friends with them, but at fourteen, I was much younger and smaller. I wondered if they looked at me like a baby with whom they had nothing in common. I wasn't sure, but I was frustrated I wouldn't even get the opportunity to find out as long as the Karolyis kept me so isolated. Sometimes I'd see my teammates in passing in the trainer's room. It'd usually be quick, grabbing a couple of ice bags and letting the trainer Saran Wrap it on our sore muscles, but I always hoped that the other girls would be there at the same time so I could share a few words with them.

Talented and intelligent, teammate Amy Chow made things look effortless. She had gymnastics tricks some of us only dreamed of throwing in competition. Her bar routine had combination after combination of difficult elements along with one of the hardest dismounts of the Olympic Games, which was called a double double (two flips and two twists in a tucked position). Amy was a force in her own right and solidified her spot on the Olympic team at the 1996 Olympic Trials when she showed true grit after a terrible fall on the balance beam. Amy slid down the side of the beam, whacking her face hard against it, but she battled through that fall and finished the routine. Talk about mental toughness! Amy was a calm yet fierce competitor on the floor and a woman of many talents off the floor as well. I wasn't sure how she managed to be both an Elite gymnast and a great pianist at the same time. It was no surprise when she went on to study medicine and become a pediatrician after she retired from gymnastics. Amy also got involved in competitive diving and competed in pole vaulting at a national level. She is truly an amazing woman.

I also always admired the relationship Amy had with her coaches, Diane Amos and Mark Young from West Valley Gymnastics club. In my opinion, Diane and Mark did an excellent job protecting Amy from overtraining and allowed her proper rest to let her body recover, so she'd be healthy and strong for competition. I remember during our team practices in the weeks leading up the Olympics, Amy was the only gymnast who did not work out twice each day at her gym back home. I found it so interesting that Amy could execute her routines so well with less training. I also admired how Amy's coaches held their ground and didn't let the Karolyis bully Amy or them into changing their training style. Marta usually tried to take charge of training even when a gymnast's personal coach was standing right there, and she usually ended up calling the shots for everyone. I remember one day during podium training a few weeks before the Olympics when Marta started practice five minutes early. When Amy and her coaches walked in the gym, Marta got very angry because she thought Amy was late.

"Amy, you're late!" Marta yelled. Amy appeared startled by how mad Marta was and she started to cry. Before Amy could say anything, Diane put Marta in her place.

"Don't you *ever* yell at my athlete or treat her that way. She is *not* late. *You* started early!" is what I recall Amy's coach yelling back at Marta. Diane was livid that Marta upset Amy by yelling at her with a nasty, accusatory tone—a tone, unfortunately, that I knew all too well and had heard daily. Wow! I'd never seen anyone stand up to Marta like that, and it was certainly the first time I saw Marta speechless. I had such respect for Diane for protecting Amy and not letting a Karolyi intimidate her gymnast. I wished I had someone to stand up for me like that.

I would often recognize Dominique Dawes's signature laugh from across the cafeteria as I sat with the Karolyis at lunch or dinner, and I couldn't help but smile. She was upbeat, positive, and movie-star beautiful. I felt good being around her. As a competitor, she was muscular and strong yet graceful. I always found the power in her gymnastics breathtaking. She executed perfectly a back-and-forth tumbling pass combination on the floor that few gymnasts even attempted. Along with Shannon and Kerri, she was one of our veterans who had competed as a member of the 1992 Olympic team.

I thought it was pretty cool that there were two Dominiques on the team especially considering that our name was rather uncommon. We'd both won titles at the 1994 US Nationals, she in the Senior division and I in the Junior division. We later posed together for the cover of *International Gymnast*, the largest circulating international gymnastics magazine. The cover line read "Dominique Duo!"

While the rest of the girls got a chance to unwind and tell stories at mealtimes, Kerri and I barely spoke at all over at the Karolyis' table. In fact, "meal" time was typically an altogether unpleasant experience. By that point, I'd been humiliated about my weight at the 1995 World Championships and at other spontaneous weigh-ins and interrogations the Karolyis conducted. I was very insecure about my body, and to have them monitor my every bite at every meal was horrible and made me that much more self-conscious. Bela and Marta would eat as much of everything and anything they wanted off heaping dinner plates, yet Kerri and I were expected to sit across the table from them and eat very small portions of particular approved foods. Every once in a while, our team physician or trainer would feel sorry for me and sneak me some food or something sweet, like a small Rice Krispies Treat, into my room after dinner.

Marta and Bela would often eye my body up and down in practice when I was stripped down to just my leotard. Their critical comments about my physique, public weigh-ins, and constant scrutiny of my food led me to believe that I was "fat" even though I was only seventy pounds at fourteen years of age. This warped body image would haunt me for years to come. The Karolyis were not the only Elite gymnastics coaches to have made me hyperaware of my weight, either. Unfortunately, for many coaches, it seems to be par for the course to keep their athletes light at all costs. Several other coaches I've worked with stressed weight in one form or another. Some were just less extreme than the Karolyis.

With little else to think about, my mind began obsessing about food, and the more I felt I wasn't allowed to have the foods I wanted, the more I craved them. On a few occasions when I was really starving, I hid food and ate it in secrecy. I was afraid for anyone to see me and tell my coaches. I had been so obedient for so long, trying to follow all of their rules to the letter, but no matter how well I listened, I was still scolded and humiliated and made to feel worthless, stupid, and, yes, FAT. What did I have to lose?

Earlier that summer, back at the ranch, Kerri and I would talk about how we were going to indulge in food once the Olympics were over. We'd lie in bed after practice—and talk about how we could hardly wait to go down the cereal aisle at the grocery store and eat every sugary cereal we were craving, listing them one by one: Cinnamon Toast Crunch, Lucky Charms, Corn Pops. At times, those small moments of joy—that wishful thinking about silly snacks and cereal—helped me get through to the next day of practice.

I think Mama was concerned that I'd be malnourished, and she ended up coming to the ranch to cook my meals that summer. It meant everything to be able to see her on occasion during the day, but Christina was rarely permitted at the ranch and usually had to stay back in Houston with Maia and Papu. I really missed Christina, who, for me, was the unknown eighth member of the Magnificent Seven because she was the closest person to me, always there to cheer me on and support me. She sacrificed as much as any Moceanu, giving full days and weeks of her own childhood, waiting around for my practices to end.

I remember when I was packing my bags for the ranch at the

beginning of summer and *Sports Illustrated* sent a reporter, E. M. Swift, to my home to do a feature story.

"Where you packing up to?" Mr. Swift asked.

"I'm heading out to the ranch—" I started to answer, but before I could finish, I was cut off by Christina.

"She's gonna stay out there . . . and she's never gonna come home."

Her words and her sad face just broke my heart. To some degree, Christina was right. Even though the ranch was only an hour's drive from our home in Houston, I wasn't allowed to come home for most of the summer.

⚜

It was July 23, 1996, at the Olympics in Atlanta. Team USA was in second place going into the final day of competition. No US Women's Gymnastics team had ever won team gold. Butterflies fluttered in my stomach as we marched out to begin the day's events. I said a few prayers, hoping that some divine power would look out for me, keep my leg strong, keep my leg pain tolerable, keep me calm, and give me the strength to deal with the pressure of perfection on this day.

Competing in the Olympics in front of our home crowd was both a gift and a constant reminder that we *had* to win gold. I was blown away by the overwhelming passionate support of the American fans, and being at home also made me want to win that gold medal that had eluded the US Women's Gymnastics team for decades. I felt there was no other option; we *had* to win—for our sport, for our country.

Our team came from diverse backgrounds—socioeconomically and ethnically—and we truly reflected the face of America. I was fortunate to be on a team I believe had the most talented female gymnasts of our generation. I knew we had the goods to win, and I felt gold was within our reach.

In Olympic competition, the rotational order of events is vault, bars, beam, and floor. I breathed a sigh of relief when I saw that our team would begin on the second event, uneven bars, because that meant that our final event would be vault. Vault had always been one of my strongest events in competition, and I had a fairly high percentage hit rate since I began competing as a child. I rarely made a mistake on vault. It was important to finish strong on a power event for me. The adrenaline coursing through me masked the pain in my leg to the point where it really wasn't bothering me. Things were starting off right.

We were neck and neck with the Russian team, who had come into the competition in first place. Initially it looked like it would be a battle between Russia and Romania for the top medals until the very end, but one by one, Team USA kept hitting, and we inched closer and closer to the top. I could tell by the crowd's reaction with each of my teammate's routines that we were on a good roll. I didn't watch my teammates or competitors. Aside from my own superstition about it, I needed to stay focused and in the zone.

Uneven bars went solidly for our team. I did one of the best routines I'd ever done, and I was so particularly proud to stick the landing at the end of my routine. I knew every tenth mattered and sticking landings was a must. It is the exclamation point at the end of a routine and, to me, if a gymnast doesn't work on sticking landings, they're missing a crucial element. It is that extra stamp of perfection.

I was second to last on our next event, balance beam, so I stayed warm on the sidelines near the podium. Again, the crowd roared with each Team USA routine. The Georgia Dome was electric with the crowd's enthusiasm. My turn finally came and with all of my teammates hitting their sets, I knew I had to nail mine, too. I could feel Marta's eyes laser locked on me. She began to pay closer attention to my beam work the prior year because I was the only

American to receive an individual medal (silver) at the 1995 World Championships on *her* event. Although she'd never admit it to me, I could tell she was proud of my beam work.

I saluted and began with my signature shoulder roll mount. It always seemed to be a crowd pleaser and I loved that. As I came out of my mount with a chest roll down the center of the beam, I stood upright, did my dance poses, and took a breath before my hardest tumbling series—back handspring three layout step-outs in a row (three flipping elements connected without using any hands for support). As I felt my feet land firmly at the end of the beam, I did the required single 360-degree turn element, I breathed a sigh of relief that all was flawless so far. I moved through the next sequence of required jumps—two acrobatic moves and my switch straddle leap—did a few poses, and prepared for my dismount. I knew if I stuck my dismount, this would be one of my best routines ever on beam, as well. As I took one last breath, I heard the warning bell, which was the indicator that I had ten seconds left to complete my exercise to stay within the ninety-second time limit. *Stick. Stick. Stick,* I said to myself as I made a powerful move into my round-off double somersault dismount. I stuck the landing. I was so relieved. I nailed my hardest event and I did it at the Olympics. *Thank you, God,* I thought as I jogged lightly down the podium and was greeted with hugs from all my teammates, then Team USA head coach Mary Lee Tracy and Marta, who was an official assistant coach for Team USA. Bela was not an official Team USA coach, so pursuant to Olympic rules, he was not supposed to be allowed on the floor. He watched from behind a nearby security wall surrounding the events area.

"Good job, little piggy," I remember Bela saying to me when I went over to him. It seemed so random, "little piggy," but he was genuinely pleased with my routine, so I figured that was his idea of a compliment—and effusive compliments from the Karolyis seemingly are reserved for the television cameras only.

I was feeling really good. I was relieved that my leg was holding up and I could gauge from the crowd's enthusiastic reaction that all the girls from Team USA were on fire. I hadn't allowed myself to look at the scoreboard to see our standing because I didn't want anything to distract me. I believed that if our team continued to hit our routines, we would win, so I didn't want to worry about the scoreboard too much. The rotation bell rang, so I quickly grabbed my gym bag and followed my team in a single-file line, like little soldiers, marching to our next event, floor.

I was looking forward to floor, the event where we could let our own personalities shine through most. I'd nailed my two most worrisome events, uneven bars and balance beam, and I was excited to perform my floor routine to the song "The Devil Went Down to Georgia" in front of the Georgia crowd. This particular song was selected by Bela. As the story goes, Bela was driving in his car when he heard this 1979 hit by the Charlie Daniels Band and immediately phoned Geza, our team choreographer. I never had much input in choosing my music, so I was quite pleased that the song was fun, upbeat, and energetic. To this day, I often meet people who comment that my "Devil Went Down to Georgia" routine was one of their favorite Olympic memories, so it was definitely a good choice.

Feeling confident, I mounted the podium for my floor routine, saluted the judges, and held my first pose, waiting for the music. As soon as the Georgia crowd heard my song, they let out a roar—by far, the best and loudest crowd of my life—and I remember thinking, *Let's do this.* I went on autopilot, letting my muscle memory guide me through my routine without really thinking much, just letting it happen and performing it to the max. I hit my fourth and final pass, which was a two-and-a-half twist backward (900 degrees of revolution twists in the air) and finished without a break or a step out of bounds. I couldn't help but smile as I danced into my final pose. I felt it was one of the best floor routines of my life.

The crowd went wild, and when I turned toward my coaches and teammates, I could see that they were cheering and happy with my performance. I was on an emotional high and felt so relieved that, again, I hit everything. A serene feeling of happiness washed over me at that point. Everything was going right—at the Olympic Games! Even the Karolyis seemed happy with me. I imagined Tata and Mama with big happy smiles on their faces.

As the rotation bell rang and we fell into a single-file line headed toward our last event, the vault, I peeked up at the scoreboard for the first time. Team USA was in first place with a razor-thin lead over Russia and Romania, our archrivals. *Yes!* I smiled to myself. Gold was within reach.

Vaulting would ultimately determine our medal color. Our team was strong and overall very consistent on vault, so I figured it was good that we were ending on a high note. For me, it had always been the least nerve-wracking of all the events. Although I had mostly avoided vaulting and hitting landings immediately prior to the Olympics due to the stress fracture in my leg, I knew I could still do this vault with no problem. I felt prepared and ready to finish strong. I was second to last in the lineup, so I waited on the sidelines near the podium. I learned early on in my career that you *never* relax in competition until you've completed the final element of your final routine. I did my best to stay focused. I kept my legs warm, running in place, doing cartwheels. One by one my teammates hit their vaults beautifully. The crowd roared with each, knowing it brought Team USA closer to gold.

Finally, I was up. I saluted the judges at 79½ feet and, like I'd done countless times in practice and prior competitions, I ran with force and attacked the vault. I had done this particular vault so many times, I could practically do it in my sleep—a Yurchenko one-and-a-half twist (540-degree twist) in a layout position.

Flump! I was stunned to find myself on the mat on my rear

end. I wasn't sure what had just happened. Embarrassed, I stood up as quickly as I could and saluted the judges. I was completely confused, and I guess my coaches were, too, because they had not a single word of technical advice for me. My personal coach on the floor, Marta, didn't say anything to me at all. She and Team USA head coach, Mary Lee Tracy, looked stunned and just stared blankly at me.

I looked around. I needed someone to tell me what they thought I did wrong. I didn't want to repeat the same mistake, and I couldn't place what had happened myself. I was in shock. I had done this thousands of times and always landed on my feet. What was happening? I had only a few short seconds to think while I was walking back to the end of the runway for my second attempt. I tried to be strong and not let any emotion show on my face even though I was going crazy trying to figure out what to do differently on my second vault. I still couldn't wrap my head around what I'd done wrong. I had done three of the most perfect routines of my life on the other events, and I certainly didn't want to finish the day this way, especially on an event that I usually nailed over and over again with no problem.

As I got to the end of the runway, I looked over at Bela behind the security wall. I was desperate for any tip or advice. Strangely, I remember feeling absolutely nothing when I looked at him. He could've been any other person in that crowd of thirty-three thousand. I felt no connection with Bela at that time.

"Stronger, Domi," Bela said, waving his hands around and making exaggerated facial expressions. *Stronger?* This didn't make sense to me because my first vault was very strong, full of power, and I ended up on my rear, anyway. I knew that wasn't my problem. Bela often said little tidbits and phrases when the cameras were rolling that I felt weren't really meant to help me, but more to make himself look like the enthusiastic, involved coach for the television audience. I guess this is when communicative coaching is crucial. I wished Alexander were there with me. He could always identify the problems and knew how to give me specific instructions for adjustments when I was struggling. I had a second shot to make things right. I think everyone, including myself, thought, *Well, that can't happen twice.*

I was somewhat numb. It felt like a slow-motion horror movie. I was terrified of failure and for my fall to define my Olympic experience. I was so disappointed in myself to have made that mistake, but I tried to put it behind me and focus on this next vault. Olympic rules stated that the highest score of the two vaults went toward the team total, so I had to keep it together. I had one more chance.

Standing on the runway, the judges were looking straight at me. The green "go" signal on the Longines scoreboard lit up and it was time. I saluted and started down the runway. I went for the same style vault as my first and pushed as aggressively as my little frame allowed. I wanted so badly to stick it this time—the only way to truly erase my first vault. In retrospect, after watching film of this second vault, I realize that it was wrong for me to focus so much on *sticking* the landing. It would've been better to focus on *making* the landing. This vault felt even stronger and higher than the first, but sadly, it ended the same. I made the same mistake and, again—*flump*—landed on my rear end. I bounced up quickly. I was stunned and devastated. The crowd felt it, too. They seemed as shocked as I was. I felt like I'd let people down: my team, my family, the fans, and myself. I couldn't believe that I worked so hard for this Olympic dream moment and in a flash of a few seconds the competition day ended like this for me. As I jogged off the podium, coach Mary Lee Tracy patted me on my back but didn't say a word. What could she say? I know she felt badly for me, but she had to move on, setting up the board for Kerri, our team's final competitor.

I kept walking and Marta stepped into my path.

"Two times? Too bad," Marta said, making sure I knew just how badly I'd messed up. She could see that I was already lower than low. She clasped the back of my neck tightly with her fingers and squeezed that trademark Marta "you messed up" squeeze. I absolutely cringed every time she did this in training when she was angry with me, but here at the Olympic Games, it was worst of all. As she held my neck with the one hand, she pressed her other hand to my forehead for a second and shot a sharp, disappointed glare into my eyes. And that was that. Marta and Bela barely said anything else to me that day or for the rest of the night. They acted as if they didn't know me, as if I were invisible. I took it hard. It was naïve of me, but I thought somewhere deep down, Bela and Marta cared for me at least enough to give me some scintilla of support after I'd fallen in front of millions.

The support was going to have to come from elsewhere.

"Don't worry about it," Amanda Borden said as she hugged me and patted my back. My other teammates each came over to hug me and offer their support. I was emotionless and empty. For several minutes, I wasn't sure if I had lost the gold medal for the team. I waited in suspense like everyone else.

In a daze, I put my wrist guards away, gathered my belongings, and turned to cheer for my friend and teammate Kerri as she prepped for her own vaults. Kerri saluted and made her way down the runway. The eyes of the arena were on her. Shockingly, Kerri also fell on her first vault. The entire arena went silent, in shock, I'm sure, thinking, *How could this be happening?* I know I was thinking it.

The two anchor vaulters for the team, Kerri and I, had just made three uncharacteristic mistakes in a row. I prayed that Kerri would land her second vault. Kerri looked liked she injured her ankle. She was assessing her ankle, rolling it around and limping after she got up. I didn't know what to think. Kerri appeared in shock as she walked back down the runway. The entire team had nagging injuries, some worse than others. As young as we were, we looked like elderly people sometimes, hobbling to our rooms after practice with bags of ice attached to our bodies with plastic wrap, but we were taught to be tough and push through. Kerri did exactly that.

As she saluted for her final vault, I whispered, "Come on, Kerri" and held my breath. Within thirty seconds, I witnessed her do the vault of her life on an injured ankle. I'd never seen anyone land a vault quite like that. At first, the entire arena was ecstatic that she'd landed the vault and not fallen a second time, but the joy was immediately followed by concern as Kerri fell to her knees in pain after saluting the judges on one foot. She stayed on all fours holding her ankle until the team trainer and Marta came onto the podium to help her off. The paparazzi swarmed Kerri to capture every single expression of pain across her face as she was carried out of the arena on a stretcher. I already knew how very tough my training partner was, and if *she* was in too much pain to walk, I knew it had to be bad.

Our team score was finally posted and the arena erupted in cheers and applause, waving American flags, chanting "USA, USA!" Team USA was on top of the leader board. We had won the team gold. We did it. A first for US Women's Gymnastics!

So much drama had occurred in that the arena in the last ten minutes of the competition, I was trying to absorb it all as I waited behind the curtain to be called for the medal ceremony. I was thrilled to have won a gold medal, but my joy felt marred. I had performed three of the best routines of my life that day on the uneven bars, balance beam, and floor and contributed high scores on those events to help our team's overall victory, yet the disappointment of my falls was hard to shake. A single nod or hug from Bela or Marta would have meant the world to me at that point, but by then they would look right past me. I had been completely erased from their minds. My emotions were bouncing all over the place— happy, sad, guilty, embarrassed. I knew they felt that I shamed them, and I wasn't sure if I deserved to smile as I received my medal. The way they ignored me made me feel like I was a ghost on the team, not truly worthy like the others.

Thankfully, as I was lost in my thoughts in the waiting area, my teammate Jaycie Phelps noticed my sadness.

"What's wrong?" Jaycie asked with a warmness that almost made me cry.

"I'm worried about my father, what he's going to say." I didn't need to say anything else because she knew exactly what I meant. Word had pretty much spread throughout the gymnastics community that Tata was a hothead with super high expectations. My teammates may not have known me well, but they knew that I feared Tata like I feared the Karolyis. I hadn't seen my parents yet, but I knew Tata would probably be very disappointed that I fell.

"Come on, Dominique! We just won the gold medal! Be happy!" Jaycie said excitedly. I wished I could feel like her and all my teammates, who were excited and truly living in the moment. Watching them hug each other and celebrate, I realized then that no matter how much I wanted to feel happy, my happiness depended on what my coaches and parents thought of my performance and whether or not *they* were pleased with me. It was hard to be happy when I felt I wasn't perfect enough for them. Maybe I didn't deserve to be happy.

As I write these thoughts now, of course, they seem absurd. I worked my whole life for that moment, to win Olympic gold. Darn right I deserved the medal and deserved to be happy about receiving it despite my performance on vault. Did I not contribute some of the highest scores on the three other events? I think that my fourteen-year-old mind had been so warped by the incessant criticism from my coaches and Tata that I actually began to believe that I had to be *perfect* to deserve any kind of happiness at all.

I will always appreciate Jaycie for trying to comfort me. She insisted that I put a smile on my face as we lined up backstage. Although it was a bit forced, it did actually make me feel better and enjoy the moment as coaches from the USA and other countries came up to congratulate our team.

I was near the end of the line as we marched into the arena to receive our medals. The arena was on fire with excitement, constant flashes from cameras, and deafening cheers from the crowd. The team final scores posted: 1. USA 389.225, 2. Russia 388.404, 3. Romania 388.246.

As we walked toward the podium, Bela appeared out of nowhere carrying Kerri in his arms. Her leg was bandaged and her foot was in a splint, but she was smiling now and she looked okay. Bela wedged himself right behind me in line. As Team USA walked up the stairs and onto the podium to receive our recognition, I waved to the crowd. Bela was still behind me carrying Kerri as our team stood on the podium. For a brief moment, I thought Bela might actually stay on the podium as we received our medals and I was horrified. I knew Bela was a publicity hound, and I wouldn't have put it past him to try and steal some of the attention away from the gymnasts. He was still carrying Kerri, looking around and smiling at the cheering crowd. Bela certainly knew how to play the part of the caring coach when the cameras were rolling. The media ate it up. I had seen the true face of the Karolyis and heard them bad-mouth many of their own gymnasts behind their backs. I didn't believe that Bela truly cared about Kerri or her leg. He was putting on a show and trying to share in the limelight that Kerri had earned with the rest of her team. I was relieved when he finally put her down and walked off the medal stand. Finally, with all of us on the stand together, I looked out into the sea of people and saw that this truly was America's gold medal! The crowd was so joyous, so supportive.

For fifty years, it was believed that the Americans could never win a women's gymnastics team gold medal because of the powerhouse of the Soviet Union and their centralized system. Their program had been state-funded with national teams hand selected based on their mental and physical makeup. They typically had a pool of thirty gymnasts and approximately twelve coaches assisting at all times. When this system collapsed and the Eastern bloc countries broke apart, there were not only seven Soviet gymnasts to compete against, there were more than twenty-one gymnasts when you included the Ukraine, Belarus, and Russia, not to mention the Romanians and Chinese. Our competition was fierce, so it was a huge feat to finally prove that the Americans were the best in the world in women's artistic gymnastics.

From the podium, I scanned the crowd right, left, then up and down. Below the podium, in the section generally reserved for media and photographers, I saw Tata front and center in his patriotic Uncle Sam top hat and his jumbo Sony camera hanging around his neck. His roll of film must have just run out because he had lifted the camera to his ear to listen to the film rewinding. Although a little embarrassed, I was impressed that Tata, in this silly hat, managed to get the best seat in the house for the gold medal moment. It made me chuckle. I knew that Mama, Christina, and my ever-supportive aunt Janice were in the audience, too, probably cheering their lungs out, but I just couldn't see them.

My teammates and I rallied in for one final team hug on the podium after the national anthem and team captain Amanda said some words of congratulations, then we did a victory lap around the arena. We were escorted to the VIP press box where our parents were waiting. It was time to face Tata and Mama. The butterflies tickled my stomach. While all my teammates couldn't wait to see their families, I wondered if there was some way to put off seeing mine—which was pretty sad considering I'd just reached a lifelong goal that they had mapped out for me and helped me achieve. I knew I wouldn't be met with the same enthusiasm as my peers would be, but I wasn't sure exactly what to expect. Part of me didn't want to see the disappointed look on their faces. Even though I had just won a gold medal, the expectations placed on me were higher.

My parents were near the front of the room along with Janice and my supportive, cheering little sister Christina. Unfortunately, Tata's and Mama's glum faces said it all. I figured they had to be proud of me on some level, and I wished they'd shown it more. They made it tough for me to feel proud of myself at that moment.

"What happened on your vaults?" was the first thing Tata said to me. I didn't answer.

Although Mama wasn't saying much, she did hug me and privately whispered, "Good job," but I saw the grief in her eyes. Perhaps it was because they both knew how hard I'd worked. If only I knew then what I know now, my entire attitude would have been different. It didn't have to be this way. Being treated like a failure or being belittled for not being "perfect" is so hurtful and damaging to a child.

That night, our team was invited to a post-Olympic party held in our honor at Planet Hollywood and hosted by Bruce Willis and Demi Moore. I was starstruck when I met the superstar couple, who I thought were the nicest people. Demi actually made an extra effort to talk with me and some of my teammates. I think she had just finished the *G.I. Jane* movie because her head was still shaven and she was wearing a bandana. I thought she was so badass!

Once the trays of appetizers and special food started to pass by, all I could think about was how hungry I was. I hadn't eaten since midday when I munched on a Rice Krispies bar that I'd snuck into my dorm room. It was already around ten and my tummy was rumbling. I was cautious and only ate a small serving of plain grilled chicken with some vegetables because I knew I would be back in the gym in the morning.

A number of my teammates and I had qualified for individual finals. I qualified for floor and beam finals; Dawes qualified for vault, uneven bars, floor, and All-Around; Shannon qualified for vault, beam, and All-Around; and Amy qualified for uneven bar finals. Kerri had qualified for events, too, but wasn't able to compete due to her injury. I was actually able to compete in the All-Around by taking Kerri's spot when she withdrew from competition. My training resumed the next day, with my teammates each going off with their personal coaches. I dreaded being with the Karolyis by myself, especially since they had barely talked to or acknowledged me after my falls, but the practice turned out to be very low spirited and uneventful, almost as if they had already written me off and were just present as a formality.

As I went into the All-Around day of competition, I had one thing I wanted to prove—my vault. My goal was to stick my vaults on this day, and this time I nailed it! I executed my vault and stuck the landing. I remember shaking my head a little after my second clean landing, wondering why I wasn't able to do it like that in the team competition. Having just missed a medal by coming in fourth in floor exercise later that week, and falling on my head during my beam routine in the event final, I didn't win an individual medal. I felt satisfied, however, that I was able to stick that vault landing at the Olympics and, of course, that as a team we had walked away with gold medals around our necks.

Heading down to breakfast the morning after the Olympic Gala exhibition, I made sure to first go to Marta and Bela's dorm room to say good morning, as I'd been taught to routinely do. I knocked on the door, waited, then knocked again. No answer. I knocked yet again. About that time, someone coming down the hallway told me that the Karolyis had left. *Left?* I thought. *Left where? To breakfast?* Bela and Marta had actually just packed up and left. No "goodbye," "farewell," or even a "good luck in life"?

I wasn't able to attend the Olympic Closing Ceremonies, which I was looking forward to since I missed Opening Ceremonies as well. Our coaches had thought our competition was too close to Opening Day and feared we'd get worn out, so we were forced to miss out on that experience. Looking back, I still regret not being able to participate in Opening and Closing Ceremonies, which are such special highlights for most of the athletes.

Interestingly, when NBC aired the women's gymnastics competition on television, it was tape delayed, so all of the commentary from Tim Daggett, Elfi Schlegel, and John Tesh was done via voiceover. The results were already in the books. The network played up the drama of Kerri's vault, which led viewers to believe that Team USA would take gold only if Kerri had stuck her vault. In truth, our team scores following my vault were already high enough to cement Team USA taking the gold medal. Ironically, it was a fan I met during a nationwide post-Olympic tour who pointed this out to me. I never bothered calculating my vault scores because the end result was gold for the Magnificent Seven. Kerri's heroic landing was certainly an iconic moment that added great drama for all of us, but the guilt I had carried thinking my vaults almost cost us the gold suddenly lifted with this realization.

This also made me realize that Tata must have known that my vault scores were, in fact, high enough to get us the team gold. Tata was good at math and always calculated the scores in his head before they were posted on the scoreboard. Later, Mama did confirm to me that they both knew my falls didn't jeopardize the gold, but they never bothered to tell me this.

I will always be grateful to have played a part in a historical moment in American gymnastics history. I have respect for all of my Magnificent Seven teammates because we each worked tirelessly toward this goal and, although we had different backgrounds and gymnastics clubs, we came together to win. This is something that will bond this team forever. We also had the first ever all-female Team USA coaching staff. Winning the gold medal in 1996 was monumental in US Women's Gymnastics on multiple levels. We changed the landscape of US gymnastics forever and, for me, reflecting back, it was truly . . . *magnificent!*

Chapter 9

EMANCIPATION

After the Olympics, the Magnificent Seven participated in a nationwide Olympic tour, which had been negotiated prior to the Games. The tour turned out to be one of the best experiences of my gymnastics career and my life up to that point. I was able to do what I loved—pure gymnastics—and perform for the public without the pressure of judges and scores and, most important, without the Karolyis barking orders at me and criticizing my every move. The tour was about gymnastics, plain and simple, and I loved that.

Bela was on the post-Olympic tour as well, but he rarely paid attention to me. I'm told that Bela watched some of my routines from backstage, but other than that, I felt invisible to him. It was difficult to reconcile that a month prior to the tour the Karolyis and I had been together around the clock, and, now he acted as if he had never even met me, sometimes passing me in the hallway without a word. It was oddly hurtful that to him I had obviously been just a tool, a means to an end. Since I felt like I'd disgraced Bela by falling and then not winning the All-Around gold medal to bring him the honor and credit he thought he deserved, I felt like I was no longer any value to him. I was relieved to be out from under his thumb. It was the first time in a long time that I wasn't walking around in fear, but it was also very confusing. As a young teen, I couldn't understand how he and Marta could just erase me out of their lives in a split second.

On the other hand, the tour itself was my first taste of freedom and boy, was it sweet. I was traveling across the country to connect with fans in each city and perform my heart out. I jokingly refer to this time as my "rock star" period because we lived out of suitcases and a tour bus for several months. It was the first time I was able to actually get to know most of my teammates, bonding with them as we went from city to city, arena to arena, in ways I had not been able to during the Olympics. It was an incredible experience, one I'll never forget.

It was also an opportunity to meet the gymnastics fans and I *loved* it. They shared a true appreciation for our sport and were so welcoming and thankful to Team USA for bringing home the gold. For me, the flowers, teddy bears, letters of encouragement, and enormous collective support I felt from these fans allowed me to temporarily forget some of my personal hardships. The disappointment and feelings of failure I felt from Tata and my coaches at the Olympics were buffered by the acceptance I received from these enthusiastic fans all across America.

It was also the little extra things—things that would seem trivial to most teenagers, but that to me made the whole touring experience a carefree, happy time. For example, I was trying foods I'd never been allowed to eat. I tried my first soda and peanut butter and jelly sandwich, and I'd order French toast for breakfast from room service in almost every hotel I stayed in. During our breaks, I'd often go shopping with my teammates or tour members. From hearing some of the other girls talk, I knew I was making a good amount of money because the gymnasts were being paid on a per-show basis and there were a lot of shows on this fifty-city tour. As someone who had basically lived in the gym since I could remember, I was content with the per diem allowance I was given by the tour managers and rarely needed more money for everyday things. I liked having some cash for food and shopping and the per diem covered those expenses.

Like everything else, Tata handled my finances and kept me in the dark about the money as well as all related business matters. He never included or informed me of even the most basic details of the contracts or appearance fees, so I had no idea how much money I was being paid for any of my events, including the tour. I just knew that it was a very successful tour and we were selling out nearly every venue. The team exceeded expectations and, from what I understand, the tour was in such demand that it was extended into spring of 1997. An additional forty cities or so were added. Looking back, I can't believe how little I knew about the money I was earning, despite my young age. I was fourteen and fifteen at the time of the tour, so I just went where I was told to go and did what I was told to do, and didn't concern myself with asking questions about my finances. I just loved performing for the fans and was ecstatic when I learned I'd be touring additional months.

After the Olympic tour came to a close, I had to return to real life. The first order of business was to find a new coach and a place to train since I basically felt disowned by the Karolyis. Tata was disappointed by Bela's complete lack of interest in my training, but he didn't know where else to take me, so he begged and begged until Bela agreed to train me for a bit. It was a mistake from the beginning; it's never a good idea to have to "beg" someone to coach you. I ended up having a couple of months of lackluster training with Bela and Marta before we called it quits. Bela didn't want to be there and neither did I. Tata asked for the Karolyis' help in finding a new coach for me if they didn't want me anymore, but they flat-out refused. They apparently kept telling him that my "body won't be able to keep up the training at this level" and that I "should just stop now." At this point I was fifteen, coming off my first Olympics, and the most recognized authorities of my sport were telling my parents and me that I was washed up, "finished." Even though it was clear to me now that Bela didn't care about me as a person, I still, for some twisted reason, craved his approval.

I worked with a number of different coaches, trying to find the right fit. Tata had me hopping from one gym to another all over the map, from Houston to Boston. We had moved to Houston in order to train with the Karolyis, and now that I was no longer with them, I lacked a "gym home." I felt like an orphan going from gym to gym asking for permission to train. The fame and Olympic credential surely didn't hurt in terms of getting me into various gyms, but Tata held the instructors to a standard they could never match, at least in his eyes. When I did get to train or work with new coaches, it was for short, irregular periods. I needed stability. Through no fault of their own, the coaches I was working with in these cities weren't a perfect match. After bouncing from gym to gym several times, I started to lose my motivation.

Tata came up with the idea of building our own gym, a place where I could train and also run my own gymnastics business as an adult when I retired from competition. I remember one night at the dinner table saying it sounded like a good idea, in an attempt to please Tata as much as anything else, and that was that. When

I was fifteen years old, Moceanu Gymnastics Incorporated (MGI) was born. What started out as an admirable plan with good intentions turned into something grandiose. Tata decided he didn't want the gym to be just *any* gym; he wanted it to be the best and biggest gym in the country. I do believe now that Tata's heart was in the right place, but he plunged in headfirst. The gym became his primary focus. He was palpably excited discussing plans for the gym. Upon completion, the gym would be dubbed the "Taj Mahal" of gymnastics by some media outlets and a buzz was created within the gymnastics community because of its state-of-the-art equipment and features. It truly was one of the finest gyms I'd ever seen, but it just seemed too unmanageably big from the start.

During construction in 1997, Tata spent endless nights at the site on Louetta Road in Spring, Texas. He really threw himself into the project day and night and was proud of how it was shaping up. It was during this time that Tata became friendly with a man named Brian Huggins, who was a salesman for RSC, the national equipment company that helped build the foundation of our gym. Tata rented large equipment, such as tractors, bulldozers, and moving equipment, from Brian. They were both big talkers and would sit for hours shooting the breeze and drinking beer late into the night at the site. Brian stroked Tata's ego in the right ways, too, and fast became what Tata considered a "buddy." Mama and I disliked it when Tata would go on and on bragging and exaggerating how much money we had and how much I'd made through my endorsements, appearances, et cetera. Mama would diplomatically try to tell him that it was giving the wrong impression, and she'd try to tone down the exaggerations and late-night stories a bit, but Tata was Tata and there was no stopping him. He had big dreams and felt like he was on top of the world while the gym was being built; he wanted everyone around him to share in the excitement.

Before I knew it, Tata—who was literally spending every waking moment at the gym site, managing all aspects of construction—

had asked Brian to help him out by taking me shopping or to eat when I was really supposed to be doing those things with Tata. Tata approved of Brian, and since he rarely approved of anyone, I figured Brian was harmless and went along with Tata's wishes. Brian was very confident, charismatic, and charming, though with his crisp Polo shirts, gelled hair, and perfectly tanned skin, he was seen by some (such as Aunt Janice, who never really liked him) as smug. He did seem a bit of a show-off—zipping around town in his flashy red Corvette—but he was polite and fun to be around, often cracking jokes. I knew very little about Brian in the beginning, except that he had a wife and a son, whom he talked about often.

I was used to being surrounded by adults more than kids my own age, so it didn't even occur to me that hanging out with Brian could be construed as anything but innocent. What began as small trips to the mall or to get a bite to eat eventually turned into all-day excursions, often on Saturdays or Sundays. It was fun to be taken places I'd never really gotten a chance to see before by this interesting and charismatic friend who seemed to know so many people and constantly made me laugh. I started to view Brian as an older brother who'd let me get away with some fun stuff that most other adults wouldn't allow. We also spent a fair amount of time at Lake Conroe on Brian's boat. Brian taught me how to wakeboard and water ski and we'd have a lot of fun being silly and goofing around. Sometimes Christina would come to the lake with us, and occasionally, Tata and Mama would come, too. If anyone enjoyed the water as much as Brian, it was Tata. He loved being on the boat, fishing and soaking in the outdoors, but more often than not, Tata and Mama were too busy with the gym to make it out to the lake.

Many times I wished that Tata had known how to spend more time with me and talk to me the way Brian did. Tata always thought he had to be so tough on the surface, even though we all knew deep down he had plenty of his own insecurities. I know that spending some quality time together could have changed our entire relationship, and I believe would have helped us avoid many problems we ended up facing. Tata asking Brian to spend time with me in place of himself was wrong on so many levels.

Aunt Janice's initial distaste for Brian had grown. As someone who loved me as if I were her own child, she was getting more and more frustrated with Tata and Mama for letting me run around town with Brian. She didn't like the idea of a grown, married man in his thirties and with a wife and child hanging out with a sixteen- or seventeen-year-old girl. She wondered on many occasions why he didn't go home to his wife and child more often. She was suspicious of Brian's intentions from the start.

Aunt Janice was the only person who had been there for my family from the beginning and for the right reasons. She made a commitment to look out for me early on and has always been true to that promise. She, in fact, stuck with all of us Moceanus through good and bad and was there for Tata, Mama, Christina, and me in ways we could not be for one another—a shoulder to cry on, a nurturing, compassionate friend, and a straight-shooting provider of doses of reality whether we wanted to hear them or not. She was the only one I was ever completely open and honest with about *everything*. I'd tell Aunt Janice how I felt—with no filter—and she never backed away, loving me whether I was exceeding my goals or falling flat and struggling. I'm so thankful she came into our lives when we moved to Houston. She was the one who told me, and still does to this day, how much Tata genuinely loved me, and shares with me the conversations she and Tata had. She is one of the very few who knew Tata's sensitive side.

"Why don't you just tell Dominique that you love her?" she'd often ask Tata.

"She knows" was always his reply. "It is something that doesn't have to be said."

"I don't think Dominique truly knows," she'd tell Tata, and she was right. For most of my gymnastics career, I felt that the quality of my performance would be the barometer of my father's mood. Unconditional love was not even a consideration to me. To hear those words from him then would have meant the world to me. Sadly, I'd have to wait until my twenty-first birthday for my father to finally say, "I love you." Through everything, Aunt Janice stayed a loyal friend to Tata and listened to all of his business schemes and cockamamie ideas because she truly believed his heart was in the right place. She was also a sounding board for Mama, who would privately reveal to Janice just how trapped and unhappy she felt in the marriage at times. We are so fortunate to have had this confidante. Aunt Janice smiles and shakes her head today when she tells me that each of the four Moceanus would confide in her things we never spoke of to one another. She always tried to get us to open up, but we were all stubborn that way—and, heck, we had Aunt Janice if we needed to get something off our collective chests.

"The first time someone meets your daddy, they love him," Aunt Janice used to tell me in her warm Southern drawl. "The second time, they hate him. I'm one of the only people I know of that actually knows your daddy *and* likes him." She was so right. Tata didn't have many genuine friends. Most of the people he knew were either business associates or people who outright feared him. But not Aunt Janice. She thought of Tata like a brother and wasn't afraid to stand up to him. She was at our house often, offering to take Christina or me places or helping Tata out with the gym. Sometimes they'd fight like siblings, especially when she was defending me tooth and nail when he was being unreasonable, which was often. I remember times when he'd be revving up for one of his scary rages and feeling so relieved that Aunt Janice was present to stand in his path and shout right back at him—cursing up a blue streak, but always in an attempt to stick up for me. When push came to shove, though, Tata still ruled the roost.

Tata's inability to listen to others and compromise was probably his downfall in a lot of ways, and eventually it was the demise of the gym. Managing a gym and all its staff of coaches and employees requires diplomatic skills, something Tata certainly lacked. He had a heart of gold at times, but he also had a heart of coal when his temper flared and he made rash decisions in anger. When someone rubbed Tata the wrong way, he'd act out of raw emotion without thinking twice about who he was hurting in the process. Words of venom would just spew out of him. It was only a matter of time until that temper would flare at the wrong time and start to destroy the gym.

Meanwhile, Mama and Tata were still searching to find me a new coach. I'd been through a long list of coaches, trying to find the right fit, and nothing seemed to work. I began to feel like my gymnastics skills might be slipping a bit and was concerned that we'd never find anyone. Bela's warnings that I wouldn't "be able to keep up the training" and that I was "done" kept flashing through my mind.

Then, like a godsend, Luminita Miscenco arrived in January 1998. She apparently had been coaching the junior national team in Romania and eagerly accepted my parents' offer to come to the United States to coach me. Tata had met with her during a trip to Romania and managed to obtain a work visa for her. She was a sight for sore eyes in the coaching department—she had a light, positive air about her, and it didn't hurt that she was youthful (only nine years older than me), with shoulder-length dark brown hair, fair skin, and brown eyes. You could tell she'd been a gymnast herself by her fit, petite physique.

I loved her right away. I had gotten out of shape and knew that I had my work cut out for me, but my motivation and enthusiasm returned under Luminita. Luminita was serious, focused, and demanding, but she also trained with compassion and care. I was shocked that she actually asked for my input in training and would read my body language to gauge my energy or exhaustion. As a gymnast herself, she understood the physical demands of our sport.

There is an unspoken understanding between most gymnasts, and this aspect of our relationship brought us closer. I responded to her training style and felt alive again in the gym. It was also the first time I was coached entirely in Romanian; Luminita didn't speak English. It was almost like a new start and I was invigorated.

Training went relatively smoothly the first eight months. Luminita worked me back into top gymnastics shape with one-on-one training sessions from January to July 1998. I had my heart set on competing at the Goodwill Games in New York in July of that year. The support of Luminita, my family, friends, and fans motivated me to keep pressing forward to reach that goal. There certainly were low points, when I was full of tears and doubted myself in the gym, but as months passed, I kept pushing myself. Luminita taught me new skills that I'd never attempted before, increasing my difficulty and helping me gain a new confidence. At the Goodwill Games, I planned to debut a new vault—a front handspring on the vaulting horse into a front layout position with a 180-degree twist. I'd also perform new routines on bars, beam, and floor exercise highlighting my newer, more mature style of gymnastics. The hunger to win the Goodwill Games grew more with each passing month.

"I foresee the competition ending with you in first place, standing between two Romanians," Luminita said to me weeks before the Goodwill Games. The fact that she had so much confidence in me and the fact that she was *telling* me how good she thought I was, even at times applauding my practice sessions, was something new to me and a tremendous breath of fresh air. It also meant that Luminita believed I was good enough to beat those "two Romanians," who happened to be two of the most accomplished gymnasts in the world at that time. Olympic and World champion Simona Amânar, who'd go on to have an impressive career, being a seven-time Olympic medalist and a ten-time World medalist, was target number one. She was a fierce competitor with outstanding difficulty and consistency. Obstacle number two was then-current European champion, Maria Olaru, who'd go on to become the World champion in 1999 and Olympic champion in 2000. The roster for competition also included Russian gymnastics legend Svetlana Khorkina. To have the chance to compete—and win—against this incredible group would prove to myself that I could do anything I set my mind to.

Due to bureaucracy, I almost didn't get the chance. USA Gymnastics, the governing body for our sport, tried to bar me from competing at the Goodwill Games. Tata had to fight with USA Gymnastics Women's Program vice president Kathy Kelly to allow me the chance to compete. As I had been kicked to the curb by the Karolyis after the Olympics, the powers-that-be in our sport didn't think I was "worthy" of a competition slot. I had trained so hard, yet Tata had to fight for me and go head to head with Kathy to even get me an opportunity to make it onto the roster. The subjectivity and politics that surround USA Gymnastics is, in my mind, the sport's worst enemy. After much battling by Tata, USA Gymnastics finally agreed to send a National team staff member, former Russian gymnast Arthur Akopyan, to evaluate me to determine if I was ready for competition. And with strong legs and stronger confidence, I was able to put on a demonstration for him that immediately showed I deserved a spot. He actually took a moment to tell me how impressed he was with my improvements and new routines. With a ticket to New York and the 1998 Goodwill Games, I felt I really had something to prove—to the world and to myself.

I had a fever of 104 degrees the evening before the Goodwill Games All-Around competition. Luminita comforted me as I shivered like a leaf through the night in the hotel room we shared. I couldn't believe how quickly these flulike symptoms came on after evening practice. I didn't want anyone to know I was sick; I had worked too hard to give any of my competitors a mental edge. Sick or not, I wasn't going to let this one slip away.

Morning practice didn't go well; I felt lethargic and my balance seemed off. I started to get frustrated and scared, but Luminita was there by my side and helped me by talking things out. The rest of my body was in great shape, she reminded me, probably the best shape of my career up to that point. I was here to win, regardless of the obstacles. When we went back to our hotel room to rest before the evening competition, my mind was racing. I was looking forward to catching a nap, because I was exhausted from being up all night with my fever. After morning practice, I passed out almost immediately. The hotel wake-up call startled me—I had slept for nearly three hours. Luminita, barely awake herself after sharing such a rough night, was leaning over me, asking me how I felt.

"Better," I said. Surprisingly, I felt reenergized. We smiled at each other and Luminita gave me that "let's go win a medal" look of hers.

I touched my head to make sure my ritualistic four dark brown hair clips I wore at every competition were in their rightful places—one on each side of my head, one on top, and one underneath my bun. I looked down at my leotard with rhinestones outlining the letters "USA" across my chest. Every shred of lean muscle I had earned over the past seven months showed through my tight, solid white leotard. I was ready. And this time, everything went right.

On July, 19, 1998, I won the Goodwill Games Individual All-Around title, topping the scores of even my most competitive Romanian and Russian rivals. It was something of a historic achievement as well, as it was the first time a non-Russian female gymnast won the title. In the end, as Luminita had predicted, I stood tall proudly on the podium between two Romanian gymnasts, tears streaming down my face and a gold medal around my neck.

I consider this competition to be one of my greatest. In seven months, I went from being an out-of-shape gymnast who'd struggled to find enthusiasm for the sport in December 1997, to upgrading the configuration of my routines from the Atlanta Olympics and competing among the best World and Olympic female gymnastics champions.

In retrospect, the fact that USA Gymnastics tried to bar me from competing at the Goodwill Games, claiming I was not good enough to make the roster, made it that much sweeter. When I did win, I was too happy to be annoyed by Kathy Kelly—now clapping her hands and telling me she was proud of me, as if she'd been my biggest cheerleader all along. I was thrilled to prove to all the naysayers that I not only could compete, but I could also still be a champion. Most important, I proved to myself that the Karolyis were wrong, that I wasn't "finished" and that I *could* win again, at the highest level, and without them. My Goodwill Games All-Around gold medal is the only award I keep alongside my Olympic medal because it means that much to me.

Before I left for the Goodwill Games, I weighed 43 kilos, or 94.6 pounds. I had a love/hate relationship with the scale—loved it when the numbers dropped, hated it when it showed I'd gained weight. In gymnastics, one's balance, form, and technique are influenced by size and weight. It's usually advantageous be smaller and lighter, hence the pressure on Elite gymnasts to be lean. The new routines I was working on with Luminita were challenging and required me to be as light as possible.

I never liked the process of cutting weight. It always brought me back to the horrible tension I felt with the Karolyis, how they'd humiliate me if they suspected I'd gained any weight. I was made to feel worthy only when I was skinny, and that certainly wasn't healthy. Although I still didn't enjoy cutting weight, I was trying to approach it with a healthier mind-set, to shed old habits and develop a better self-image, but it was difficult to change. I still had plenty of emotional scars and a warped perspective of my body. I'd look in the mirror and no matter how thin I was, I'd always manage to find a piece of skin to pull away from my body, which I thought of as fat even if it was skin. I always thought I could be skinnier.

I had a major growth spurt of nearly eight inches after the Olympics. I went from being the smallest member of Team USA at 4' 4" and 70 pounds, to 5' and 98 pounds, which may still sound small, but it was considered pretty tall for a gymnast back then. I've often wondered if that growth spurt was a result, in part, of finally being able to eat. From the age of ten through fourteen, my caloric intake was extremely limited even though I spent the majority of my days working out in the gym. The Karolyis always seemed to think the less food, the better. I can't help but think that my growth was stunted to some degree during that period from malnourishment and, now, my body was making up for lost time. I also allowed myself to eat some of the forbidden foods that I had always craved, like bread, sweets, and even pizza on occasion. I was never educated about counting calories or understanding the difference between and function of carbohydrates and proteins, so I never approached my weight or weight loss in a healthy way.

When I started gaining weight, I tried to make myself purge on a few occasions, but, thankfully, I was never any good at it. Instead of bingeing and purging, I found myself in a cycle of bingeing and starving, especially when training for the Goodwill Games. I'd eat freely on the weekends, most often overdoing it until I was uncomfortably stuffed, and then I'd starve myself during the week. Sometimes, I wouldn't eat any dinner even though I was doing two long training sessions per day. I'd often run a few miles at the track after the last training session to make sure to burn off everything I'd binged on the past weekend. When Friday evening came, I'd start the bingeing cycle all over again. I didn't realize at the time how unhealthy this was for my body and my mind.

I was obsessed with seeing the numbers drop on the scale, but I had my weak moments like when I'd go through the Dairy Queen drive-through on my way home from morning practice and gorge on a burger and fries, sometimes even an ice cream cone. I'd feel horrible afterward and would work out extra hard at the afternoon session and wouldn't eat anything the rest of the day. Other times, I'd buy Gummi Bears and snacks at the gas station on the way home from the gym and keep them as a secret stash in my car. When Christina and I begged Mama, she would sometimes give in and allow us to indulge in a low-fat frozen yogurt at TCBY. Aunt Janice was the only adult who didn't monitor my food constantly and because of that, she was the only adult I felt I could eat freely in front of. She was the first to let me try mac and cheese when I was a teenager, which I loved. In the end, I'd be disgusted with my-self when the scale would show I'd gained weight, and I'd be angry and frustrated for being stuck in this unhealthy cycle.

When my daily weigh-in showed I'd gained a pound, Luminita would take me to the track to run and burn some extra calories after my afternoon training. One day, as we drove to the track, she discovered my secret stash of treats in the car. She was angry and disappointed with me and made sure that I knew I'd be running extra miles that night and probably the rest of the week. It put me in a bad mood, and I got more annoyed when Luminita phoned Mama to come join us at the track. I didn't like mixing my train-ing with family time, and it bothered me when Mama would come run with us, which was becoming more frequent. Mama loved any opportunity to exercise, and she got such joy from walking and run-ning around the track. I usually had to sit there and wait because Mama always wanted to do "extra" laps no matter how many we'd already done. Other times, I'd get too impatient and go home, leav-ing Mama alone at the track for hours—she was a runner at heart. I understand now that the exercise helped her decompress and balance the stress at home; it was her only outlet to release the tension, and I should have been more understanding, since she was kept on such a very tight leash by Tata and rarely allowed to go off to exercise by herself. Tata controlled her even more than he controlled me, yet she was a grown woman. Looking back, I still don't know how she dealt with that kind of control in a marriage. I promised myself I'd never marry someone who wanted that type of control over me.

After my successful performance at the Goodwill Games, I immediately started training for US Senior Nationals in Indianapolis the following month. No flu this time, but I broke out in hives all over my face the week before the competition, probably from the stress of a hyperextended knee that occurred during vault practice one afternoon. I had to stay off the knee for a couple of days and did what I could to allow it to heal, but there just wasn't much time. At Nationals, I made errors on my bar routine both days that put me out of contention to win the All-Around. Luckily, even with my wobbly bar performances, I managed to place third in the All-Around, and I won two golds—for balance beam and vault in the individual event finals.

By the time we came home from Nationals, we desperately needed a rest. It took some heavy convincing from Mama, Luminita, and me, but Tata miraculously agreed to let the three of us go to Cancun for a few days. Tata agreed that it would be good for me to have some time to rest and figured I'd come back rejuvenated and ready to train. An actual vacation? I was beyond excited. Those were the fastest days of my life. Being near the beach, having downtime, really served us all well, including Mama, who I rarely saw sit down, let alone relax at home.

Training went well the month following Cancun. Since I had no major meets on the horizon, we took things slowly and trained in the pits on the soft surface. I should have known that things wouldn't stay calm for long. In mid-October 1998, Tata and Luminita got into a huge argument that would be the turning point in my relationship with both of them. During practice one afternoon, Tata came to my private training area in the back of the gym. Tata enjoyed watching me train, and he'd stop by now and then, so at first I thought nothing of this particular visit. He knew it distracted me when he stayed too long, so he usually watched for a short bit, then shoved off. This time, Tata stayed.

I cringed as a few comments flew back and forth between Tata and Luminita. It was never good when they talked during my training; it distracted all of us and it sometimes turned into Tata listing one thing after another of what I was doing wrong. The topic of conversation that day, however, was not me, which made things even worse. Within a few minutes, their discussion got heated, and by the middle of my vaulting session, it was a full-blown argument. They had recently begun butting heads, mostly about money. From what I understood, Luminita had been asking for a raise for some time. I heard rumblings from Tata at home about how Luminita was getting "greedy" and "too demanding." It was awkward hearing from both sides and being caught in the middle. I was having my own issues with Tata trying to control me and my finances, so I could appreciate Luminita's perspective, but I also saw how much my parents had helped Luminita. So I tried to stay out of it, but that was nearly impossible.

I stood frozen by the end of the vault runway watching this argument escalate. Soon they were both yelling uncontrollably. Tata, face red and arms waving, kept shouting that he did too much for Luminita, that she wasn't appreciative. I'm not sure what else he said to her, but something clicked in Luminita and she lost it. She let it rip, giving Tata a piece of her mind, holding nothing back. This was bad. I finally had a stable, positive coaching situation and then this. All the security we had established in my training the past year began to crumble before my eyes. I felt sick to my stomach.

"Okay, you're fired! Get your things and leave!" Tata barked.

Enraged, he also yelled something about having her deported and sent back to Romania. Tata always hit below the belt when he was in the heat of an argument, and people never knew whether he was serious about his threats. I knew Tata was fed up with Luminita and he meant what he said. He'd felt for some time that she was ungrateful for all that he and Mama had done for her—they had completed all the paperwork and paid the expenses for her to get her visa and come to the United States, moved her into a house with other coaches, given her a car and a job coaching me, among other things. When Luminita asked for more money, Tata told her the arrangement was fair for now.

After Luminita darted out of the gym, Tata turned to me.

"She has to be patient to build a life in this country. She'll get more money. . . . She can't expect to have *everything* she dreams of the first year of coming here!"

Tata said he was paying her a decent salary, as much as he could afford during these beginning stages of the gym when most of the revenue went to cover bills and operating costs. He was working hard to increase enrollment and actually had intended to give Luminita a raise, but on his terms. For now, he was trying to meet her needs as best they could. I know Tata and Mama were even starting the process to bring Luminita's boyfriend at the time over from Romania just to keep her happy.

Apparently, it was a relative who had been stirring the pot from the beginning by repeatedly encouraging Luminita to ask for more money. I overheard Tata and Mama talking about it one evening when I was on the balcony debating whether I should sneak downstairs to the kitchen for a quick late-night snack; I was starving. I never found out who this family member was, but Luminita later implied that someone in Tata's extended family was telling her to make these demands. It was a shame that my own family was whispering about Tata behind his back and causing problems for our family.

"Tata, Tata, what are we going to do?" I gasped after I heard the gym door slam behind Luminita.

"You'll be fine. We'll find you a new coach," he grumbled before storming out the opposite side of the gym as Luminita. He said it so matter-of-factly, as if it were as simple as buying a new pair of shoes. Did he not remember how difficult it was to find Luminita in the first place? I was furious with Tata for ruining everything that was finally right in my life. Why couldn't he hold on to the one person who'd brought me stability that year and helped rekindle my fire for gymnastics? She not only helped me achieve my big win at the Goodwill Games, but we had bonded in the gym like no other coach I had had before. Outside the walls of the gym, she was like a big sister to me. I confided in her and she in me. We were inseparable over the course of those ten months when she first came to Houston, and I depended on her.

I knew this was the beginning of the end. What would follow that argument in the coming months would change the course of our lives forever. It literally tore my family apart—almost for good. That day was a huge turning point in my life and marked the beginning of my independence, though not in the way I had imagined.

Watching Luminita explode at Tata released my floodgates, too. All my anger and resentment had been building for some time; I just hadn't realized how bad it had gotten. My relationship with Tata was already on thin ice. I was fed up with him trying to control my every move, not giving me any freedom of choice or opinion in the gym or at home. I was tired of putting on a front and pretending that our relationship was fine when it really wasn't. I was tired of being Tata's workhorse and having everyone depend on me but never having a voice in anything.

I think Tata sensed that he couldn't stop me from growing up, but he wasn't ready to release his control over me. I think it scared him that I now had my driver's license and I wanted to do things with other kids my own age. I remember one of the very few times

I invited friends to our house earlier that year. Tata got into one of his moods and started loudly berating me for something in the downstairs kitchen. Luminita was there, and she and Mama were with us in the kitchen. I was so embarrassed because I knew that my friends could hear him yelling at me. That was another thing about Tata: he didn't care whom he acted out in front of. These public rants also served as fodder for gossip throughout the gymnastics community, making people whisper about how crazy, unstable, or belligerent he was. I was so angry with Tata for humiliating me in front of my friends that I somehow had the nerve to answer back and our voices got even louder. I'm sure my friends were terrified listening from upstairs. Tata was shocked and ticked off that I stood up to him, and he started to charge me with his hand raised ready to strike me.

"Dimitru, calm down! What's come over you?!" I can still hear Mama saying in Romanian as she reached for his raised hand.

Tata yelled that he'd never said I could invite friends to the house. Mama tried to calm him, telling him she had given me permission, but that only fueled the argument as Tata then exploded at Mama because *she* hadn't asked him for permission, either. I was mortified that my friends were listening to Tata scream at both Mama and me for inviting them over. I wanted out. Tata turned toward me, and I recognized the rage in his face and knew I had to get out of the house before he hit me. I inched backward away from Tata as he got closer and closer to me until my back was against the kitchen door leading outside. In a split second, I grabbed for the doorknob, threw the door open, and took off sprinting down the driveway and into the street as fast as I could. My heart was pounding as I turned my head to see if Tata was chasing me. Thank God, there was no one behind me.

I kept running until I was a safe distance from the house and then I collapsed in tears on the curb. I didn't know what to do. I sat in the darkness crying and cursing Tata's name. The last thing

I wanted to do was go back to the house, so I stayed there on that curb and fumed . . . until I could see Mama and Luminita walking down the street looking for me. I knew I had to go back and apologize to my friends, who were still in the house. It had been more than an hour since I'd run from Tata. I felt so embarrassed, yet I had to go face them and Tata. It was yet another reminder that Tata was as determined as ever to control me, like he controlled Mama, for as long as he possibly could.

I was seventeen years old and the primary breadwinner of the family, yet Tata still treated me like a ten-year-old, and he certainly didn't think I needed to concern myself with finances. I, however, felt that if I was capable of earning the money in the first place, then I should be at least involved in decisions and have some input on how that money was going to be spent and invested. Tata got annoyed if I even asked about how much I was earning, how much we'd spent or saved.

"You don't have to worry about that, we'll take care of it," was Tata's standard answer. But I did worry. I wanted to keep track and know what was happening with the money I'd made from my career—the endorsements, print ads, the Olympic tour, appearances, and so on. Tata had big ideas, many of which were great, but he was also a risk taker, and I was nervous that he'd spend all my savings. Tata also didn't always understand how things worked in this country. I remember he didn't think twice when he began accepting the USA Gymnastics monthly stipend money offered after I'd made the National team. At the time, Tata didn't understand that accepting that stipend would strip my NCAA eligibility, meaning I would be forever barred from competing as a college athlete. All my parents knew was that they could barely pay their bills and accepting that $1,000-per-month stipend would help keep me in gymnastics. For me, I would have liked to better understand my options, but how could I blame them for not explaining it when they didn't fully understand it themselves? Misunderstandings like these were warning signs that I needed to be more involved in such decisions. I tried to wedge my way in, but Tata usually stonewalled me.

"What about college?" I asked Tata about one week before he fired Luminita. "I want to go to college and get my own apartment. I'll need my own money."

"Don't worry, we'll pay for it. I will send you money," he replied, but this time it wasn't good enough for me. I'd seen how he'd take away the car keys from Mama or me when he got angry or in one of his moods. Even though it was childish, it was his way of reminding us who was in control. I could easily foresee him withholding my own money from me when I needed it. I knew I couldn't trust that he'd send it to me on time every month.

"What if I have to pay my bills or apartment rent, or buy books?" I challenged him. "You expect me to wait for you to send the money?"

Tata was furious that I was pushing and made a show of anger instead of answering any of my questions. Deep down, what I really wanted to know, but was still too afraid to ask, was, *"Where is all the money I earned?"* I feared that all, or most of it, was sunk into the construction of the gym and spent on bad investments. I didn't have any idea how much it cost to build the gym, but it was the grandest gym I'd seen, so I knew it was a lot. I just kept praying that it didn't eat up all of my savings because I needed that money for college, for my future. I know Tata had envisioned the gym as a family business, one I could run one day, but with any business, there is risk. Tata was learning quickly just how much time and money were required to build a successful gym even *after* the construction was complete. Operating expenses were high, we were desperately trying to build a decent enrollment, and we were a long way from being profitable.

Standing alone in the gym after Tata fired Luminita, I could feel that everything was spiraling out of control. I had worked so hard the past year, and the sudden instability put me over the edge. As I drove home, I became more and more upset. The reality of the situation was sinking in. By the time I reached our house, I had worked myself up into a rage. I was hysterical imagining how I'd live without Luminita as my coach and a part of my life. I made up my mind that if Luminita was leaving, I was leaving, too.

I ran to my bedroom in the back of the house and thrashed through my closets searching for luggage. I knew I had less than ten minutes before Mama and Tata would be home to check on me, so I needed to pack my stuff and get out as fast as possible. I didn't have any idea where I was going, but I had my mind set on leaving and never coming back. I threw as much of my life as I could fit into a few duffel bags and then ran to my car. In a state of hysteria, I just kept repeating to myself, *I've gotta get out of here, I've gotta get out of here.* I'm sure I looked like a madwoman, moving feverishly, tears streaming down my face, and talking to myself as I ran out of the house. I did feel horribly guilty leaving Mama and Christina behind. I also couldn't stop thinking about what Tata would do to me when he tracked me down. It certainly wasn't the way I envisioned leaving home.

I drove straight to the house where Luminita lived with other coaches from the gym. As I drove, I called Brian and my loyal cousin Spiros, whom I had grown close to, asking both of them to meet me at Luminita's. This little makeshift support group huddled with me in Luminita's room, trying to help me devise a plan. Luminita was freaking out, too, and wanted to make sure we were out of the house by the time Tata came looking for me. The coaches' house would be one of the first places on Tata's search. For one thing, he owned the property, and, second, he'd surely know that I'd likely be with Luminita. Tata was already calling repeatedly on my cell phone and for the first time in my life, I ignored his calls.

Brian made some calls and arranged for me and Luminita to stay in a room at a hotel near I-45 in Houston. Luminita and I stayed up most of that night talking and trying to figure out what we should do. It was all very surreal trying to plan the next stage of my life when up to that point I hadn't had much freedom at all. My mind was jumping from one idea to the next and in between. All I could think about was how angry Tata was going to be if I went back home.

Tata kept trying to reach Luminita on her phone as well, and she started to worry that he would call the police and try to have her deported. I briefly called Aunt Janice the following morning to let her know I was okay. I didn't want to involve her and put her in an awkward position with my parents, so I didn't tell her where I was. Aunt Janice told me that my parents reported me missing to the police when I didn't come home that evening. I knew they were worried about me, so I was glad that Aunt Janice could at least let them know that I was okay, but that was it. I really wanted to hear Mama's voice and let her know where I was as well, but I knew she'd tell Tata.

Tata was a determined man and it didn't take him long to track me down. He discovered our hideout after following my cousin Spiros to the hotel when he came to see me on day two, which was right about the time the media caught on to my story. I was terrified when Tata left messages on my phone letting me know that he had found me and that he could come to get me if he wanted. I expected Tata to barge through the door and drag me out screaming. Instead, Tata left another message pleading for me to come home.

I never in a million years imagined that I'd run away like I did and certainly would never encourage any other seventeen-year-old to do the same, but at the time I felt like things would have gotten even uglier if I had stayed home—especially that night. Things had reached a boiling point in my family. There was no reasoning with Tata and instead of him giving me more autonomy as I was nearing eighteen and becoming an adult, it felt like he was tightening the reins even more. It still had to be *his* way always and with everything. He wouldn't accept that I needed a voice in my own life, in my own matters. He was so used to giving orders to all of us that he didn't stop to think that I would want to be my own person who made decisions for myself one day.

I certainly wasn't going to be like Mama—a grown woman who let Tata run her life. At home, Mama took the brunt of Tata's abuse. I'd get so angry at times that I just wanted to lash out and physically hit Tata for all the hurt he'd caused Mama and me over the years, but I knew more violence was certainly not the answer. For Tata, violence and bullying seemed to be the only way he knew how to release his anger, and I hated that. He was so quick to raise a hand, yell, and hurl harsh, hurtful words at us. Witnessing Tata go off on Mama for something that wasn't her fault made me so angry and, after all those years, that pent-up anger was starting to show. I'd begun answering back to Tata when he was arguing with Mama and, on occasion, I stepped in to break up a fight between the two of them. Everything I'd bottled up for so long had finally started to boil over, and I knew things would never be the same again. As I sat in that grungy hotel room off the interstate with Brian, Spiros, and Luminita, I knew one thing for sure: I wasn't going back.

Many of the details from the next few days are a blur, but I ended up hiring a lawyer to help me become emancipated. Emancipation, in simple language, was a ruling by the courts that declared me an adult (even though I was only seventeen) and gave me, instead of my parents, legal control of my own finances. When I left home, the only form of money I had in my possession was a check for $10,000 made payable to me for a professional competition I'd done months prior. It was one of the few checks that had actually been hand delivered to me instead of Tata. That check was the foundation for my independence. I started my new life with that $10,000.

Through the emancipation process, I learned that by age seventeen, I had earned nearly one million dollars. Perhaps not a ton of money by today's endorsement standards, and not the "millions" Tata sometimes exaggeratedly boasted of, but for me and my family—immigrants who had fled the oppression of Romania—it was an enormous amount of money. I also learned that by the time I was emancipated, Tata had already spent virtually all of it on the gym and a number of other investments, as I'd suspected.

"Spoiled Brat Divorces Parents" was just one of the many headlines in the media at the time of the emancipation. Many other magazines and tabloids, from the the *National Enquirer* to our local *Texas Monthly*, ran equally judgmental and mean-spirited headlines. I was embarrassed to read them as I stood in line at the grocery store, and I wanted to flip every one of them around and hide them, and me, from the world. I wished I could just disappear. I had been a public figure since I was young, and the hope of going through a legal battle privately was a pipe dream, especially when the papers could run juicy headlines about the greedy pixie gymnast and her tyrannical father. Some stories had bits and pieces of the truth, but most often, they were poorly investigated and loaded with misinformation. The situation created a huge burden on my parents as the paparazzi staked out their home and would snap the most unflattering photos of them to sell to the tabloids.

In my heart, I believed that I was entitled to have a say in what to do with my earnings. I'd worked extremely hard since I was unusually young, and I didn't understand why people would label me spoiled and crucify me because I wanted to take control of my life, which, yes, included taking control of what was left of my earnings. I had sacrificed nearly all of my childhood for these earnings, but the public and the newspapers didn't seem interested in that. While most seventeen-year-olds are still dependent and asking their parents for money, I was merely asking for some straight and honest answers regarding where the money even was. All I had wanted from Tata initially was to be included in the decision-making process for my financial future, but he refused. He had been so pumped with pride after he built his "Taj Mahal" that it was going to take something drastic to bring him down to earth. Throughout the entire legal process, he never once acknowledged that he made any mistakes in dealing with me or handling my finances, even though he burned through most of my $1 million earnings and had only this enormous gym structure to show for it. My attorney at the time agreed that emancipation was a necessary last resort.

So much of my childhood was devoted to bringing honor to my family and making sure I never did anything that would in any way shame the Moceanu name. My parents had drilled into me very early on that a child must never disgrace his or her family in any way, and whatever happens inside the walls of the home is no one else's business. Until now, I had lived my life with this mind-set, applying it to my home life *and* to my life inside the walls of the gym. I had never complained publicly about the struggles and abuse I met in my home with Tata or at the gym with some of my coaches. It was very painful that I had followed these rules and tried my best to be an honorable "good" daughter only to have it end this way, on the eve of becoming an adult.

During the trial, it was heartbreaking to see Tata and Mama sitting across the courtroom, looking as if they were losing everything that ever meant anything to them. They both seemed so sad and so hurt. I broke down in tears whenever I looked at them, and I literally fell apart bawling on the courthouse steps after I had to testify. I dreaded taking the stand because I had to admit that Tata abused me and physically hit me, which I'd never said publicly before then. I was ashamed to have to say those words, but it was the truth. It was the worst day of my life, and I couldn't even look at my parents afterward, knowing that I must have hurt them so, so deeply. My heart was broken. Despite these conflicting emotions and enormous feelings of guilt, I didn't see any other way to break free from Tata. I needed this for my sanity—so I could live and grow—and I prayed one day we could all look back and understand one another in a different light.

Before the trial started, I was contacted by William ("Bill") J. Hickl III, a CPA who had read my story in the *Houston Chronicle*. He offered to help get my finances in order, and I accepted, since I was amassing huge legal fees by the day. Bill's plan from the get-go was straightforward and simple: gain control of the gym without a court battle to keep my legal fees low, so I wouldn't wind up spending more on fees than the equity in my gym. Bill was confident that he could accomplish this without involving attorneys. I was surprised when I first met Bill because, for whatever naïve reasons, I was expecting a serious and somewhat detached banker type, but Bill was the opposite—a warm, kindhearted gentleman and a father of three, who approached me with compassion and professionalism.

Bill did what he promised and immediately focused on gaining control of my only real asset—the gym. Of course, getting control of the gym meant taking control *away* from Tata. Bill managed to set up a series of face-to-face meetings with Tata. He knew Tata would be a tough nut to crack and instead of trying to challenge and overpower Tata, he aimed to prove that he was an honest guy who wasn't going to take advantage of me. What was said in those meetings—Bill empathizing with Tata and sharing that he was a father himself—worked. Surprisingly, Tata ended up trusting Bill, which proved to be instrumental in getting Tata to sign over the trustee papers and title of the gym without another painful court battle. Per Tata's design, the gym was originally held in trust, but what startled me was Tata designed it so I wouldn't become eligible to receive the gym in my name until I was thirty-five years old. Did Tata really think it was okay to bar me from my own gym for that long? Was that the age he was finally going to let me start making my own decisions?

Aunt Janice was in the room at the courthouse hearing when Tata had to sign over the gym, and she has shared with me just how painful a moment it was for him. He was crying, telling her that if he signed the papers, he was would lose me forever. It was one of the most difficult things Tata had to do, but he knew he had no choice. The gym was losing money after I'd left home, and Tata didn't want to see the building go into foreclosure after he'd worked so hard to create it. He knew we'd lose everything I had earned and he had invested if we didn't try to salvage what we could, and fast. Once Bill gained control of the building, he was able to help me avoid foreclosure by engaging the right real estate broker, who found me a stable, reliable non-gymnastics-related corporate tenant who signed a ten-year lease. When the market permitted, I'd be able to sell the building and hopefully regain some of my earnings by cashing out of the gym. Bill also began helping me manage what little was left of my life's earnings at that same time. I was by no means wealthy, but I was finally free to make my own choices, free to hire who I believed had my best interests at heart, and free to start building a new dream.

Closing this chapter of my life, I honestly believed my darkest days were behind me. Little did I know, there were plenty waiting for me ahead, some right around the corner.

Chapter 10

DARK TIMES

My emancipation was a double-edged sword. It lifted an enormous weight off my shoulders by finally giving me the financial and personal freedom I had sought, but it also left me with a heavy heart. I felt awful that my family suffered through a very public trial that aired our dirty laundry. I know it devastated all of us on a personal level, and I didn't know how to recover from it. I was torn between feeling guilty for what I had done to my family and feeling excited and invigorated by the prospect of starting a life of my own. The wounds were too fresh and too deep for me to enjoy my freedom.

Everything had happened so quickly that most of my time after the trial was spent in a state of confusion, guilt, and pain. I had been sheltered my whole life and was suddenly afforded immediate liberty without any preparation, and I made mistakes—lots of them.

Looking back, the one thing I did right was get a place of my own. As I sat in my apartment, I realized for the first time why people referred to home as a "sanctuary." I cherished the peace, the quiet, and the safety that little apartment brought me. It was the first time in my life I was able to come home and truly relax, letting the security and privacy of home envelop me. I didn't have to worry about Tata erupting into one of his rages or that he and Mama would get into a fight that I'd have to break up. I often thought of Mama and Christina and wondered how they were coping with the stress following the trial. I hoped that my absence made home a better place to be, but I knew Tata was upset that I had left and feared that it possibly made things worse. When I'd phone Mama to check in on her and Christina, she always sounded so beaten down; I attributed a lot of it to how much she missed me, like I missed her. She'd also tell me that Tata said he wanted to disown me.

Moceanu Gymnastics Incorporated began folding quickly after the emancipation trial. The gym was struggling, and the stories about our family that continued to run in the newspapers and on TV didn't help matters. Families and coaches began to leave the gym, and without my presence and the unity of the Moceanu family, it couldn't sustain itself. Within a few months, all of my gymnastics memorabilia was taken from the glass cases in the entry and the family business shut its doors for good. I felt tremendously responsible for this loss and wished it had ended differently. I continued to pray that one day Tata would see my point of view and we'd reconcile.

After everything that had happened, the very notion of working things out with Tata was to be a difficult challenge—especially since he still blamed the loss of the gym solely on me and told anyone who'd listen that our family's world came crashing down because I ran away from home and started listening to others who were a bad influence on me. By "others" he meant Brian and Luminita, two people he had brought into my life in the first place. He was convinced that Brian and Luminita were out to take advantage of me and had pressured me to leave home. I was definitely an impressionable seventeen-year-old, but I didn't leave home because of Brian or Luminita; I left because of a turbulent family life and a growing disconnect between me and Tata that came to a head with the firing of my coach. Tata made it very clear in public interviews that he disapproved of "those people" and was afraid they were out for financial gain. He thought Brian and Luminita were trying to take the gym from me and that I was just unable to see it.

I think in desperation, Tata began harassing me—he'd call many times a day, leaving messages about how I'd ruined everything and when he caught me live on the phone, he'd pressure me to tell him where I was living. I wanted my apartment to remain a private, safe place, so I told very few people my address, and Tata was not one of them. His calls became relentless. I ended up obtaining a short-term restraining order prohibiting him from contacting me. Here I was emancipated, but I was hounded constantly by Tata. I didn't want to abandon my family; I just needed Tata to leave me alone for a while so I could get things sorted out in my own head.

Tata was never intimidated by authority, so I shouldn't have been surprised that the restraining order didn't faze him one bit. He was still going to see and talk to his daughter whenever he wanted regardless of some piece of paper. To prove this, Tata staked out my school, Northland Christian High School, one morning and stayed there all day in order to follow me home to see where I was living. I remember it like it was yesterday—sitting in my classroom looking out the window and noticing Tata's car across the street. I froze when I saw him sitting there behind the steering wheel. The classroom windows were tinted, so I could clearly see Tata, but he couldn't see me. A wave of terror washed over me.

I was embarrassed to tell anyone that Tata was across the street, but a couple of friends noticed that I'd turned ghost white and were concerned. My family already had more than enough negative press and I didn't want to cause any more, so I tried my best to downplay the situation. I was so tired of being the girl with the crazy life. I just wanted to be a normal teenager. As far as I knew, none of my other classmates ever had to deal with their fathers stalking them! Besides, I really didn't know what to expect from Tata at that point. He was still so angry and crazed, I wasn't sure if he wanted to hug me or strangle me.

My school wasn't big, so chances were that Tata would spot me pretty quickly after school. I wanted to slip out immediately after the final bell in the hopes that I'd be hidden in the crowd of exiting kids. I'd switched cars after I left home and had my fingers crossed that Tata hadn't yet discovered that I was driving a forest green Ford Mustang. I kept peeking out the window during the day, each time spotting Tata sitting there in his car. Was he planning to follow me to see where I lived? Did he want to talk to me? Did he want to hurt me? My mind was racing. This was why I obtained the restraining order in the first place, but I couldn't bring myself to call the police.

When school ended, I did my best to blend in with the crowd and swiftly get to my car. As I pulled out of the school driveway, however, Tata immediately started tailing me. I felt like I was in a low-budget movie as I tried pathetically to lose him without getting into an accident. There was no way I was going to lead him toward my apartment—that had to stay sacred—so I randomly zigzagged through some streets, making quick turns. I realized that Tata wasn't letting up, so I finally pulled into the parking lot of a shopping center. I parked in a very publicly visible spot, locked my doors, and waited for Tata.

Tata was capable of a lot of things and I knew to never, *never* underestimate him. I didn't want a confrontation, but I wasn't sure what else to do. My stomach was in knots and my adrenaline pumping as Tata pulled beside me and approached my car. I hadn't spoken to him since I left the courthouse at the close of the trial.

Tata motioned with his huge hands for me to roll down the window. I looked straight at him and shook my head no. He jiggled my car handle and tried to open the door, but I wouldn't unlock the door, either. We stared at each other through the glass for a minute, then Tata started talking to me, going on and on about how I'd made a big mistake by leaving home, how I'd lost the gym for us, and how he wanted to know where I was living.

"Dominique, open the door," Tata said in Romanian.

I cracked the window so he could hear me.

"No, Tata, I don't want to do this. Just leave me alone . . . please."

"Why are you doing this, Dominique? You want us to lose everything?" His voice quavered as he spoke; he sounded broken. My guilt overwhelmed me. The next thing I knew, I was climbing out of my car. He told me he wouldn't hurt me, and for some reason I believed him.

I saw Tata get choked up with emotion as he looked at me. I could see the hurt in his face, but I could also see love . . . a love that had always been unspoken and buried beneath so much anger, so much drama. Tears rolled down my face. I couldn't speak and neither could Tata. As he hugged me, I could feel and hear him crying. We sat there, holding each other tightly. It was an honest moment between us, one that I will never forget.

As oddly as the whole encounter started, it ended. Not wanting to ruin the moment, I climbed back into my car and before driving away, I told Tata not to worry about me, that I was okay and safe. I had hoped that maybe this was a new beginning for us.

When I got home, I plopped down on my sofa to let it all soak in. I was lost in thought when I heard loud knocking on my front door.

Oh, my God. Did Tata follow me? I thought as I slowly crept to the peephole. Three police officers in uniform were peering back at me. I was relieved it wasn't Tata, but it was still scary. The policemen banged on the door again and said they needed to speak to me right away. I was still trying to settle myself after my encounter with Tata and now this.

"Can we speak to you for a moment?" one of the officers asked, as I showed them inside. I was trying to act like I knew what I was doing, but inside I was scared to death, and I had no idea if I should even be talking to them without an attorney. I didn't know what this was about, but I'd seen in the movies that people asked for an attorney before talking to the police.

The officers explained to me that they had become aware that Tata had hired a private investigator to follow me and that this hired PI had gone to the police after Tata started talking a bit crazy. *A bit crazy?* I thought, wondering what was crazy by their standards. Apparently, the police were investigating Tata for some serious charges. The PI had become concerned and come to the police after Tata started talking specifically about hiring people to "take out" Brian and Luminita.

I couldn't believe what I was hearing. I'd just had this beautiful, hopeful moment with Tata in the parking lot—a possible fresh start—and now they were telling me he was trying to have Luminita and Brian killed. The PI was concerned with Tata's mental state; he wondered if Tata was losing touch with reality from all the stress his family was under. As part of the subsequent investigation, the PI had started recording his conversations with Tata for the police. I knew Tata was distraught, but I couldn't imagine him going that far. It was all so bizarre. I wondered if Mama knew about any of this craziness.

The officers wanted more information about my "friend Brian" and my "coach Luminita," as they had been referred to in the recorded conversations. I told them that Luminita was out of town, I believed in Las Vegas with friends, and that as far as I knew, Brian was in Houston with his family. Brian ended up coming to my apartment to talk to the officers in person. Brian paced the floor as he listened to this story of "contract hits" and private investigators. I remember thinking that Brian looked so much calmer than I did, sipping his Dr Pepper and easily answering the officers' questions. It made me realize just how much older he was than me.

I was at a loss for words as the officers explained that Tata was only one step away from carrying out his plan. They were just waiting for Tata to make the payment for the hit, and once this "exchange" occurred, they would arrest him. I had been through a lot in my seventeen years, but this was the most insane of all. I was freaked out enough that Tata was following me and waiting outside my school the entire day, but now there was this.

Has Tata gone mad? I wondered. I just kept thinking back to that moment we had shared in the parking lot. Despite the circumstances, that had probably been our most normal father-daughter experience, with actual shared emotions, actual expressed feelings. This man who was, for better or worse, a part of me and whom I loved was capable of a murder plot? And Brian and Luminita—who had been friends of our family, friends and colleagues of Tata's, were the targets. I just couldn't bring myself to believe it. Tata was a big talker who would often shoot his mouth off and make threats that he didn't intend to carry out. I tried to convince myself that it was all a misunderstanding and someone must have taken Tata seriously when they shouldn't have. Yet the police sounded so certain, I just didn't know what to think anymore.

I knew I'd heard it all when the officers suggested that Luminita, Brian, and I leave town immediately and "disappear" for a while. They said it was for our own safety and to make sure we didn't jeopardize the case before an arrest was made. I thought the police only said those things on television shows, including their parting line about them letting us know when it was safe to return to Houston. I couldn't believe this was my life.

"My dad has officially gone crazy!" I gasped once the police officers left.

Brian's wheels were turning, and he started to make some calls on his cell phone as we sat on my patio trying to figure out where to go. Brian lit up a Marlboro Light and I reached for one, too. I never thought I'd want to smoke a cigarette because I'd always thought it was a disgusting habit. Tata was a big smoker, and I couldn't stand how he reeked when he'd come in the house from smoking on the porch. Nonetheless, there I was, picking up a Marlboro like I'd smoked my entire life. I figured it would settle my nerves.

Brian just kept shaking his head in disbelief at the thought of Tata putting a hit on him. I know he was in shock, but in typical Brian fashion, he tried to lighten the seriousness of the situation by joking he'd "get a bullet in my ass" if Tata had his way. We laughed, which made the whole scenario that much stranger.

"Where can we go?" I asked. "This isn't going to look good in the media, either, you know!" The stories of my emancipation and family were still fresh in the newspapers. I was doing everything I could to fly under the radar and avoid more public scrutiny. Meanwhile, Brian was a married man hanging out with a teenage girl. How were we going to "disappear" together without causing more rumors?

We talked for hours, weighing our options, and in the end, we decided to follow the officers' advice and leave town. Through one of his friends, Brian was able to the get use of a private jet and within twenty-four hours we were flying to the Cayman Islands, where that same friend offered up his vacation condo for free. I didn't expect to be hiding out on a resort island in a gorgeous home, but since we had nowhere else to go and all of our expenses were paid, we went.

I was really worried for Tata and kept praying that this whole situation was a misunderstanding—that Tata was just making threats out of anger and that he never intended to actually have anyone killed. Even though I was truly afraid of him and wanted to keep a safe distance, he was still my father, and the last thing I wanted was for him to go to prison. Brian was more understanding of Tata's behavior than I would have expected and was almost sympathetic to the fact that Tata, like any father, must have felt like he was losing everything and was acting in desperation.

The Cayman Islands looked beautiful, at least from what I could see from the condo windows. It was anything but a vacation. I was miserable and anxious during our stay, too paranoid to leave the condo for fear that I'd be seen by the media. The last thing I needed was to have more tabloid headlines about me vacationing in the Cayman Islands with this older married man. Even amidst the chaos of my life, my moral compass was still intact, and I wasn't going to ruin Brian's marriage by letting some misleading headlines get out. Besides, I never viewed Brian in a romantic way at all. I admired his confidence and his charismatic way with people, but he was like an older brother to me and someone I felt I could trust as a friend. Despite Brian's efforts to make it tolerable in the Cayman Islands, I just didn't feel comfortable being there, so we packed up after a few days and left.

The police advised us to stay away from Houston for another week, so we decided to go and see Luminita in Las Vegas to explain in person the situation with Tata. We hadn't talked to her since we left for the Cayman Islands, and aside from telling her to stay away from Houston and lay low for her own safety, we hadn't given her the specific details about Tata.

It was good to see Luminita, even under the stressful conditions. My life had spiraled out of control so quickly that seeing her and hearing her voice again made me miss our time together training in the gym and working toward a goal. Gymnastics seemed so far away at this point, like another lifetime, even though it had been only months since I last competed.

Luminita completely flipped out when we gave her the full story. Refusing to hide any longer, she immediately reached for the phone to call Tata to confront him about the "hit." By making that call, in one fell swoop she exposed our whereabouts and ruined the officers' case against Tata. Tata and Luminita got into a yelling match. I couldn't keep track of everything she was saying in Romanian, but she was hysterical and letting Tata have it, again. Inside, I was relieved that this was happening—it meant that whatever his intentions, Tata's "plan" would not be taking place and there would be no case against him. Contrary to what the police were assuming at the time, I honestly don't think Tata would have ever gone through with it. I prefer to believe that Tata was just making threats out of anger. Much to my relief, that chaotic episode of my life was over and I wasn't even contacted by the police after we returned to Houston.

Just before I had become emancipated, Tata and I had signed with a new agent, Janey Miller of Gold Medal Management. Having just joined with us, Janey was taken aback by how suddenly I'd left home and broken away from Tata. I'm sure she was wondering what kind of mess she'd gotten herself into by taking me and all my baggage on as a client, but to her credit, she stood by my side before and after the process, when most of my friends, colleagues, and sponsors had become afraid to touch me with a ten-foot pole. There continued to be some sponsorship and other opportunities on occasion, but not many. I was disappointed with USA Gymnastics for not offering me certain appearances and promotional events

I thought I had rightfully earned. I watched helplessly as those opportunities were passed directly to other gymnasts. Janey saw that I desperately needed all opportunities to support myself, and she worked hard and never gave up on me. Thankfully, I still had my stipend money for making the US National team in 1998 and that $1,000 per month helped me survive that first year on my own.

It was Janey who eventually landed me and Luminita a gymnastics home at the US Olympic Training Center (USOTC) in Colorado Springs in early 1999. I was thankful that the USOTC took a chance on me, allowing me to become the first female gymnast to train there. For almost a year, it was ideal as Luminita and I housed together at the USOTC campus. It gave both of us a safe place to live rent-free, with three meals a day, and a local gym to train in until I figured out a long-term plan. I still wasn't sure of the direction of my life, but I knew I wanted to continue gymnastics. I just needed to get back on track. I'd put on some weight and was struggling to get back in shape. Finally having freedom, I'd let myself eat everything I wanted, from Big Macs to Dairy Queen whenever I felt the urge during the trial. The mistake of adding alcohol to the mix meant I was taking in more calories than ever before. It was just a matter of time before I blew up. I was depressed from everything that had happened with my family, and I turned to food for comfort. I also went through puberty that same year and parts of my body were beginning to change and expand. Before I even knew it, I'd put on fifteen pounds in a couple of months.

To shed the weight, I increased my workouts, and Luminita had me running outdoors again in addition to training. She brought out the plastic sweatsuits, the kind wrestlers use to make their weight class by sweating off those last few pounds. In an attempt to get back to a high level of training faster than I probably should have, the sudden and strenuous workouts took a toll on my back. At first, I tried to push through it the best I could, but it turned out that I was suffering from a stress fracture in my lumbar spine (L4 and

L5). The doctors advised me to stop gymnastics altogether for several months to let my back heal. I ended up spending the majority of the day in physical therapy during recovery.

It was around this time that Luminita and I came to realize that we were far better as coach and athlete than as roommates. Being together day and night, we started getting into terrible arguments. I could see that she was still hurt and angry with Tata for everything he'd put her through, and I felt she was taking it out on me. I was already feeling down that I was injured and frustrated that I wasn't able to train, so I didn't handle it well when Luminita started "mothering" me and angrily asking where I was going at night. I had been staying out of our dorm room more and more often to avoid arguing with Luminita and, understandably, she was concerned when I wouldn't return until very late or, sometimes, not at all. I was making new friends and exploring opportunities to party, and Luminita did not approve. Her intentions were good—and certainly justified, since I shouldn't have been where I was most of those nights—but I resented her for asking at all. Later, of course, I realized she was just being a caring friend and doing the right thing by checking up on me, but at the time I didn't want to report to her or anyone else. I had been controlled my entire life and was desperate to be free from everyone—and to exercise that newfound freedom.

Clearly, Luminita couldn't just sit around hoping my back would heal and that one day I'd regain my competitive edge. We both knew it was best for her to move on. I regretted the way things ended, and I'd wished we were both more patient and mature to make sure our good-bye was filled with the respect it deserved. I felt an enormous loss when she moved out of our dorm and stepped out of my life. She was one of the few people I had ever fully trusted. Following her departure, I slipped into a dark and often dangerous time of my life. For a long time I wasn't even sure where Luminita had moved on to and, sadly, we rarely spoke.

Eventually, I'd heard that she got a full-time gymnastics coaching position at Colorado Aerials and married one of the wrestlers from the USOTC. I was happy that she'd figured things out and made a good life for herself.

All of the emotional baggage I'd carried into training that year in Colorado was just too heavy to ignore, and it affected my attitude. I'd lost my drive and fire to train to be the best, and nothing seemed to help. I had hoped it would be the right transition for me to be surrounded by other athletes who were goal oriented, and I was hoping it would inspire me to train again. It did for a while, but, like any elite-level athlete, that desire has to come from within, and I was still struggling in that department.

I turned to partying to numb my pain and to forget all that I'd gone through the past year. It certainly wasn't the right thing to do, but I experimented with drugs and alcohol as an escape from the depression I was feeling. I gravitated to new friends who knew how to party, so drugs were readily available. Within a short time, I was exposed to a wide array of drugs. I exerted no self-control and was willing to try anything simply because I had the freedom to. I lived on my own, so I had no curfew and no boundaries. I had gone from one extreme to the other.

In terms of drugs, if it grew from the ground, I tried it. Marijuana and alcohol were my staples, but I tried other recreational drugs. Thankfully, I never used needles or anything that required them. I felt that the drugs I did abuse were powerful enough to put me in a state of euphoria, allowing me to forget all of my problems. There was no need to reach further.

The rave party scene was popular at that time, so I dabbled in that, too. Raves were a haven for recreational drug use, especially ecstasy. My first rave party was at a huge warehouse in the middle of nowhere in some Colorado field. I remember feeling like I was finally part of "the glamorous life" as I waited in the dark in a long line of strangers to get in. A few months prior, I would have been at home tucked into bed by that hour, yet there I was partying with kids from all walks of life. I could hear the echoing throb of techno music as I walked inside with my friends. We went from one section to the next checking out the scene: in one area, kids were liquid dancing (a dance craze); in another area, they were jumping up and down into a frenzied sweat while waving glow sticks; and in a third section, people were sitting Indian-style massaging each other's backs in a single row. I thought it was all very bizarre, but for someone so sheltered for so long, it was a world of intrigue.

My friends were moving from person to person at the party looking for a "hookup" to score more drugs. I was pretty clueless and had no idea what we were looking for, so I just followed along. I remembered one of the older girls in our group showing me a tiny white pill with a clover on it. I had no idea what it was, but she said it was "fine" as she swallowed it, so I figured she knew what she was talking about. I not only took one, I swallowed a second for good measure, having no clue how powerful they were.

My senses were heightened, and I could feel my jaw clench as my first roll of ecstasy kicked in. Ecstasy, the "love drug," made me feel warm inside and unnaturally drawn toward everyone around me. In the moment, this chemical effect made it easy to make new friends and feel instantly connected to strangers, which I particularly wanted then. I was constantly hugging my friends and telling them I loved them. I could feel the music pulsing through me. I wanted to stay in this euphoria forever. Once my second roll kicked in, I started to feel a bit nauseous and realized that I'd probably taken too much, but it didn't stop me. I ignored my body's signals and continued to party as we left the rave and moved on to a house party, invited by someone we had met at the rave. By the time I got home in the wee hours of the morning, I was pretty out of it. I remember my friends' faces were morphing into scary images, like a lion and the old woman from a beer commercial that I'd seen on television. I was lucky to have ended up home, safe in my own bed.

After Luminita left, I'd started hanging out mostly with athletes I'd met on campus. I was still seventeen years old and a lot younger than most of them, so there was always the dilemma of trying to get into bars with fake IDs in order to be with the group. I'd accept their invites to parties or to just hang out and drink beer because I was lonely and I didn't want to be in the dorm room by myself. Any distraction from my real life was welcome.

I was inexperienced when it came to romance. Tata would barely let me go out with my girlfriends, so boys were completely out of the question. Now, with my newfound freedom, I could socialize with whom I pleased. This was all new territory for me. I wasn't sure how to handle my feelings of attraction toward some of the guys I had befriended, especially when I found myself craving affection from one in particular. My parents had never talked to me about the birds and the bees. Sex and dating were pretty much forbidden topics in our home. I cannot imagine my grandparents broaching these topics with Mama or Tata when they were growing up, so it's no surprise my parents avoided these awkward talks with me as well.

I remember questioning Aunt Janice to some extent, sometimes with such honesty that I'd make her blush, but I was still rather clueless about sex, romance, and relationships. Aside from a "first kiss" in high school, I was completely inexperienced. I naïvely thought that any affection from a boy meant that he had genuine feelings for me and that, perhaps, he was interested in a real relationship. I remember being quickly jarred into reality when I saw my crush flirting and then passionately kissing another girl outside my dorm after he'd acted like he was interested in me. It was a very confusing time. I was living on my own, acting like an adult, but I was still a little girl in many ways.

Physically injured, without a coach, and testing dangerous waters with alcohol, drugs, and boys, I was in a million pieces and had no idea how to put myself back together again.

Off Balance

It was Easter 1999 that I finally stepped foot in my parents' home again after running out six months earlier. It was a reunion I was dreading. I was afraid to see Tata, especially in his own house. I could hear him in my head already, yelling at me about leaving home and ruining everything the family had built. I didn't want to go, but Mama and Aunt Janice kept insisting I come home to visit the family. Mama had become my main family liaison since Tata and I had not spoken during those six months, except for our "moment" in the parking lot.

"Easter is a time to forgive, and you both should try," Mama said. I was dying to see her and Christina, but I didn't think I could handle another confrontation with Tata. I agreed to come on the condition that Tata wouldn't bring up the gym.

As I entered the house through the back staircase, I felt a small surge of adrenaline upon seeing a clear view of Tata through the glass patio doors. He was planted on the couch watching television—basketball or the evening news, I figured. Christina, Mama, and I hugged tightly as I walked through the door. It struck me just how deeply I'd missed them. We had a few private minutes to talk in Christina's room before Mama went downstairs to get Tata. I was nervous. Mama begged him for a peaceful day and to go easy on me, but I knew Tata was still hurting from all that had happened between us. I had no idea how he was going to react to me. I told myself to be strong and not give in even if he was looking for a fight.

Christina was in the middle of showing me some of the collages she'd made at school when Mama walked back in, followed by Tata. My throat choked up as I looked at him—he looked so old. It was clear that the emotional hell we'd just gone through had aged him so much in a short period of time. His eyes were tired and worn, his head mostly bald with tufts of gray hair on the sides. He didn't have that Tata fire. I couldn't speak, so we just stared at each other without saying a word for what must have been five minutes at least.

"Okay, are you two going to talk?" Mama asked in Romanian.

Mama pushed the two of us together to hug, and Tata squeezed me hard for a really long time. He was trying to hide that he was so emotional, but I could feel his body move up and down as he sobbed. It was one of the longest hugs we'd ever shared and the tears were streaming down my face uncontrollably. I knew that tight squeeze was Tata's way of showing me what he was unable to say in words.

It took a while for the lump in my throat to go away. I tried to get control of my emotions because I wanted Tata to start viewing me as a strong independent woman, not as a little kid bawling her eyes out.

"Why did you have to go?" Tata asked me point-blank as soon as he caught his voice again. "We almost had everything set up and in place for you."

I looked at Mama. So much for Tata's promises not to discuss the gym. Perhaps he wanted to hear me say it again in my own words, but I didn't want to rehash everything and ruin our Easter together.

"Tata, stop. I don't want to talk about it," I said quietly.

Mama chimed in, too, begging him to stop in Romanian.

"Tata, I don't want to go there. I needed my freedom. Are we going to start again?" I asked.

Tata bristled, some fire and anger returning.

Tata and I went back and forth a little, then he stormed out of the room. I stayed for a little while longer talking to Mama and Christina in the bedroom, then I left the house. We clearly needed more distance and perspective to understand each other.

❧

Mama worried about me alone and without any family in Colorado for some time, so in August 1999, she and Christina came to live in Colorado Springs for a stretch. I was shocked at first that Tata allowed them to rent a small apartment on their own, outside of Houston. They loved the fresh mountain air and beautiful scenery, and it felt like a new beginning for us in a way. Tata was busy back in Houston trying to set up his own car dealership, but he'd come to Colorado Springs to visit on occasion.

During one of Tata's visits, he and Mama got into an explosive argument late one night. I didn't even know what started the fight, but it escalated super fast. I stepped in to try to calm Tata down, which only opened the door for him to yell at me for everything wrong I'd ever done. It got ugly. Tata said he was moving Mama and Christina back to Houston. Mama, who was usually the calm, quiet one in the room, started to lose it and argued back at Tata in Romanian. Tata grabbed Mama's car keys and headed outside to Mama's car, saying something about driving to Texas. Tata was screaming in front of our apartment building at the top of his lungs, and I was convinced the neighbors would call the police any minute. Somehow we ended up sitting in the car—Tata and Mama in the front seats and Christina and I in the back.

I thought things might settle down once Tata realized the craziness of the situation—a family of four screaming loudly at one another in a parked SUV in the middle of the night—but Tata was undaunted and proceeded to complain about Texas and how we needed to be there. He was just getting started, it seemed. With one quick lunge, I dove over the front seat and grabbed the keys from the ignition. I opened the car door and dashed for the apartment, looking back to see Christina and Mama scrambling along behind me. We got into the apartment, and I locked the door before Tata could enter. Mama looked taken aback that I had the courage to lock out an enraged Tata.

"Dominique, open the door!" Tata demanded in Romanian as he pounded loudly on the door. "Open the door right now!"

"No," I said, literally shaking in my boots, hoping that that flimsy door could hold Tata back. Mama was afraid, too, but was worried what the neighbors would think of our ordeal. The pounding on the door continued. "Don't you dare let him in," I kept telling Mama before I finally picked up the phone and dialed 911. It was the first time I'd ever actually called the police, but I was fed up with feeling terrorized by my own father. I wasn't going to wait until Tata broke down the door or got into a fight with neighbors coming out of their apartments. He continued pounding on the door and swearing at me, saying what a bad person I was.

Two male officers responded to my call. They made sure we were okay, then took Tata to the airport, so he could fly home to Houston. Tata was a great talker, and even though he had just tormented our entire apartment building with his ranting and banging on the door and walls, he managed to convince the officers to take him to the airport when any bystander would think he was headed straight to the local jail.

The quiet in the apartment lasted only a short while, as Tata started calling Mama's cell phone nonstop from the airport. My jaw dropped when Mama answered the phone to talk to him, so I quickly grabbed it from her and hung up on him. It was pointless, since she answered immediately when he called back again. A few minutes later, Mama was grabbing her keys to go pick up Tata from the airport like he'd asked. Apparently, Tata was sitting with his head drooped downward on an outside bench when Mama pulled up. His tail between his legs, he knew he was in the wrong. I was still too angry and didn't want to see him, so I left the apartment before they returned. He never apologized to any of us, and life carried on like nothing had ever happened.

This was the kind of craziness that confused me while I was growing up. We had finally come to a place without rage and violence, only to invite it right back in. I knew it was a cycle I didn't want to continue when I had my own family one day.

Sadly, 1999 came and went with a lot of pain and angst, but not a lot of gymnastics. For the first time in my life, I didn't compete in a single competition the entire year. I had struggled with several new lows that year and I had started to question if I'd ever be able to compete again. I felt defeated. Luckily, my agent, Janey, one of the few people who hadn't given up on me, recognized that deep down I wasn't ready to retire, and she stayed positive, looking for new opportunities.

Chapter 11

JENNIFER: FLASH FORWARD

It had only been a few months since the mind-blowing revelation that I had another sister. And even though I hadn't met Jen in person yet, I felt like I was rapidly growing closer to her. We shared a tireless series of stories over the phone and provided midday updates through text and sometimes email. Despite the fact that I had just given birth to my first child and was consumed with the joy and daily discoveries that come with that, I still couldn't get enough news from Jen. I felt fortunate to have been able to support her as she began her journey into aerial acrobatics, which she'd later turn into a promising career.

It was during one of our early phone conversations that Jen mentioned an interest in getting back into gymnastics herself. She was living in Orlando and working at Disney World as an operations cast member for the park's parades and shows. She loved watching the stage shows with acrobatics and aerial work, and she felt with her strength and agility, she could perform those routines if given the chance. She had been such a powerhouse in tumbling and gymnastics when she was younger, so I thought it was a great idea for her to try it. She'd already proven to be a champion tumbler—despite having no legs—so why couldn't she be an acrobat?

I was impressed to see how quickly Jen moved to make this dream a reality. One minute she was telling me she "just knew" she could do what these acrobats were doing, and by the next time we spoke, she was already lining up a professional partner. One of her Disney managers had given her the name of an aerial gymnast, and Jen was arranging to meet with him. I was so impressed by her focus and determination. Boy, when she wanted to get something done, look out.

I looked forward to Jen's updates about her training sessions with her new partner, Nate. I could tell from the pure joy and excitement in her voice that she'd found a new challenge—one she absolutely loved. Her enthusiasm was contagious, and I even got excited hearing about her strenuous workouts and how they'd make her so sore she could barely lift her wheelchair into her car afterward. She hadn't worked out hard for the past four years, but she was doing all the right things to get back into shape. I remember when she talked about being a bit nervous to train on "silks" since many of the tricks required the use of legs for support, but a week later when we spoke, she reported that she was already doing "roll-ups" on the silks, which typically only male acrobats are strong enough to do. I could barely keep up with her progress because she was moving ahead so quickly. It was very rewarding and inspiring to follow her path as she achieved a succession of goals. My "new" sister was growing into a real superhero to me. I couldn't wait to meet her in person, yet I was still a little nervous. I didn't want to rush into a meeting too fast and ruin what we had built so far.

Jen and Nate shared gym space with soccer and volleyball players, so they would warm up and practice stunts on the trampoline while they were waiting for their floor time. These trampoline "stunts" soon turned into a full-length act that got the attention of other gym patrons and promoters. Before they knew it, they booked their first gig, center stage at the Amway Arena in Orlando with more than five thousand people in the audience. I remember Jen was over the moon describing how they had "knocked the performance out of the park."

I liked it when Jen bounced ideas off of me and asked for my input or feedback on training and performing. I was desperate to do something more for her, my sister. I tried to give Jen every bit of advice that I thought could possibly be helpful with her career. I'd been burned too many times by people I thought I could trust, who'd claim they wanted to be my friend or help me, when they really just wanted to use me for their own gain all along. I didn't want Jen making the same mistakes I'd made over the years. I already felt that we were close enough to talk about those things honestly.

Christina, Jen, and I began to brainstorm about where and when the three of us should meet in person. I think we all knew that we'd maximized our "getting to know each other" period over the telephone and it was time to take the next step. My sisters took mercy on me as a new mom and agreed that it would be easiest if the two of them came to my home in Cleveland.

I finally met Jen in May 2008. As she wheeled herself through the elevator doors at the airport, she was exactly what I'd pictured—beautiful, spirited, confident, and independent. She'd traveled from Florida to Ohio and arrived midday, an hour and a half before Christina's flight from Texas. I hugged her tightly, then handed her the rose I bought on the way to the airport. I wasn't sure if it was what one gives a long-lost sister, but she seemed to like it.

"This is your auntie Jen," I said to Carmen, who was watching us from her stroller. Jen smiled from ear to ear as she cooed with Carmen.

It was surreal, yet stingingly real. Having her in front of me, I could see she was a Moceanu through and through. I'd already seen lots of her photos, but it was much more obvious in person. She reminded me so much of Christina and myself—not only the striking physical similarities, but the way she talked and laughed, even the way she moved her hands when she was describing things. I just kept staring at her. We had a chance to talk and get comfortable in each other's presence as we ate and waited for Christina.

Once Christina's flight arrived, I became even more emotional. It seemed like our circle was complete, and I tried my best to hold back tears as the three of us hugged. Jen and Christina seemed to be keeping it together, and I didn't want my crying to distract them from their own first moments together. Back at my house, we sat in the living room for hours, talking about our childhoods, sharing photos, and trying to fill in the gaps. I asked her to retell stories she'd already shared on the phone, just to make sure I didn't miss any details.

"I just can't believe we're all really here together, and I'm finally meeting you and Christina in person!" Jen repeated a few times that first night, almost in disbelief. She had dreamed of us coming together for so many years, I think it was a bit overwhelming that it was actually happening at last.

We avoided talking about Mama and Tata at first, but we all knew we'd have to discuss them at some point. It was like the elephant in the room that everyone pretends doesn't exist. Tata and

Mama were what bound the three of us together. They were our parents, at least sort of. How do you reconcile one sister being put up for adoption? By that time, we all understood the circumstances surrounding Jen's adoption, and it was pretty clear that Jen's childhood was a lot more stable and happier than mine and Christina's had been, but it still had to be addressed. I took a deep breath and told Jen that Tata and Mama had been asking a lot about her and that they were supportive that we were building a relationship. I told Jen that Tata had become quite ill recently, but that he and Mama hoped they would be able to meet Jen one day, too, even though they were nervous about it. Jen listened to my words. She seemed so gathered and mature, I had to remind myself she was only twenty years old. I knew she had prepared for this moment—meeting her biological family—for a long time, and I'd hoped she was getting the answers she needed. I looked forward to Jen ultimately meeting Tata and Mama because I thought it might give her more closure about her birth and how she ended up with her family, the Brickers.

Those few days together were magical. We were able to open up and share our feelings, cry, laugh, and bond in new ways, and the fact that we did all this within the walls of my home made it even more special for me. As we hugged good-bye, we all promised to get together again sooner than later. I had no worries; I knew we'd make it happen.

Jen and Nate's first performance at Amway Arena in Orlando gave them immediate media attention. They started to land trampoline and silk performances, first in Florida, then all around the world, including the modern dance arena with the world-renowned Heidi Latsky. It all happened very quickly and in 2009, Jen was invited to join the biggest tour in the pop world at the time, the Britney Spears tour. Nate had been hired onto the tour and once he showed the producers video of Jen performing, they invited her to become part of the cast. What performer doesn't dream about doing their thing alongside a world-famous pop icon? Heck, I would've loved to have gone on tour with Britney Spears myself! And to think that Jen had only been involved in aerial gymnastics for one year at that point was mind-boggling. I remember telling her how proud I was and how she deserved it all as she set off for the second leg of the US and Australian tour.

I was fortunate to see Jen and Nate perform when the tour stopped in Columbus, Ohio. Jen and Nate's routine on the trampoline electrified the arena and left fans screaming for an encore. I had chills up and down my arms. It was a richly satisfying, emotional experience for me to see Jen perform on this grand stage.

In the short time I'd known Jen, I'd watched her break boundaries and do things most people with all their limbs only dream about. I looked forward to seeing what other tricks she had up her sleeve as she ventured out to Los Angeles to pursue her solo career. One thing I'd learned so far was that when Jennifer Bricker sets her mind to something, you'd better believe it will be happening.

Chapter 12

ENTER
MIKE CANALES

Who would have thought that the boy I bumped into in the hospitality room at the 1994 US Nationals would end up being the man I'd marry? I was only twelve years old and he was sixteen at the time, so it was merely the start of what would evolve into a long yet persistent love story.

I had just won my first All-Around title at the Junior Nationals in Nashville, Tennessee, and my coaches Alexander Alexandrov and Jackie McCarter and I were over the moon with the victory. The following day during the men's competition, I made my way to the hospitality room, a private place where gymnasts can rest or grab something to eat between events. I was done competing and my next objective was to get some food in my stomach. I'd barely eaten that past week preparing for the meet. I was so focused on grabbing snacks that, at first, I didn't notice my future husband pacing around the room. Michael Brian Canales stood about 5' 5" with a thin, lean physique—the typical build of a male gymnast in the 1990s.

"How ya doing?" I asked, surprising myself by striking up a conversation so easily.

"I'm okay," he replied quietly and without much enthusiasm. I could see that he was preoccupied and figured he had his mind on the men's competition, which was still going on in the main gym.

"Well, hang in there!" I said, looking him straight in the eye, giving him my best "you'll be all right" look of supportive confidence. I spoke with conviction, like I was a coach or some kind of expert. I could see the wheels in Mike's brain turning as he looked down at me, wondering who was this four-foot pipsqueak giving *him* a pep talk. I looked more like someone's kid sister than a fellow gymnast. He looked at me for another few seconds and then smiled warmly before turning toward the door.

Mike and I still laugh about that first meeting, both amazed at my gumption considering how sheltered and timid I was at the time. There I was, trying to counsel and advise a boy four years my senior. Turned out that Mike had gone into the hospitality room that day to clear his head. He was competing against some of his longtime gymnastics idols for the first time at Nationals that day and was feeling a little overwhelmed. He had no idea who that supportive little kid was, but I ended up providing him with a bit of perspective . . . and a smile. Apparently, someone pointed me out to Mike later as the winner of the women's All-Around, which we also laugh about now—"So that kid really did know a thing or two about gymnastics."

Mike and I eventually had a proper introduction and became friendly as we crossed paths at a number of gymnastics meets and exhibitions over the next four years. The visits were intermittent and never long enough. We'd get a chance to talk and catch up on gymnastics and then we'd have to say good-bye. He was so down to earth, kind, and respectful to everyone, and I always looked forward to seeing him. His generous spirit and genuine concern for others was quite an inspiration. Due to training and travel schedules, it's difficult for most Elite gymnasts to keep in touch with one another, and it was especially challenging for me as I had no downtime leading up to the Olympics. Also, this time predated Twitter, Facebook, and teenagers toting cell phones and laptops in their backpacks, so staying in touch was a lot more challenging. I did see Mike after the Olympics when our Magnificent Seven tour stopped in his hometown of Columbus, Ohio. He was the local guest gymnast who performed with us that evening and I still have a photo of the two of us that was taken after the show. In that photo, you can see that Mike is wearing an old US Nationals T-shirt—a red shirt with my picture on it.

I never was able to spend long periods of time with Mike, but each time we saw each other, we just picked up where we left off. Quick conversations in passing were really all there was time for, but I always enjoyed seeing him, however briefly. It was almost as if destiny kept bringing us back together, but I was still young and it would be some time yet before I developed feelings for him that went beyond friendship.

We reconnected at the US National Championships in 1998. I was still clueless about romance at that time and, to me, he was a special friend whom I wanted as my pen pal. I remember sitting at my desk when I returned from Nationals and writing Mike a short note on a smiley face notepad a fan had gifted me. Years later, Mike surprised me by pulling that same smiley notecard out of a box of belongings. He had guarded that first piece of mail alongside his other treasured things for years, and that touched me to no end.

I next saw Mike during the summer of 2001 and by then, I felt like a different person. I had been through hell with my family, suffered sidelining injuries, and veered down a dangerous path of alcohol and drugs to try to mask my pain. I viewed people and life in general through a whole different lens. I remember I was sunbathing in between camp sessions at the International Gymnastics Camp (IGC) summer camp in the Poconos in Pennsylvania when Mike appeared out of nowhere. I looked up from my towel by the pool and saw him standing over me. He was with his good friend Raj Bhavsar, an Olympic gymnast whom I'd known since I was seventeen.

Mike was a sight for sore eyes—and these eyes certainly saw him in a new light this time around. I took in his bronzed skin and fit, muscular body under his white T-shirt as I got up to give him and Raj hugs. When I got closer, I saw that Mike had silver circular piercings in his ears and a silver stud piercing in his labret—the area just below his lower lip. I thought it was an unusual place for a piercing, but somehow he pulled it off and it actually looked good on him. For the first time, I felt drawn to Mike in a romantic sense and I remember feeling a bit self-conscious standing there in my burgundy bikini, feeling less fit than I had been before. Mike's warm smile and friendly way was such a ray of sunshine and I just couldn't take my eyes off of him. Perhaps I was finally in the right place and right time to notice him in a different way. We couldn't talk long as they were on their way to meet up with Raj's gymnastics team from Ohio State University. Mike had already graduated from Ohio State and was coaching his former team as they trained for the US Nationals later that summer.

I could hardly wait to see Mike later that night at the cabin house, where the gymnasts and some staff would hang out. As we sat outside in the fresh air, it was the first time I was able to have a long, in-person, uninterrupted conversation with Mike. We'd known each other for years and had written back and forth now and again, but we'd never had a decent chunk of time to talk face to face. I was intrigued by Mike—here was this stud gymnast who was intellectual and educated with well-thought-out opinions and ideas on so many things, yet he was humble, sincere, and easy to be around. The hours flew by as we talked and laughed. I felt a new and stronger connection with Mike that evening, and there was no doubt in my mind that he was special.

We were inseparable for that week at camp until I had to pack up and move on to my next camp, which was what I typically did during summers. I'd travel from one camp to another, so I really didn't know when I'd see Mike again, especially since I lived in Texas and he was from Ohio. Oddly, we didn't exchange phone numbers or talk about when we'd see each other again. We had always come back into each other's lives and I figured it would happen again.

The year 2001 was yet another time of transition for me. Following my last attempt to qualify for a spot on the Olympic team in 2000, I was forced to step aside due to repeated injury and surgery. Having officially retired from gymnastics, I was left wondering how I was going to fill the void. My life had been consumed by my sport for as long as I could remember. On top of the sudden free time on my hands, retirement was bittersweet because I felt it was premature due to injury. I had two surgeries on my right knee (one in 1997, the other in 2000), then surgery on my right shoulder in early 2001. I was injured, but I wanted more and felt I still had it in me to compete. Heck, despite the gymnastics mileage I'd put on my body, I was still only nineteen years old.

I attended the 2001 US National Championships as a spectator instead of a competitor for the first time since retiring. The competition was held in Philadelphia, and I decided to go with two girlfriends. I was looking forward to the meet and thought it would be a good distraction since I was already going a little stir-crazy in my newfound retirement. My friends and I were waiting at our hotel to catch the shuttle to the gymnastics arena, but for a number of different reasons, we kept missing the bus and we'd have to wait for the next and the next. It was getting late and I was in the middle of asking someone about the next shuttle when the revolving doors in the hotel lobby turned and in walked Mike!

It was so unexpected that my stomach was doing flips. I was out-of-my-mind happy to see him. We hadn't spoken since summer camp in the Poconos, and here he was strolling through the lobby and back into my life as if we'd planned it for months. The timing couldn't have been more perfect.

I tried to walk over casually to greet him, so I didn't look like a total dork, but it was no use—I couldn't stop myself from sprinting toward him and practically tackled him as I threw my arms around him. I was so surprised to see him. He had hitched a ride to Philadelphia with some friends from Ohio State and was there to support Raj and the men's gymnastics team. He still hadn't connected with Raj to find out where the team was staying.

"Why don't you stay with us? Hang out with us!" I blurted out. I was practically bouncing up and down as I ran with Mike to drop his stuff in our room before grabbing a cab to the competition. *Thank God we missed those earlier shuttles,* I thought to myself as we made our way to the venue.

Nationals flew by quickly and, quite honestly, I was more into Mike than the competition. He was so knowledgeable about gymnastics and could practically predict what would happen next just by analyzing a gymnast's entry or moves leading into tricks. I loved how passionate he was. I was impressed by his knowledge of and respect for women's gymnastics as well. Most male gymnasts I knew didn't know nearly as much about the women's events, especially the technical and historical aspects. Mike was like a gymnastics encyclopedia, and I found myself captivated by his rich love for the nuances and artistry of our sport. I even learned a few things just listening to his comments as we watched the women that day.

I learned of Mike's goal to be a foot and ankle surgeon during our time together at IGC. He had taken a year off after graduating from Ohio State University with a degree in molecular genetics and was getting ready to start the long journey through medical school and residency. He had volunteered that summer helping the Ohio State Men's Gymnastics Team prepare for Nationals and made his way to the meet to support them. He had also tutored many players on the Ohio State University football team during past years, wanting to help his alma mater as much as possible before burying his head in medical school.

Sunday morning came, the meet was over, and I dreaded having to say good-bye to Mike yet again. As he helped me into a taxi to the airport, I realized I didn't even have his phone number. This time I wasn't leaving until I got it. As we exchanged information, I leaned in and gave Mike a warm hug and planted a firm kiss on his lips. He kissed me back. I was complete mush as the taxi carried me to the airport, and I had no idea when I'd see him again.

We started talking on the phone regularly, often for three hours or more on any given night. I never knew I could talk so much and still have more to say. During one of our marathon conversations, I shared how I'd always imagined myself going to college, but so many things had happened in my life and college kept getting postponed. I was beginning to wonder when I'd be able to make it happen. Mike repeatedly encouraged me to enroll in college sooner than later and thanks to his persistence, I enrolled at Montgomery Community College in Texas in the spring of 2002. I had always dreamed about being the first in my family to graduate from college, and it was starting to look like I could. Mama and Tata never had that opportunity, and I wanted to do it for all of us. I completed my first semester of college with a 4.0 grade point average. I felt great.

I had boarded a flight and departed New York the morning the World Trade Center was attacked on September 11, 2001. I didn't learn about that horrible news until my plane landed and was immediately grounded in Pennsylvania, not too far from where the third hijacked plane crashed that morning. There were no flights anywhere, so I knew I couldn't get home to Houston. I managed to use the voucher I was provided by the airline to pay for cab fare to Cleveland, where I could stay with Mike until the airlines were operating again.

Mike and I were horrified as we watched the 9/11 stories unfold on the news. I ended up spending the next five days in Cleveland. It was an emotional, dark time for our country and we, like most, were overtaken by grief. I felt closer to Mike as we talked about life and death and war and how much being American means to the both of us. I felt our relationship strengthen during my stay and there was no denying that my love for him had become strong and genuine.

Growing up under Mama and Tata's turbulent union, I couldn't believe I was already thinking he was "the one," and I felt in my heart with great certainty that I wanted to spend my life with Mike. He understood me like no one ever had, and I never felt like I had to hide my skeletons or water down my rocky past. He loved me for who I was *now* and nothing else seemed to matter.

Looking back at that time now, I had become a bit chubby. In fact, I was the most full-figured I'd ever been when Mike and I began dating seriously in 2001. Having been hyperaware of my weight and a topsy-turvy relationship with food my entire life, I felt self-conscious at first, but Mike always made me feel beautiful. He loved my curves, embraced them, and helped empower me to feel more confident about myself in every way. I knew I was falling deeper and deeper in love and I wanted to spend every waking moment with Mike. Every time we said good-bye, I was more certain that there would come a time when we wouldn't have to separate.

It took eight more months of flying back and forth between Cleveland and Houston until I took the leap and moved to Cleveland to be with Mike as he continued in medical school. My parents were not happy that I was leaving, especially to "chase a boy," without being formally engaged, but I knew in my heart it was right.

Tata and I had been slowly rebuilding our relationship. There was never a moment when he or I formally apologized for any of the things that had gone on between us. It was more that the fighting and rehashing of the past had died down and we began to realize it was pointless to argue when we both still felt we were in the right. We learned to accept each other for who we were and move forward little by little.

Mike came to Houston to meet my family during Christmas 2001, five months before I moved to Cleveland. I really wasn't sure how Tata would react to Mike. Despite the improved condition of our own relationship, he was always a tough critic when it came to my friends or anyone I'd shown interest in dating the past two years. I couldn't imagine him ever "approving" of someone I wanted to follow to another state. Tata grilled him with what seemed like hundreds of questions, and Mike calmly and respectfully answered each one and was able to win Tata over in the course of the conversation. I remember Tata even asking Mike what he knew about goat cheese, of all things.

"How much a pound?" Tata asked.

"I don't know, Mr. Moceanu, I just eat it," Mike replied with a smile.

Tata laughed and really got a kick out of Mike, which was a huge relief. I knew Mike was "the one" and nobody was going to convince me otherwise, but having Mama and Tata approve of him certainly instantly made my life easier. It also provided me with hope as we moved into this next stage.

Off Balance

In May 2002, I stuffed my Ford Explorer with my personal belongings and set off on my 21-hour trek to Cleveland. In contrast to the last time I had left Texas, Tata was warmly supportive, even helpful. He even generously offered to bring my furniture and larger items in a moving truck a few weeks later. I was thankful for his blessing and support. Mama was supportive as well but reluctant to let me go in the end because of the distance. I promised I would return home often and be in regular touch.

Mike opened a door for me to work as a coach at Gymnastics World (GW), a gym where he had trained since he was a junior in high school. GW owners Ron and Joan Ganim welcomed me with open arms and have continued to be an extended family in Cleveland to this day. While I coached, I also attended Cuyahoga Community College and John Carroll University, to complete my business degree.

Mike remained passionate about gymnastics and even after he retired from competition, he stayed competitive by participating in the annual Ohio State University Alumni gymnastics performance each January, despite his heavy course load as a full-time medical student. It was inspirational to watch Mike deftly balance his various commitments. I also admired how he was so disciplined about getting to the gym to train. He used the January performances as a personal goal to keep in shape and stay involved in gymnastics while he navigated through medical school, residency, and beyond. Precision conditioning for our sport is demanding, and most gymnasts I know are unable to perform at an Elite level even *one* year after retirement, yet Mike was continuing to wow audiences years and years after he'd retired. He has actually earned quite a reputation at Ohio State for his impressive Alumni performances. I have never known anyone who loves gymnastics as much as Mike does, from the inside out. January 2012 marked his 17th consecutive alumni performance.

In 2004, I was spending a lot of time in the gym training for a post-Olympic tour and Mike started making comments about me getting back into competitive gymnastics.

"You should train again. You could do it," he'd say.

His words intimidated me at first. I wasn't sure that I could do it, or that I had it in me to push myself through the mental and physical aspects of training again, but he had me thinking. I had often felt my retirement was premature, and leaving the sport because of injury had felt like I didn't leave Elite competitive gymnastics on my own terms. My heart still ached when I watched others perform. I definitely missed performing competitively. There were so many things that could have been done differently, and I certainly was intrigued by the thought of competing on my own terms. Mike was consistently encouraging and wanted to help me feel fulfilled with my gymnastics career, so slowly but surely I started training more seriously. By 2005, I was in full-blown training mode. However, this time, we followed Mike's strategy to "train smarter, not harder," so we could preserve my body and limit injury. I felt strong and motivated and trusted Mike's approach, but it was at first a challenge for me to change the mind-set that had been hammered into me all those years. For most of my career, I was conditioned to believe I had to be in the gym forty-plus hours each week and that I couldn't miss more than one day a week to perform at my best. Mike helped deprogram those notions and showed me that this smarter approach was just as effective. I trained a few hours every day, went to college full-time, and coached young gymnasts at GW part-time three days a week. I was taking on a lot, but I felt balanced, empowered, and determined. I'd always loved gymnastics, but for the first time I felt like I was doing it for *me*.

With Mike's guidance, I decided to become a "specialist," meaning that I would focus on two events only—vault and floor exercise—as opposed to training for the All-Around like I'd always done in the past. I was learning new skills and it was challenging, but very exciting, too. I was enthusiastic to train, so even when Mike wasn't able to meet me at the gym, I would videotape my sessions, and we'd review the footage together later that night. I'd never studied my training sessions like this before, and it was an eye-opening experience. I learned so much from this approach because I could actually *see* what I didn't always *feel* as I was doing certain skills. It opened up a door to finally being able to clearly identify the things I was doing right and the things I needed to correct. Watching film certainly was not an original idea, as I'm certain the Soviets and others have been utilizing it for years, but I had seldom seen it during my training throughout the United States, and we never recorded training with the Karolyis, aside from media footage. I wondered why more coaches didn't incorporate it in their training as it surely seems every gymnast could benefit from watching and critiquing her own routines.

Mike continued to coach and encourage me, and before too long I felt confident enough that I set my mind on doing what I never thought would be possible . . . training for an Elite competition at the age of twenty-four.

There were skills that still came naturally to me, like the Tsukahara element on floor exercise named after legendary Japanese gymnast Mitsuo Tsukahara. The skill is two flips in a tucked position with one 360-degree twist in the first flip. It's a skill I'd been doing since I was nine years old and mastered by my twenties, so it came back to me relatively easily once I got in shape. I loved flipping again and it was exhilarating to learn new skills and prove that I could get better with time.

Everything was clicking, so with Mike as my coach, we set our sights on me competing at the US Nationals in 2005, knowing full well it would be an uphill battle considering all of the rules and restrictions our governing body placed on gymnasts attempting to come back after retiring. It was widely believed that USA Gymnastics was then almost entirely controlled by Marta Karolyi, who was National Team Coordinator for Women's Gymnastics and who didn't appear to be a Dominique Moceanu fan by any means. As National Team Coordinator, Marta oversaw the US National team, having a powerful say in selecting the gymnasts for international assignments, as well as World and Olympic teams. We were well aware that she had the power to easily put a stop to my gymnastics comeback at any moment by simply stating "she didn't qualify" or "didn't meet the criteria." Selections for the World and Olympic teams, as well as scoring, are very subjective, and Mike and I were fully aware of the politics of Elite women's gymnastics going in. I'd seen at least a few gymnasts magically appear on the National and even World team without qualifying through the normal process. These gymnasts were selected for these teams without any explanation, not that anyone would ever question Marta. We decided to move forward anyway, feeling that if I performed well enough, I might have a chance of breaking through the politics and earning the right to compete again.

I was coming back to my sport for different reasons this time— and I moved toward my goal with a different attitude. I was wiser, mentally tougher, and totally focused on my main goal: to compete at the highest level one last time, 100 percent on my own terms.

On July 2, 2005, that sixteen-year-old boy I had met in the hospitality room eleven years earlier asked for my hand in marriage. "Yes!" couldn't come out of my mouth fast enough. The pieces of my life that had been scattered far and wide for too long were finally coming together and settling in their rightful places.

Chapter 13

THE COMEBACK
TRAIL

A gymnast in her twenties is considered geriatric, so my "comeback" at twenty-four was virtually unheard of, especially since I'd been out of the Elite scene for a good five years. If I were younger, I would have been deterred by my critics, and at this point there were plenty of those. Haters and naysayers seemed to come out of the woodwork when I announced I was training for a comeback. By 2005, however, I was older, wiser, and definitely more thick-skinned, so the negative comments and mean-spirited barbs didn't sway me.

Fortunately, as I trained for my comeback, I had the support and sponsorship of Woodward Gymnastics Camp in Pennsylvania. The gym offered to cover my training and living expenses during summers in exchange for my coaching at their camps. I loved working with young gymnasts, so it was a win-win for me. I lived at the summer camp lodge and had access to the cafeteria, but I elected to bring my own food to make sure I stayed on my regimented diet. For once, I was eating a sensible, well-balanced meal plan and I didn't want to mess that up. The Woodward facility had top-of-the-line equipment with foam pits for vaulting and floor exercise, which was key to sparing my body from the heavy pounding and overuse that is exacerbated with older equipment.

The facility was about a four-hour drive from Cleveland, so I had the freedom to come home to spend time with Mike on weekends and during my off time. While I was at camp during the week and Mike was knee-deep in his medical residency in Cleveland, we had to be creative about my training. Mike would write out my daily training plan, then email it to me each morning. It was an unorthodox method, but it worked for us. As a seasoned gymnast, I was able to stay on task and push through workouts on my own. I'd get odd looks and comments from people when they'd see me in the gym alone—no training partners, no coach. Just me and my video camera. I'd position the videocam on a tripod and review each turn as I completed it. A far stretch from how I'd trained in the past, but the video didn't lie and held me accountable. I'd make corrections and repeat each skill until I got it right. Mike's training philosophy, medical knowledge, and pure love for the sport helped me see gymnastics in a new light. I was training more effectively and even as a "geriatric," I felt refreshed and more motivated than ever.

As word got out in the gymnastics community that I was training again, I'd find spectators, sometimes coaches from gymnastics clubs who had gymnasts at camp or collegiate gymnasts and coaches, would watch my workouts from the sidelines. Sometimes these observers were very supportive, but there were always those few who watched with a critical and judgmental eye. This was to be expected and basically unavoidable since I trained in an open facility. I remember two specific occasions when bystanding coaches made personal, derogatory comments as they stood there watching me train, as if I were a circus animal there for their viewing and criticizing pleasure. The expressions of pure shock were priceless when I later learned what they had said and confronted them, telling them how their rude, inappropriate comments were disrupting my workouts. Both of these guys immediately began backpedaling and stumbling over their words after I'd confronted them. It was liberating to stand up and not be intimidated, knowing full well that I would never have had the confidence to do so earlier in my career—least of all with those who held themselves out as coaches. Thankfully, for every naysayer viewing me as a "has-been" came hundreds of supporters, and I focused on the letters, emails, and cards of encouragement that I received from fans and the gymnastics community overall as I pushed toward a comeback.

By July 2005, I was exceeding my goals and sticking my landings. Right when things were moving along so well, however, I started suffering from an intense new pain in my right Achilles' tendon, which Mike diagnosed as Achilles' tendinosis. We immediately slowed my trainings, but the pain persisted. Easing up on my workouts seemed appropriate to me, but I was surprised when Mike told me to take four days off for physical therapy and rest. Four days was the equivalent of forever in my mind. I still wanted to compete at the US Classic in late July, and the injury was already slowing me down. I didn't think I could afford to put training on hold altogether. Mike was adamant, explaining how the body would attempt to repair itself, but not if I continuously tore it back down by working the muscles and tendons where I was hurting. By this point, Mike had become a foot and ankle surgical resident, so I wasn't about to argue with him. He was convinced that my Achilles' required time off from the repetitive pounding in order to avoid a complete rupture of the tendon, which could end up requiring up to a year of recovery time. Mike thought that stretching and reviewing training videos was more beneficial than being in the gym and risking a rupture.

Mike also asked his mentor, world-renowned foot and ankle surgeon Gerard Vincent Yu, DPM, to examine my Achilles' tendon. Before the MRI and X-ray results were even back, Dr. Yu confirmed that the Achilles' tendon had degenerated and that I indeed had tendinosis of the Achilles', and there was already a slight tear in the tendon. I also had a condition called Haglund's deformity—a bump of bone at the back of the heel that pushes against and irritates the tendon, which added to the pain.

Instead of competing at the US Classic at the end of July, I was in the operating room, as Dr. Yu and his resident team, Mike included, performed surgery on my right Achilles'. They utilized an innovative, less invasive surgical procedure that would allow me to heal faster. Dr. Yu also shaved down the Haglund deformity in my heel and removed a bursa sac of fluid. The surgery was a success, and I was able to return to Woodward Gymnastics Camp to finish my summer coaching obligations, albeit with cast and crutches. My recovery was swift, though. In October, just eight weeks after the operation, I was able to perform at the Hilton Ice Skating and Gymnastics Spectacular Show with an all-star group of Olympic ice skaters and gymnasts. I viewed my Achilles' surgery as a mere bump in the road—my tendon was mending quickly and was almost back to normal. I was still determined to push ahead.

In the meantime, Mike was dealing with a less than welcoming USA Gymnastics, going back and forth trying to simply determine the correct protocol to allow me to compete at the Elite level again. We were finally told that in order for my petition to be granted to compete at 2006 US Nationals, I had to do two things: first, I had to attend a National Team Training Camp at my own expense, and second, I had to compete in at least one event at the 2006 US Classic. Mike and I carefully submitted all of the information, documents, forms, and membership fees asked of us in order to comply with these two requirements. We paid our expenses to attend the National Team Training Camp, which was to be based at the Karolyi ranch, where I'd trained with Bela and Marta all those years—a place that held more than its share of unhappy memories for me. We had done our part and awaited the green light from Marta for admission into her training camp.

The National Team Training Camp at the Karolyis' ranch was where gymnasts would basically "try out" to compete at the Elite level and, ultimately, for the National team. To attend the Karolyi camp, a gymnast had to submit a video demonstrating her skills, and if Marta, the National Team Coordinator, approved of the video performance, then that gymnast could enroll (and pay the $240 weekly fee per coach and gymnast). Once the gymnast was at camp, Marta, and sometimes a panel of National team staff members under her supervision, would evaluate that gymnast's "physical abilities" and skill level and determine if she would be allowed to compete in an Elite meet. Gymnasts who were not given high enough marks at camp, or gymnasts who were denied enrollment to the Karolyi camp altogether, were less likely to secure roster spots at subsequent Elite competitions unless they qualified at one of the Elite qualifier competitions. In essence, the Karolyi training camp was the gateway to becoming an Elite gymnast in the United States, and if the gatekeeper, Marta, didn't believe in you, or disliked you for whatever reason, then your chances of moving forward at the Elite level were very slim.

The entire process was extremely subjective and contrary to the methods used to select athletes in other national sports. In the United States, a female gymnast's future, in large part, teetered on

Marta's opinion of her skills, her physique, or her opinion of the gymnast in general. I didn't know of any other Olympic sport that was controlled so subjectively, and it seemed crazy that gymnastics' governing body allowed Elite women's gymnastics to fall under the control of one person: Marta. In my opinion, there seemed to be very little oversight and no legitimate system of checks and balances. The governing body and Marta seemed to arbitrarily apply "official" criteria and standards on an ad hoc basis simply to justify their selections at the time.

A number of weeks had passed and I still hadn't heard if I could attend the Karolyi training camp. It was drawing closer and I needed an answer, so I phoned Marta directly to inquire and make sure she'd received my video and the other mandatory materials.

"What Olympics were you in, again?" Marta interrupted me. This was Marta's way of making sure I knew my place and that I was nothing special.

"The 1996 Olympics! The ONLY time our country has won team GOLD! Does the Magnificent Seven ring a bell?!" is what I wanted to yell into the receiver. Marta was so transparent, dismissively feigning that she couldn't remember which Olympics I was in, when I knew full well that the 1996 Olympic Games was among Marta's most memorable moments since she defected to the United States. It was the first *and* only time she could say that the US women's team was the best in the world.

"Um, excuse me?" is what I coughed up.

"What Olympics were you in?" Marta repeated, coldly.

Were you not my personal coach? I thought to myself. Marta may have wanted me to feel like I was one in a vast sea of Olympic gymnasts she'd coached over the years, but we both knew perfectly well that she and Bela handpicked only a few Elite gymnasts to personally coach every few years. And of those handpicked gymnasts, only a select few went on to win Olympic gold.

"The 1996 one, remember?" I calmly replied. Once she finally gave me the final approval to attend camp, I couldn't get off the phone fast enough.

Mike and I headed off to the National Team Training Camp the week of July 4, 2006. It was hard to believe that I was voluntarily returning to the Karolyi ranch, one facility I had tried to put out of my mind for years. I knew I had to pass through this nightmarish place in order to compete again, however, so I figured I might as well make the best of it. I was a different person with a new perspective driving down that dirt road toward the ranch, and I was hoping that confronting this aspect of my past might free some of the hurt that still lingered.

After conditioning circuit training on day one, I noticed Bela enter the gym. As I'd been taught the moment I arrived on the ranch as a ten-year-old, I went straight over to greet him. I approached Bela, smiled, and before I could get a word out of my mouth, he shoved right past me, literally inches from my side, and went into his office. He kept his back turned to me inside the office. For a second, I wondered if maybe he didn't recognize me, but when I looked back at Mike, he was shaking his head in disbelief at Bela's rudeness. I had become less than a stranger to him; I was invisible. When I walked back to continue my training, Mike gave me the best advice of all.

"Ignore him. He's not worth being upset over." Mike was right; I was here for gymnastics this time. Not for Bela Karolyi.

During the mock competition, I was placed in a group with some of the most recognizable young names in gymnastics, including Nastia Liukin, Chellsie Memmel, and Alicia Sacramone. It was enjoyable getting to know these girls and sharing with them stories from my career. My first vault was a Podkopayeva, named after the 1996 Olympic All-Around champion from Ukraine, Lilia Podkopayeva. My second vault, which I planned to perform at US

Nationals, was a Tsukahara in a layout position with a 1½ twist. I wanted to showcase this skill because it was one of the higher difficulty vaults in the world at the time, and I thought it would give me an edge since no one at camp was attempting this type of vault. I was proud of both vaults as I executed them cleanly with little error.

When we moved on to floor exercise, I was one of the few gymnasts who performed her entire floor routine on the standard floor mat, not exercising any tumbling passes in the softer pit. Some gymnasts did "timers," which are watered-down, simplified versions of the most difficult passes, and other gymnasts did *all* of their passes in the pit to protect their ankles, or because they lacked the endurance to do all the passes on the center mat. Mike and I contemplated using the softer landing pit for my first pass, like many of the other gymnasts were doing. If I'd used the pit, I would've upgraded that first pass to a double layout (two flips in a layout position), which would've upgraded my difficulty and increased my overall floor score a bit. However, we felt it was a trade-off because we also figured that Marta would use the pit against me, claiming I was not fit or skilled enough to perform my routine on the center floor. So I completed my floor exercise in its entirety on the center mat. Ironically, here I was the oldest gymnast at camp and one of the few to do my entire routine, including all four of my passes, on the center floor. I certainly wasn't going to knock a gymnast for making the smart decision to use the softer landing mat, but we felt I didn't have that luxury with Marta evaluating me.

At the end of training camp, Marta would approach each gymnast and her coach to discuss areas the gymnast needed to work on. While we were all stretching and winding down on the final day, Marta was in the gym, moving from one coach and gymnast to the next. Marta met with every single gymnast and coach in the building that day *except* for Mike and me. Mike was helping me stretch as we waited for Marta to give us her constructive criticism, like she'd given everyone else in the gym, but she never came.

"She skipped us on purpose," I said to Mike as Marta left the gym. "She doesn't want me to feel like I am a contender here."

"Don't worry about it," Mike said. I could see he was a little irked by Marta's pettiness, too. Mike, being Mike, made the perfect next move. He reached into his pocket and pulled out a photo of a silly cat we cut out from the *SkyMall* magazine on our plane flight from Cleveland. We called this cat Fred, and Mike had pulled Fred out of his pocket to make me laugh throughout camp whenever he thought I needed it. It was an inside joke that lightened the situation and made me smile when I got frustrated. He was right. I couldn't let Marta's mind games get to me.

During the final dinner at camp, Kathy Kelly, vice president for the Women's Program, approached my table. I remember the moment distinctly because I had just decided to grab a kaiser roll from the bread basket right before she walked up. I was one of the few who had been brave enough to eat anything from the bread basket all week. I smiled, thinking that the bread basket was still taboo and that some things never change. Heck, I was at my optimal weight and felt I'd deserved a simple roll with my dinner on the last night of camp.

Kathy hadn't said a single word to me during the entire time I was at camp, but she felt it necessary to approach me during dinner in front of all the gymnasts at my table to tell me what areas *she* felt I needed to work on. I believe she was acting on Marta's orders. She had long been Marta's right-hand woman and it seemed she didn't do anything without her blessing. I didn't trust her. I had learned long ago not to tell her anything. She was also the one Tata had had to battle with to get me a spot to compete at the Goodwill Games in 1998, and then was all smiles after I'd won the All-Around gold there, pretending that she'd been my friend and supporter all along.

"Well, I guess you know what *you* need to work on" were the first words out of Kathy's mouth.

"I think I did great!" I said immediately. I know I took her off guard by answering so quickly and so confidently. She seemed to forget what else she was going to say, because she just stood beside me a few more seconds before walking away.

I wasn't going to let Kathy Kelly, or anyone else, belittle my accomplishments. I was proud that I'd turned in Elite-level performances on floor and vault. I'd survived camp alongside current greats Nastia Liukin, Chellsie Memmel, Shawn Johnson, and Alicia Sacramone, among others, while attending college full-time, coaching part-time, and planning my wedding. Just *being* at camp at twenty-four and holding my own among these amazing young gymnasts was an accomplishment. I achieved what I set out to do that week.

After camp was over, Mike and I waited on an outside bench at the ranch for Christina, who was picking us up and bringing us to Houston to take engagement photos before we headed home to Cleveland. As we sat there, Bela came riding up the dirt road on his tractor. He obviously saw us there but never stopped or even slowed down. Just as he passed, however, a few feet in front of us, it seemed he couldn't help himself. He waved, flashed a big grin, and said, "Bye." Mike and I turned to each other and burst out laughing. The situation was so bizarre.

At the onset of my comeback, USA Gymnastics stated in writing that my petition to compete at Nationals would be granted if (1) I attended a National Team Training Camp at my own expense, and (2) I competed in one event at the US Classic. A few weeks after camp at the Karolyi ranch, I indeed competed at the US Classic, thereby fulfilling both requirements of my petition. Even though USA Gymnastics stated that I needed to compete in only *one* event at the US Classic, I decided to compete in two, the floor exercise and vault. Mike and I wanted to take advantage of the forum and practice both events in preparation for my comeback at Nationals. I performed a recently upgraded floor routine, which included five passes instead of the four I had done at the training camp.

My competitive gymnastics career ended on August 1, 2006, just two weeks before I was to make my official, planned "comeback" at US Nationals. We were notified that I would not be allowed to compete. Mike and I were stunned because I had done exactly what USA Gymnastics required of me. I attended training camp and competed in "at least one event" at the US Classic. I had satisfied the requirements *they* set out for me and now I was told I couldn't compete at Nationals. Mike and I wanted an explanation and to see if maybe there was a misunderstanding of some kind.

Apparently, despite my compliance with the stated criteria, a three-member committee voted unanimously to deny my petition. This committee was made up of Kim Zmeskal-Burdette (the athlete representative), Steve Rybacki, and Marta Karolyi (National Team Coordinator). I wasn't surprised that Marta voted against me—her dislike for me was palpable, but the other two panelists' votes gave me pause. Steve Rybacki had actually seemed impressed with the difficulty of my vaults at training camp and had commented positively to me. The fact that Kim Zmeskal-Burdette was on the panel at all surprised me. Kim wasn't present at the training camp or the US Classic competition, yet she was representing one-third of the panel's voting power. I didn't understand how she would evaluate my skills. I felt cheated.

My entire comeback hinged on competing at US Nationals. I had done everything USA Gymnastics required of me to compete at that meet, yet at the eleventh hour, they were changing the rules on me. I knew I was in trouble when they started backpedaling on their original criteria and began talking about scores. For the first time, after we demanded an explanation, USA Gymnastics claimed I had needed to obtain a combined score of 28.0 on *two* events at the US Classic in order for my petition to be granted. *What?* They explicitly told me in writing that I need only compete in *one* event—and now they were saying I needed a specific combined score in *two*. This was crazy-making. I wasn't originally even planning to do two events. I was going to only do vault, but Mike and I figured I might as well do floor exercise to get an additional competitive practice before Nationals. We were never told that my combined scores would factor in my petition. Had I known, I would've strategically done my four-pass routine (not the five passes), just to be on the conservative side and make sure my scores were solid. It seemed they were arbitrarily coming up with new criteria just to keep me out.

If USA Gymnastics was now requiring a combined 28 on two events, I'd actually already satisfied that benchmark at training camp a few weeks prior when I received a combined 28.80 on vault and floor. "Banking" scores from a training camp or another competition is a regular, sanctioned practice in gymnastics, yet USA Gymnastics refused to consider those scores for me.

It quickly became clear that whatever Mike or I presented or proved to USA Gymnastics, they'd come back with some newly introduced wrinkle to deny me the chance to compete at Nationals. All my training and hard work invested for that opportunity to compete at Nationals was washed away by bureaucracy. I was deeply disappointed, but I was also taken aback at how unfair the whole process was and how easy it was for the system behind the Elite level of our sport to block anyone from competing. I knew my shot was over, but I wanted to stand up for the gymnasts following me, the hopeful young girls I'd met at camp, the kids I'd been coaching in Cleveland and at Woodward, and future generations of young athletes who would possibly face this biased, closed-door selection process one day themselves—after they'd been chewed up and spat out by the system.

On August 2, 2006, I filed a grievance with USA Gymnastics, the first of its kind by a female gymnast. Few gymnasts dared to challenge the governing body, especially Marta Karolyi, because it most surely meant they would be blackballed down the road. And since most gymnasts eventually coach or own a gym themselves, everyone is afraid of burning bridges. USA Gymnastics also lines up many paid performances, tours, and events for the gymnasts, current and retired, so butting heads with them is never in a gymnast's best financial interests, either. I was well aware of this, and I assumed I'd be stonewalled, but I still wanted Marta, the selection committee, and the governing body to be held accountable to some extent.

As expected, the grievance committee confirmed the selection committee's decision to bar me from competing at Nationals in a 2–1 vote. I had my final opportunity to argue my case during a conference call that was supposed to simulate a court hearing. It was my sole opportunity to talk to and question the selection committee about their votes to block my petition, yet Steve Rybacki was the only member of the selection panel to participate in the hearing. The other two-thirds of the voting panel, Marta Karolyi and Kim Zmeskal-Burdette, didn't even phone in. Mike, as my coach, was on the grievance call with me and did an amazing job outlining how we'd complied with all of the requirements. He methodically outlined how patently unfair it was to throw a new requirement our way *after* the fact, when there was no time or venue in which to correct it. He also asked a number of questions, which were met with awkward pauses as the grievance panel clearly didn't have answers. But what they did have, in the end, was all the power. USA Gymnastics attempted to make the entire process seem official and "by the book," but it was obvious to me that they were winging it, seeming to improvise as they went along.

This was the state of US Gymnastics in 2006, and, sadly, the situation has not improved. Instead of making the selection process more open and objective, US Gymnastics has gone in the opposite direction. I believe Marta Karolyi now has even *more* subjective control and power. In 2011, the US Olympic Committee named the Karolyi ranch the "official" training site for US Women's Gymnastics, as well as women's tumbling, trampoline, and acrobatic gymnastics. Now Junior and Senior Elite gymnasts who train in gyms across the country with their own coaches must attend Karolyi ranch camps throughout the year to be monitored and evaluated by Marta, the National Team Coordinator.

While it's understandable that USA Gymnastics would want to emulate the successful Soviet and Romanian practice of "centralized gymnastics," there is, in my opinion, something innately wrong and very un-American about one person holding nearly all of the power over a national sport. With little published criteria and few guidelines outlining how gymnasts are to be evaluated, ranked, and selected, there is no accountability and no safe and effective way to appeal a determination by the selection committee. I believe that filing a grievance against the committee is, in essence, filing a grievance against Marta, the National Coordinator, because she seems to have a stranglehold on every aspect of Elite women's gymnastics, including, ultimately, who makes the Olympic team.

Making decisions and naming World and Olympic team members in "closed door" sessions seems to contradict the notion of fair play. If I were in charge of USA Gymnastics, I'd go back to the tried-and-true system of selecting World and Olympic teams through public competitions, such as Olympic Trials. Not too long ago, we relied on Olympic Trials to determine which gymnasts were peaking at the right time and were primed for international competition. Top scores at Trials would qualify gymnasts for a World or an Olympic team—much as they would in other events such as track and field, swimming, and diving.

I also think there needs to be a petition format in place for those gymnasts who may be struggling with an injury at the time of Trials, whereby the gymnast could qualify for the team based on the strength of National Championships or similar meets. This was the system in place in 1996, and it seemed to work well enough to create a team of us that earned Team USA the gold medal at the Olympics.

The gymnastics community needs to start asking why we've

moved away from that selection process, which is still utilized in most other national sports in the United States. Bela and Marta pushed US gymnastics toward a semi-centralized system for years, and since they are the most successful coaching duo in gymnastics' history, it's no surprise that USA Gymnastics has accommodated them each step of the way. But we must remind ourselves, and the Karolyis, that we are not in Romania, where Bela and Marta were able to pluck prospective gymnasts from school yards, public parks, and gyms across the country and house them in a year-round gymnastics boarding school. Back then, the Karolyis selected the gymnasts themselves and, in turn, produced Olympic medalists, so it's no wonder that they sought the same control here. It is up to USA Gymnastics, the Olympic Committee, and the public at large to tell them, "No, in the United States, we have a more democratic process, which gives every athlete an opportunity to compete and to be judged fairly—and not by one or two people."

In a twisted way, one has to admire the gumption of the Karolyis and how they are able to hypnotize people with their Olympic medals. Why is it that the gymnastics community doesn't question the conflict of interest created by having the National Team Training Center *and* the National Team Training Camps based on property personally owned and operated by the National Team Coordinator, Marta Karolyi? Do we really want someone who financially benefits from hosting training camps telling us we need *more* of these camps throughout the year? Shouldn't an unbiased individual, one who doesn't have a financial stake in the property or the camps, be making those decisions? Or do we just continue to look the other way and ignore the damage as long as the Karolyi system brings home a medal? I love the actual sport of gymnastics too much to give in to that line of thinking. I believe that Team USA can win World and Olympic medals by instituting a fair selection process and adopting guidelines designed to protect our athletes from injuries and abusive training techniques along the way.

Even though I wasn't allowed to compete at the 2006 US Nationals, my comeback was still a success in my eyes. For the first time in my career, I was a gymnast on my own terms—and I proved that women can still have a place in "women's" gymnastics and that the sport is not only for malleable prepubescent girls, as many would like us to believe. I faced some childhood demons by returning to the Karolyi ranch with a new perspective, and proved I could hang with the best of them at the national training camp.

Even my grievance filing and dispute was a blessing in that it gave Mike and me a platform to expose USA Gymnastics' dubious and secretive selection methods. I sometimes wonder if that was meant to be my mission all along. I received loads of phone calls and emails from people in the gymnastics community who were grateful and excited that Mike and I were demanding answers from USA Gymnastics and Marta. These gymnastics insiders, many of whom I'd known for years, and others I'd never met, gushed their support from behind the scenes. They were afraid that speaking out publicly might jeopardize their own positions in the sport. I appreciated where they were coming from. Heck, I lived in silent fear of the Karolyis and the USA Gymnastics system for years, but I was done being afraid. Despite any backlash or criticism I'd face, I decided that enough was enough and that the sport I love was too important for me to continue to look the other way like so many have done for years. If I sat back and did nothing, then more of the same would occur and change would never come. My grievance proceeding motivated me to stop being silent and be more proactive and outspoken for positive change within Elite women's gymnastics.

My comeback taught me that sometimes your impact may not be in the form of a medal, but it may be just as meaningful. I hope that by sharing my story, I inspire others to stand for what they believe in and know that their voice matters, even if change doesn't occur overnight.

Chapter 14

FAMILY

On November 4, 2006, I married Michael Brian Canales. Standing at the altar, exchanging vows with a man I view as "golden," was one of the most meaningful moments of my life. I'd navigated some dark waters to get there, and I wasn't about to let any of the magic of that day slip by unnoticed. I savored it all. With Mike—my partner for years and now, finally, my husband—I felt at peace and excited for our life together.

The heavens must have been listening to our whispers about wanting to start a family, because a year after we married, we were blessed with our firstborn, Carmen Noel. She arrived on Christmas Day in 2007, giving her dad and me the best and sweetest present ever. A little more than a year later, in March of 2009, we welcomed our handsome and loving Vincent Michael. Becoming a mother changed my world and instantly reshuffled my priorities. Watching my children take their first steps, hearing them say "Mama" and "Dada" for the first time, rocking them to sleep in my arms—these are the things that melted my heart and made my days complete. Sleepless nights, potty training, and endless worry when they're sick are a far cry from the life of a competitive gymnast, but I cherish every minute and wouldn't trade being a wife and mother for anything.

I am thankful that I was able to further reconcile with Tata before he passed away from cancer in 2008. I cannot recall a single time in my childhood that I saw Tata sick, even with the flu, so his being stricken with cancer was a devastating blow to him and our family. For the first few years he dealt with it fairly well, was positive and determined to conquer it. He had a rare form of eye cancer—cancer of the lacrimal gland—and, unfortunately, there wasn't an abundance of research on the condition. He received care from some of the best oncologists in the country at MD Anderson Cancer Center in Houston. They were able to prolong his life with the most current treatments available at the time.

Tata's illness was a constant battle for the five years he had to live with it, but if anything positive came of it, it was that Tata began to open up to his family for the first time. As I imagine many do when facing the end of life, Tata began to express his feelings and show emotion, which was a complete revelation for all of us. My father, who made me wait twenty-one years before telling me he loved me, was finally tearing down the barricades he had built around his heart and was trying desperately to pull Mama, Christina, and me inside before it was too late. I saw another side of Tata as I watched him cry and expose his vulnerabilities. He regretted so much of the past, and carrying that guilt and remorse had been a heavy burden. We began healing our battle wounds together, understanding each other, and really forgiving. I was relieved that he and I could finally each release our anger and guilt and forge a tighter bond.

As strong as Tata fought during the first four years, the final year was the toughest, and it seemed like my family was getting hit from all sides. In the midst of Tata's decline, my parents' house in Houston almost burned down to the ground. Mama was running herself ragged taking Tata to his stream of doctors' appointments and also tending to Maia, who was also ailing in her older years. It was a full-time job for Mama to care for both of them, leaving little time to rest or even slow down. On the day of the fire, Mama was in such a rush to get to the doctor with Tata that she left a candle burning in her prayer room. Mama's prayer room was her private sanctuary, filled with religious figurines she'd collected from the holy land in Jerusalem and from the many monasteries she'd visited throughout her life. She prayed in that room every day, often lighting prayer candles.

The fire destroyed the entire second story of their house and a large part of the first floor. Mama's prayer room and Christina's bedroom were reduced to a pile of ashes. It was heartbreaking to see them lose so many of their treasured possessions. I certainly wasn't about to cry that my wedding dress went up in flames when my poor sister lost her entire bedroom and nearly all her belongings inside.

Tata, Mama, and Christina spent the following day inspecting the damage and rummaging through ashes, trying to find any valuables spared in the fire. By the time they packed the car with the recovered items and drove to a local hotel for the night, they were so exhausted, physically and emotionally, they didn't have much energy left to unload the items from the car. They carried what they could as they staggered into the hotel and never made it back out for a second load. Tata was usually the one to put some extra muscle into such tasks, but his cancer was beginning to spread and he didn't have the strength or stamina that he used to.

In some cruel twist of fate, a thief broke into their car during the night and stole every last item they'd salvaged from the house that day. Among the stolen items was Mama's jewelry, including her Rolex watch, which was a special anniversary gift from Tata. He had saved for many years to buy her this watch to celebrate the twenty-seven years they'd been together. Christina's laptop, one of her few items not burned in the fire, was also taken. Tata did his best to stay strong and worked with Mama to repair the fire damage to the house, so they could sell it and move to a new home. It took a lot out of them when they were already beleaguered to start with.

Tata continued to get weaker, and he was now operating with only one eye, having lost the other entirely to the cancer. I'm grateful that Tata was able to walk me down the aisle at my wedding. After all we'd been through, to have him escort me as I moved to the next stage of my life made that day complete. The fact that he was also able to later meet and hold his first grandchild, Carmen, was a blessing as well.

In fall 2008, during the second trimester of my pregnancy with our son, Vincent, I packed my bags and went to Houston to support Tata, Mama, and Christina as the cancer was now rampant and it was clear Tata was losing the battle. He was admitted to the hospital, and we were told that he was nearing the end of his life. His impending passing was beginning to sink in for all of us, especially Mama. Tata was all she'd ever known; she'd never been on her own, having gone straight from her parents' home in Romania to marrying Tata and starting a new life in America. I never doubted Mama's strength; she was a survivor. But I could feel her pain. Tata had put her through hell a million times over, but she still loved him and she knew in her heart that he loved her with everything he had. In those final years, he had come to terms with his own mistakes and asked for forgiveness.

"Will you ever forgive me for all that I have done?" he asked Mama.

"Yes, of course I will," Mama said, not thinking twice.

I tried to stay strong to comfort Mama and Christina. As I was a relatively emotional person to begin with, being pregnant made it even more difficult to keep it together. I'd find myself crying more times than not. It was heartbreaking to see Tata's withered body once we moved him to hospice just waiting for the end. He was so frail; he'd lost so much weight, I didn't recognize his body at all. His mouth was dry and I could sense no life coming from him. He was barely hanging on.

Our last coherent conversation was at the hospital the week before he moved into hospice care. Dementia was setting in, so I'd have to repeat things, which I didn't mind. It was the least I could do for Tata. He kept asking me what "hospice" was, and, sadly, I'd explain again and again. It was very difficult to move him to hospice, since it was basically an admission on all our parts that the end was near, but at this point he required care around the clock. I remember we took a family photo in the hospital: Tata, Mama, Christina, and me, the three of us huddled around Tata in his bed. It would be our last.

Mama was making herself sick staying by his side all day long those final weeks. She wanted to be by Tata's side when he took his final breath. I literally had to pry her from his bedside just so she could eat and get a breath of fresh air. Christina and I were with Tata every day those last few weeks in hospice. It was excruciating watching him fade before our eyes. I'd talk to him as much as I could, standing at his bedside, holding his hand and sharing memories. I prayed he knew we were there.

When the telephone rang in the middle of the night on October 12, 2008, we all knew what it meant. Just days after his fifty-fourth birthday, Tata passed away.

I know he loved us and did the best he could to be a good father and husband. Now, as a parent myself, I understand that more than ever. Forgiveness is purifying for the soul, and I'm so thankful that the four of us were able to forgive one another before Tata left this earth.

With every ending comes a new beginning and, for me, I was lucky enough to have two beginnings after Tata's passing: Vincent and Jen. Tata never met either of these "new beginnings" as Vincent was born just months after his passing, and Tata was too ill by the end to meet Jen. Christina, Jen, and I had continued to build our relationship and get closer over the next year. By winter 2009, all three sisters knew it was time for Jen to meet Mama.

Mike and I decided to host Christmas at our home in Cleveland that year. We figured it would be the perfect time and setting for us all to come together. Mama, understandably, was nervous and anxious to meet Jen. She'd already heard so much about her from Christina and me and knew she'd had an amazing family and up-bringing, but Mama still carried remorse and guilt about putting Jen up for adoption. Even though Mama was scared and worried that Jen might be resentful and angry, she knew she owed it to Jen to at least meet her.

Within minutes of Mama arriving at my house, she was hugging Jen, long and tight. I had a lump in my throat the size of an apple. I immediately welled up as I watched Mama squeeze the daughter she never was given a chance to hold at birth. I caught Mama staring at Jen, just like I'd stared at Jen when I first met her. I'm sure Mama was taken aback at the similarities between all of us, and I remember Mama nodding her head when I mentioned it. I couldn't imagine what it must have been like for Mama to have given up a baby at birth, and now have all three of her daughters in the same room having an early Christmas dinner. I wondered if Mama noticed Jen's resemblance to Tata, in particular. The shape of her face, her nose, the color of her skin—it was all Tata.

"Did you wonder what ever happened to me? Did you ever think about me?" Jen asked Mama.

My heart pounded and I could feel the tears building up. I was so proud that Jen asked Mama these questions right away. Mama told her that she'd thought about her often. I could see that Mama was emotional and on the verge of tears, but she did her best to be honest and give Jen the answers she deserved. I remember Jen also asked if Mama had any photos of herself when she was pregnant with Jen. I was surprised when Mama said yes, that she had found one when she was looking through old photos to share with Jen. She said she'd give it to her. *Man,* I thought, *I want to see that one, too.*

Mama went on to ask Jen about her childhood, her parents, her siblings. Jen was very generous to Mama, reassuring her that she had a wonderful childhood and that Mama shouldn't feel badly for what had happened. She told Mama that her parents taught her to never judge her biological family, because there was a reason that things happened the way they did and, in the end, their family was blessed with her.

We sat together until one in the morning, talking and sharing stories. We also brought out the camera and snapped a few shots to mark the beginning of our new chapter together. I remember Mama brought a Christmas gift for Jen—a white zip-up Guess jacket and a matching white wallet, which Jen tried on and was wearing in the photos. It made me think back to the rose I'd given Jen at the airport the day I first met her and how all of our lives had changed so much since then.

As for gymnastics, people ask me all the time, *Will you let your kids be gymnasts?* Of course I will! Heck, they already are! I love my sport with all my heart. It was never the *sport* that harmed me, it was the self-serving adults surrounding the sport at the Elite level who harmed me. I'm excited for my children to experiment with gymnastics, and I won't lie: I'll be thrilled if they share my love for it, but, more important, I want them to be exposed to many different sports and activities so they're able to identify their own passion in life. Whether it's gymnastics, another sport, music, art, or something entirely different, Mike and I will support and encourage them to fulfill their own passions.

Gymnastics will always be a part of my life (past, present, and future), and I am grateful for the life lessons and confidence it has given me. Whether joined by thousands or standing alone, I will continue to be an advocate for my sport and push for fairness in women's gymnastics across the board. I am eternally grateful and proud to have found my passion in what I believe is the greatest sport in the world. As the next generation of young gymnasts reach new heights and stick their landings, I'll be supporting them and promoting our sport . . . every step of the way.

Acknowledgments

There are many individuals who made this book possible. First, I'd like to express my deepest gratitude to my husband, Michael, who has always been a pillar of strength. You truly are my knight in shining armor. Your support and understanding empowered me to take this leap of faith and write my story. I couldn't ask for a better partner. You're my best friend. I love you.

To my co-authors, Paul and Teri Williams, the dynamic duo! Not only are you my A-Team, you are dear friends I adore and greatly respect. My sincerest thanks for all of your dedication and guidance over the years—and especially with this project. It was long and tedious at times, but your patience and efforts are truly appreciated. Thank you for believing in me.

To Michelle Howry, and the entire Simon & Schuster team— thank you for your enthusiasm and encouragement from day one. Your expertise, support, and care throughout this process have been invaluable.

To my agent, Stephanie Abou—thank you for helping me connect the dots to make my story a reality.

To Aunt Janice, my sounding board—I thank you for being such a loyal and loving friend to me and my family over the last twenty-one years. I look forward to fifty more!

To my sisters, Christina and Jennifer—with the release of this book comes a new chapter in our lives. My life is better for having the two of you in it. Now I have not one but two sisters to love, protect, and share my life with. I love you both and look forward to our future and the new memories we will make together.

To Mama, I want to express my love and appreciation for your unwavering support. You have loved me unconditionally, taught me right from wrong, and done everything in your power to provide me with the best. I am forever grateful for the sacrifices you made for me. I love you today, tomorrow, and always.